T0034947

PRAISE FOR
AN UNSPEAKABLE HOPE

"Ford takes us on a path that leads from rage through rehabilitation, all the way to redemption."
—Rob Kenner, *New York Times* bestselling author of *The Marathon Don't Stop* and Founding Editor at *Vibe*

"*An Unspeakable Hope* offers a remarkable demonstration of resilience, grace, and forgiveness. With powerful and insightful vulnerability, Leon provides a raw and riveting account of the arduous journey navigating life after injustice."
—Cyntoia Brown-Long, NAACP-nominated author of *Free Cyntoia: My Search for Redemption in the American Prison System*

"If there is one voice, one story and one person the world needs to hear from, it's Leon Ford. This powerful and moving memoir will take you on an emotional roller coaster. As Leon tells his story of healing, triumph, and resilience, you will find yourself crying and rejoicing."
—Shaka Senghor, bestselling author of *Writing My Wrongs* and *Letters to the Sons of Society*

"With searing vulnerability and insight, Leon Ford reveals his compelling life story, reminding us that the gift of hope often comes in not-so-pretty wrappings of pain, loss, and forgiveness. *An Unspeakable Hope* illuminates Leon's inspiring journey as a Black man, a father, and a community leader, transforming his story of tragedy and injustice into a triumphant invitation for America's racial healing and repair. Read it and you'll certainly reap from Leon's unflinching love and light."

—Shawn Dove, author of *I Too Am America:
On Loving and Leading Black Men & Boys*

"Ford moves beyond reflexively hating cops or uncritically advancing Black Lives Matter and modern social justice organizing to formulate a blueprint for the life he must find a way to live, and a new way forward for our country."

—Deborah Douglas, author of *U.S. Civil Rights Trail:
A Traveler's Guide to the People, Places, and
Events That Made the Movement*

"A timely book about resiliency that will find both advocates and detractors but is well worth hearing out."

—*Kirkus Reviews*

AN UNSPEAKABLE HOPE

BRUTALITY, FORGIVENESS, AND BUILDING A BETTER FUTURE FOR MY SON

LEON FORD

with Jeffery Renard Allen

ATRIA PAPERBACK

New York London Toronto Sydney New Delhi

ATRIA
PAPERBACK

An Imprint of Simon & Schuster, LLC
1230 Avenue of the Americas
New York, NY 10020

Copyright © 2023 by Leon Ford

All rights reserved, including the right to reproduce this book
or portions thereof in any form whatsoever. For information,
address Atria Books Subsidiary Rights Department,
1230 Avenue of the Americas, New York, NY 10020.

Some names have been changed.

First Atria Paperback edition April 2024

ATRIA PAPERBACK and colophon are trademarks of Simon & Schuster, LLC

Simon & Schuster: Celebrating 100 Years of Publishing in 2024

For information about special discounts for bulk purchases,
please contact Simon & Schuster Special Sales at 1-866-506-1949 or
business@simonandschuster.com.

The Simon & Schuster Speakers Bureau can bring authors
to your live event. For more information or to book an event,
contact the Simon & Schuster Speakers Bureau at 1-866-248-3049
or visit our website at www.simonspeakers.com.

Interior design by Lexy East

Manufactured in the United States of America

1   3   5   7   9   10   8   6   4   2

Library of Congress Cataloging-in-Publication Data

Names: Ford, Leon (Activist), author.
Title: An unspeakable hope : brutality, forgiveness, and building a better
future for my son / Leon Ford.
Description: First Atria Books hardcover edition. | New York : Atria Books, 2023. |
Includes bibliographical references and index.
Identifiers: LCCN 2022055228 | ISBN 9781982187279 (hardcover) |
ISBN 9781982187286 (paperback) | ISBN 9781982187293 (ebook)
Subjects: LCSH: Ford, Leon. | Victims of crimes--Pennsylvania--Pittsburgh. |
Social reformers--Pennsylvania--Pittsburgh. | Discrimination in law enforcement--
Pennsylvania--Pittsburgh. | Racial profiling in law enforcement--
Pennsylvania--Pittsburgh. | Mistaken identity--Pennsylvania--Pittsburgh. | Police brutality--
Pennsylvania--Pittsburgh. | Social change--Pennsylvania--Pittsburgh.
Classification: LCC HV6250.3 .U53 P584 2023 | DDC 362.8809748/86--dc23/eng/20230513
LC record available at https://lccn.loc.gov/2022055228

ISBN 978-1-9821-8727-9
ISBN 978-1-9821-8728-6 (pbk)
ISBN 978-1-9821-8729-3 (ebook)

To my baby sister Leona Tawnae Ford,
I love you and miss you dearly.
You will forever live through me.
Thanks for being my guardian angel.

A man only begins to be a man when he ceases to whine and revile, and commences to search for the hidden justice which regulates his life. And as he adapts his mind to that regulating factor, he ceases to accuse others as the cause of his condition, and builds himself up in strong and noble thoughts; ceases to kick against circumstances, but begins to *use* them as aids to his more rapid progress, and as a means of discovering the hidden powers and possibilities within himself.

—James Allen, *As a Man Thinketh*

BAPTISM OF FIRE

That night I was driving along, bumping music, feeling the sounds vibrate through my body, on my way to my grandmother's house, not a care in the world. All my loved ones would meet at my grandma Peewee's house for Sunday dinner to enjoy her smothered pork chops, fried cabbage, and mashed potatoes. Knowing that I didn't eat pork, she would make a pan of her famous baked chicken covered in her special barbecue sauce. I felt the steering wheel moving easy under my hand, the world passing by at a steady clip, autumn clear and bright but chilly. We called this hoodie weather, and I comfortably sported a Jordan sweat suit. Each moment carried me more into the song until I started to spit the lyrics of "Sideline Story."

Rapping along with J. Cole, I turned the music down a little when I saw a police cruiser driving up the one-way street the wrong way, coming right at me. No headlights or anything. The cruiser pulled to a stop.

I looked at the car, two officers inside, and they were looking at me. I thought, *What the hell are they doing? They don't have the headlights on or anything.* Once they turned, I sped up to the stop sign, made a left, sped up that street, made a right, doing my best to get way ahead of them. I knew they were going to pull me over, so I wanted to save myself the frustration and stop before they forced me to. It was an unwritten rule that if you see a police cruiser and think they may pull you over, stop the car, park, and get out. If they don't see you get out of your car, they don't have probable cause to search your car; that's why I wanted to get ahead of them. I didn't want to get stuck on the side of the road for nothing, again.

I've done this several times before and found it to be an effective way to avoid being harassed. I'd been harassed by cops many times before and found the practices of the "hop out boys" to be quite the inconvenience. They'd stop you for no reason, search your car, and sometimes even pocket any money they found on you. They'd threaten you, sometimes even beat you up, then let you go, most times doing so without any resistance. Losing a couple hundred bucks didn't seem so bad; we were just happy not to be shot or thrown in jail.

I was going across the bridge when I saw them in my rearview, speeding behind me with no lights on. Later I would learn that they were going ninety-three miles an hour on a residential street.

As soon as they put on their sirens, I became annoyed and wished I had stayed home. *Damn*, I said to myself, knowing from experience that some bull was about to happen. I pulled the car over at the next stop sign and killed the music. Although I was irritated, I tried my best to keep my composure. Having an attitude would only make things worse so I took a deep breath, then I put my seat belt on. I thought about my grandma, her chicken, and all the love that would await me at her home once I got through this traffic stop. I could hear my aunt Barbara call me "Handsome." I could imagine the warm welcome from my cousin Shy, who would tell me that I had a million-dollar smile. Perhaps that million-dollar smile could get me out of this ticket.

I rolled my window down, allowing the cool fall air to blow in. I remember seeing the orange glow from streetlights in the dark, the red and blue police lights fluttering through my rearview. I tried to figure out why I was being pulled over in the first place. I mentally traced my steps and could not put my finger on it. *Maybe it's my tinted windows*, I thought. The officer was soon at my window looking in at me, breathing deeply as if to detect the smell of weed. But I didn't smoke. He looked all around the car as if he were trying to find a way in.

I felt something familiar: these officers were messing with me because they could, and I was pissed. I had enough sense to know when you're young and you're Black, police officers can do what they want and say what they want without consequence.

"What did I do?" I asked.

He didn't answer, only snatched my driver's license. I could feel his energy: intense, brute, full of privilege. He had no regard for me as a human being. While he went back to the cruiser to run my license, his partner walked toward my car and stood by my window. At least this officer had a mild temper. I could tell a lot by his body language. His shoulders were relaxed and soft, while his partner was tight and poised, as if he were getting ready for a brawl.

"Where are you going?" he asked.

I said, "To my grandmother's for Sunday dinner."

As he stared me down, I felt the heat start to rise in the car, a crushing pressure in my head. Although his body language was more relaxed, he still had an air of disdain and superiority that I could feel rolling off him. I tried to find the right words to let a little air in.

"Look, I'm not a bad guy. I'm not a wild street dude." I pulled out my phone and showed him pictures of me painting and detailing cars. "I'm a working man just like you."

"That's him," the second officer yelled from his cruiser behind us.

I tensed up. In my side mirror, I could see this second officer walking toward my vehicle from his cruiser. I thought, *What does he mean, "That's him?" I haven't committed any crime. I haven't hurt anyone. What could I have done?* My stomach flooded with nerves.

The initiating officer reached my car again. Now both officers were standing next to my door. The initiating officer asked me if I knew someone named Lamont Ford. I told him I'd never heard of him. There were a lot of Fords in Pittsburgh; my family was mainly from the eastside, Larimer and Homewood. There is a Ford family from the Mon Valley area, but I never heard of any relation to them or anyone named Lamont. He told his partner to go back to the cruiser to look at the photo of Lamont Ford. His partner obliged.

The first officer asked me if I was Lamont Ford. I said no.

"Are you sure you're not Lamont Ford? Have you ever met Lamont Ford? Have you ever been shot before? Where are you from? Is he your cousin? Do you have a brother named Lamont Ford?"

I said no. No. No. No.

"You know you're Lamont Ford," he said. "Why the fuck are you lying to us? If you're lying about being Lamont Ford, it's going to be real bad for you. We're going to kick your stupid black ass."

I gave him my birthdate and address. "You got my driver's license, you got my registration, you got my car insurance. Everything is in my name. What's going on?"

The other officer stomped back from the cruiser. "Yeah, he kinda looks like him. I can't really tell." Then he said, "Why the fuck are you lying to us, scumbag?"

The other officer said, "How did you buy this car?"

"I work. I work just like y'all work."

"Just tell us the truth," the second officer said. "We don't want to make it bad for you."

It was at that moment I became afraid. My whole body tightened with fear, tense as if my skin were shrinking around my flesh. I had to get away. Not because I had committed a crime, but because I knew my life was in danger. I had been harassed by police officers many times over. But this time was different. These officers couldn't hear me. I knew I was not Lamont Ford, but they would not believe me. On top of that, they were relentless. If I could just make it to a gas station or a family member's house, some place where there was light, I would be safe.

The first officer told me to step out of the car and come back to the cruiser to look at the photo of Lamont, which I thought was strange. I've never heard of a police officer asking anyone to go to their cruiser to do anything, especially look at a picture. His request made me more uncomfortable. I thought, *They're trying to get me out of my car to beat me up.*

"No. I know what I look like. I know I'm not Lamont Ford. I don't need to know what he looks like. I don't need to go to your car."

Then the first officer said, "You know what, get your black ass out of this car before we pull you out and whoop your ass."

I was shocked. "What? What do you mean?"

The officers still hadn't told me what I'd done wrong, they were making me out to be someone that I knew I wasn't, and now they were threatening to whoop my ass. My body froze, the pit in my stomach grew more intense, my eyes watered with anger, fear, and confusion. He reached his hand through my window, unlocked the door, and opened it. Now they were on me, their hands trying to yank me out of the car.

"What are you doing? Why are y'all doing this to me? Get off me, man."

They kept yanking and pulling. I firmly wrapped my arms around the steering wheel. I did not want to leave my car. I felt like if I let go, I would never see my family again. The officers had guns to match their overzealous behavior and I did not want to be shot. My biggest fear was these officers pulling me out of the car, saying they thought I had a gun, and shooting me in the back. If I stayed inside of my car, I would be safe.

The officers struggled while pulling me out of the car. I held firmly on to the steering wheel, put the car into drive, and pressed the gas as hard as I could. Not two seconds passed before I heard gunshots.

Pop pop pop pop pop.

I felt bullets exploding in my body before I lost control of the steering wheel. The smell of gunpowder saturated my vehicle. I lost consciousness and crashed. The airbag mushroomed up into my face and body. What had just happened? Where'd the gunshots come from? With my face mashed into the airbag, head pounding from impact, I tried to put two and two together, question and question. I didn't know that a third cop had jumped into the passenger seat next to me. He'd shot me, five times.

I felt them pulling me from behind the wheel of the car. Felt myself being slammed into the concrete facedown. Heard the clink of handcuffs and felt metal biting into my wrists. The pain from the bullets drowned out the pain from the handcuffs.

They were shouting at me. "Fuck! Where's the drugs? Where's the guns?"

One officer knelt right next to my head and said, "I hope you fucking die."

Truth be told, I wasn't sure if I wanted to live or die. I was only nineteen years old, but I'd taken so many beatings in life that I figured death couldn't be so bad. If my ten-year-old sister could die, so could I. Had she felt pain? Had she been scared? Was I? If anything, I was afraid that no one would know the facts: that these officers wanted to kill me, although I'd done everything I could to show them that I was innocent. I did not want my life to end with lies tarnishing my legacy. I wasn't crazy, I wasn't a criminal, I wasn't violent. I didn't want to hurt anyone.

I remember lying there, facedown on the ground, taking slow deep breaths, inhaling, exhaling, slow and deep. I could smell my hoodie burning, could feel blood pouring out of my body. Me, Leon Ford, inching closer to death. I was so afraid of dying that I stopped feeling pain.

"Where's the guns? Where are the fucking drugs?" they repeated, over and over.

Tears slid down my face. It was hard to get the words out.

"I have no weapons or drugs." I said it again: "I have no weapons or drugs."

Would I die?

"Why did y'all shoot me, man. Y'all shot me!" I could feel warm blood oozing from my chest, could taste blood in my mouth. I spit it out on the concrete. The lights from the squad cars blinded me, an exploding whiteness. I could not hear myself scream beneath the sound of the sirens, only the voices of the officers shouting "Fuck!" as they rummaged through the trunk of my car hoping to find guns, drugs, something. I tried to move, but my body was stiff, heavy, taken over by a tingling sensation. God, please let the ambulance come. My parents couldn't bear losing another child. I wanted to live.

I continued to breathe, even counted my breaths to make sure that I stayed conscious. Still, my mind began to drift, my conscious-ness moving in waves, going in and out. Soon I lost count of my breaths. Had I ever started counting or was it merely a thought? My eyelids felt heavy.

When I closed my eyes, I could feel myself leaving my body. When I opened my eyes, I could feel myself back in my body. Each time I closed my eyes it felt like an hour had passed, a day. I saw a vision of my unborn son. With every blink, a new vision came. Then my eyes shut, and I felt my spirit leave my body, a strange sensation of peace. I stood looking down at my corporeal form lying there on the sidewalk. The police, the lights, and sirens gone now, only this other form of me, pure consciousness. A feeling of peace that I'd never experienced. It was a feeling I was to have again many times in the days, months, and years to come.

At some point my eyes closed and I drifted, finding my-self looking down at a white casket with gold trim, looking at my corpse dressed to the nines in an all-white suit, a gold chain around my neck. My mom stood there crying, my father next to her with murder in his eyes. All my siblings were present, along with my grandmother and my cousins. My child's mother rubbed her swollen stomach, sobbing for her unborn, fatherless child. Deep sorrow soaked the room, everyone was screaming or shedding tears or lost in their thoughts. My aunts did their best to console my parents for the loss of their second child. My aunt Terri held my mom's hand while my aunt Nicky softly rubbed my dad's shoulder.

My father whispered, "You know I had to send my little nigga out in style."

While my family grieved for me, I grieved for them.

I closed my eyes and saw police officers surrounding my dad as he emptied the clip of his semiautomatic, striking all of them dead. I could not allow that to happen. If my father did that, he would be dead, too. Then who would raise my son? The possibility of my father being hurt forced me to open my eyes. Although death felt more peaceful, I decided to live, to keep my eyes open and continue to breathe. I sacrificed eternal peace to prevent my family from experiencing even more heartache.

More officers swarmed the scene. The sirens got louder and the lights brighter. Finally, I felt a warm hand on my neck, checking my pulse. It was the EMTs. They rolled me over onto my back, but I could see nothing beyond the bright lights. I felt them lift me inside the ambulance. They cut my clothes off and asked me for my name. I heard words fall from my mouth: "My name is Leon Ford. My birthday is 3-16-93." Then I repeated the information again, and still again, and kept repeating it, over and over, to stop myself from drifting out of consciousness. I even gave them my mom's name, dad's name, and grandma's name along with their phone numbers and addresses. The light on the ceiling of the ambulance glowed brighter and brighter into nothingness. No police, no sirens, no lights, no breathing or counting, only darkness.

In many ways, my life started that night.

It was November 11, 2012, when a Pittsburgh cop shot me five times and left me paralyzed below the waist. Know this: I have always been a person of importance. I have always been resilient. My life has always mattered.

I am Leon Ford, phoenix who rises from the ashes.

ONE
ASHES

1
LITTLE BIT'S SON

The mortician had done his best, but Darnell didn't look real to me lying there in the coffin, that velvet-cushioned box. Recently released from jail, he had been shot in the head at a dice game. Standing there looking down at him, all I could think about was his big bright smile. I was five years old. My earliest memories are permeated by death. It made me and everyone in my community anticipate a short life. The fear of dying young loomed over all of us.

I took my place on the pew next to my grandma Peewee, my mom, and my aunt Terri, three women dressed in black. And crying. Sobbing. What could I do to comfort them? I started to pass tissues out. Gave my grandma a tissue, my aunt a tissue, my mom, and even my sister Shalaia, who was four years older than me. Like me, she was experiencing death for the first time. As Lil Bit's son, it was second nature for me to be a comforter. I watched my dad comfort the women in my family and figured I should do the same. I was a compassionate child, a giver, quick to share my food, even if I had already taken a bite. My mom would affirm me by smiling and marveling at my cuteness. "Aww boo, you're so thoughtful," she would say, then take a fake nibble. Although I wanted to cry with my loved ones, I had to be strong for them. Looking at the casket, my eyes welled up, but I refused to let a tear fall. I sat there on the hard pew, looking at all the mourners and the bright flowers, listening to the organ player, the loud sobs, the pastor preaching.

That was my first time in a church. Although we were believers, we were not a churchgoing family. My mom would often say that it is not about the religion; it's about the relationship.

Darnell's dad, my uncle Teddy, circulated through the mourners, cheerful, smiling, trying his best to make sure everybody else was comfortable although he had lost his son. I'm sure he was heartbroken, grieving. However, he was a strong man, one who could suppress his pain to comfort his family, our family. If you had not known Darnell was his son, you would not have assumed he was burying his child. He was clean-cut, charismatic, and loving. I didn't know how a man should grieve. I figured there would be more tears. I watched Mr. Rogers almost every day and often he would talk about feelings and loss. He would use words like "sad," "lonely," "angry," and "frightened." My uncle Teddy didn't show any of these emotions. Mr. Rogers would say "look for the people who are helping." Even though my uncle had lost his son, he was still able to be a helper. I too wanted to be a helper and learned a valuable lesson that day: even if someone hurts me or a loved one, even if I am angry, sad, or frightened, I could still be a helper.

After the service was over, I ran up to my father. For me, he was a tower I could climb and a god I could look up to: strong enough to hold me up to the sky but scary enough to make bad men stay away.

"Dad, guess what?"

"What's up, soldier?"

"I didn't cry."

He opened his mouth and grinned his approval, his gold tooth flashing. "My man."

I was so proud of myself.

He always told me, "Big boys don't cry." Although I'd felt my tears building for Darnell, who I'd just played football with a few days earlier, I had pushed them down.

I was happy I had proven that I could be strong like him and my uncle, two men who could both stand in the face of adversity without losing the essence of who they were: loving, charismatic, joyous. I longed to be like them one day.

Born Leon Ford but known on the streets as Little Bit, my father was an infamous drug kingpin in Pittsburgh, a mastermind who could do business in any neighborhood in the city no matter what gang controlled the turf. This mobility allowed him to make a lot of money and earn respect. And where we come from, cash is king, and respect is God. After that day, I knew I wanted that respect. I would live for it.

———

A week or two after the funeral, my father made me breakfast as he usually did when I stayed at his house. I woke up to the smell of crisp bacon, scrambled cheese eggs, French toast, grits, freshly cut fruit, and orange juice. The light from the morning sun shined through my bedroom window. I stretched my arms to the ceiling and got out of bed, then stumbled to the kitchen to eat. My dad was already there, full of energy. He was always upbeat, especially when he made other people happy, and that day I would be the lucky recipient of his joy.

"Yo, dawg, you're going to be G'd up today. I want you to wear your suit to school." He chuckled and smiled.

I quickly ate my breakfast and went to my dad's room where he had my clothes laid out.

"Did you brush your teeth?" he asked.

I whispered, "No, I was—"

He cut me off. "Listen, dawg, you got a million-dollar smile, you don't want teeth like crackhead Larry. His shit all fucked up. All the girls gone call you shitty mouth Lee."

We both laughed.

I brushed my teeth in his bathroom in one sink while he brushed his in the other. "Dad, why do you have two sinks in your bathroom—and that big tub and a shower?"

"Luxury, son. When you work hard you deserve to treat yourself to the best life has to offer. That's why today you're wearing a tailored suit. You worked hard and got on the honor roll, and this is your reward."

Then he dressed me up in a shiny blue suit.

He asked me, "Yo, dawg, which car do you wanna drive today?"

This was our routine. Each morning, he would let me choose the car we would take to my school. For a five-year-old, the choice was empowering.

At the time, he owned four cars: a Mercedes, a nice BMW, a Land Cruiser, and a Corvette, all brand new. I picked the Mercedes, mostly because I found the logo appealing. Plus, it was the same car DMX drove in the movie *Belly* I had watched with my older brothers Reese and Dale. I thought it was cool that my dad could afford the same cars as rappers. To me, my dad was cooler than any rapper on TV.

We were soon on the road, me buckled up safe and secure in the front seat as the Lenny Williams classic "'Cause I Love You" spilled from the speakers. Our song. Each morning during the ride, my father would play the song so that we could sing it together. I screamed from the top of my lungs "Girl you know I, I, I love you." My dad laughed hysterically. I could see the joy in his eyes. Once the song ended, he turned on the radio to WAMO, the R&B station. He loved R&B music, his favorite, but we both loved the comedian who had a morning program on the station. The guy talked in a funny voice, and my father and I would crack up at his jokes. Whenever my father opened his mouth, I could see his gold tooth sparkle. One day I would have a gold tooth just like him.

We stopped at a small bakery to buy me some donuts and chocolate milk, also part of our routine. I loved chocolate milk. I would shake it up so that it had bubbles at the top when I opened it. To me, shaking the milk made it have more flavor. Finally, we pulled up outside my school, Fort Pitt Elementary in Garfield, which sat on the top of the hill across from the projects where many of my family members lived and where my mother had an apartment. We would stay there when we weren't with my father in the suburbs.

My father said, "Here, dawg, give these to your teacher." He reached over the seat and passed me a bouquet of roses, bright and fragrant. I hopped out of the Mercedes.

The teachers standing outside the building started complimenting me. "Oh, look at you, little spiffy man. He's spiffy right there."

I felt like a superstar in my tailor-made suit, hopping out of a brand-new Benz. I knew something was different about my life compared to people around me. None of my friends' parents drove a Mercedes or had an inground pool and I never saw any kids wear tailored suits to school.

Once inside the classroom, I presented the roses to my teacher. She buried her face in the flowers to imbibe their smell. Then she thanked me and gave me a hug. I took my seat.

Sometime after lunch, I remember doing my work in class then looking up and seeing my mom and dad peeking at me through the window of the classroom door. They would randomly pop up at my school sometimes. They opened the door and entered the room in matching Coogi sweaters. I knew that they lived in different homes, but here they were at my school dressed in matching, designer clothes. Normal parents don't show up in your classroom wearing expensive sweaters. My mom with her pretty round face, high cheekbones, and big eyes. Her hair sculptured in finger waves. Gold chains encircled her neck, and huge gold door-knocker earrings hung from her ears. My dad rocked a gold Cuban link chain with a Mercedes-Benz charm, the same model that he drove. Both my parents wore Rolex watches.

I smiled as my classmates marveled at my parents. They came over and hugged me.

My mom gave me flowers and candy, while my dad presented the class with a gift, a box of twenty cupcakes, one for each classmate. Everyone became raucous and happy as my dad started to distribute the treats.

My mom said, "We love you so much, Leon. We'll see you later, boo."

I knew my mom meant what she said. I could deeply feel her love. My mom was a beautiful woman, not just her looks, but her presence radiated warmth. She made me feel safe in a way different from my dad. While my dad was a protector, outspoken and edgy, my mom had a calming spirit.

The entire class applauded my parents' departure. I was already a popular kid, but the cupcakes made my classmates love me all that more. I felt special, and my teacher and classmates treated me special because of the way my parents treated me.

Once the class settled down, I gave the flowers to Rihanna, the pretty smooth-skinned girl with pigtails who sat next to me. I had a crush on her.

She smiled. "This is nice." Shy, she looked at me without making eye contact.

I thought one day her and I would show up to our son's class with nice clothes, jewelry, flowers, and cupcakes. The thought made me smile.

After school, I walked out the building with the other kids then hooked up with my cousins from the Garfield Projects. I liked being in the suburbs with my dad, but the hood was more exciting. Everybody knew me and I knew everybody and had the liberty to go anywhere I wanted and explore. I was Lil Bit and Tawn's son. People affirmed and respected me. People loved me. Some called me Professor because of the way my dad dressed me and because I was so talkative and curious. People would compliment me: "Oh, you're so handsome, you have the best smile," they would say. "You're Lil Bit's son, right? You're going to be something great one day." Or, "You have a big smile just like Tawn."

The projects were home: a relative or a friend of the family lived in almost every row of the projects. My grandma Peewee's house was on one row. My grandma Flo's house was about three rows away. My mom's house was across the street. My grandma Peewee's sisters all lived in the projects: my aunts Barbara, Kim, Linda, and Diane. And her brothers, my uncles Robert, Teddy, and Harry, all shared one house with their many kids. Even if they didn't live there full time, I would see them often because we were a close-knit family. I would find my aunts and uncles either cooking in their homes or outside either drinking or just chilling and relaxing. Summertime in the projects smelled like charcoal, fresh cut grass, weed, and beer.

My cousins Tawana and Tyrone would babysit me when my mother needed them, too. Tawana always wanted a son and would dress me up and take me all over the neighborhood. Tyrone loved boxing and would always teach me how to throw my hands. He would say, "Let me see your guard, Lee," and I would put my hands up and throw bunches. My cousins Luv, Robbie, and Raymon were all older than me and were always up for an adventure. They had to put up with my running behind them and trying to get into the mix. We would play football, chase girls around the neighborhood, and even sometimes crunch up old leaves and smoke them in rolled up paper. We could play outside well past sundown without fear. Occasionally drive-bys would have us ducking bullets, but it was a norm we quickly adapted to. My favorite time of day was right before dark: when I could watch my grandma play spades with my aunts and uncles around the dinner table or my cousins shoot dice on the stoop of the weed lady's porch. A couple dollars were always destined to come my way.

I could hear Anita Baker's "Caught Up in the Rapture" playing in the background. My grandma Peewee smiling as she showed me her hand of cards. I didn't know what the cards meant, but I knew she was going to win because she was happy. "Come on, mutherfuck-aaa," she would say to my aunts and uncles. Usually if she was losing, she wouldn't be this excited. "I got you, Grandson. This is the one right here. After this game I'm going to give you a couple dollars."

My grandma always kept money in my pocket. Even if I had money, she would give me more. The spades game with my grandma and her crowd was calmer than the dice game. In the distance you could hear the dice game, the older guys arguing as usual, red flags hanging from their pockets. My aunt Barbara told me, "Stay away from them, Handsome. Them fools ain't got no sense."

Although we stayed in the projects, we never lacked for anything. My family members in the projects didn't have money like my dad, but I never looked at them as being poor because they had everything they needed. *We* had everything we needed. We always had something to eat, somewhere to eat, and something to do. Not to mention the love. My grandma Peewee would say "We're rich in spirit." I believed her because life was always good and love was always present. Even among those in my family who struggled with alcoholism or drug abuse. They were still happy and thriving off our most important possession: family.

I didn't realize until I got older that many of my aunts, my grandma's sisters, were on drugs or that my grandma Flo and my uncle Sonny were alcoholics. It was as if a generational curse had been placed on my family. A firecracker, my grandma Flo drank a lot and cussed people out. As my father says, "She was crazy as hell. Nobody would or could talk crazy to her, but she would talk crazy to every-motherfucking-body else." I remember the way she would say, "When I die, bury me upside down so you all can kiss my ass." Although many things she said hurt, we still found humor in her feisty behavior.

Uncle Sonny, my grandma Peewee's uncle, smelled like liquor, coming through his pores. Although a wino, he was a funny dude. He walked around singing and dancing like Michael Jackson. He would slap his thighs and knees, chest, and even mouth while singing, "Hambone have you heard, momma's gonna buy you a mockingbird. If that mockingbird don't sing, momma's gonna buy you a diamond ring. If that diamond ring don't shine, momma's gonna buy you a gallon of wine."

My grandma hated this song, but Uncle Sonny would always make me and everyone in the projects laugh.

"Hambone went to the sto. He pissed on the counter and shit on the flo. He wiped his ass with a piece of ham. Made the preacha man say goddamn."

Tears of laughter would pour down my face. Everyone loved Uncle Sonny and he made everyone laugh, even at the expense of being kicked out by my grandma for a few hours.

When Uncle Sonny came over to Peewee's house for a cookout or some other family gathering, it was my job to follow him to the bathroom and make sure he didn't go in nobody's room to steal something. I would spy on him through the bathroom door keyhole and see him going through all the cabinets and shelves, but I never told anyone because I didn't want him to get beat up.

In Garfield, I was raised by survivors who taught me how to see the world, how to resolve conflict, how to provide for myself and others, and how to rise above circumstances beyond my control. My paternal relations managed to survive with hustler's ambition, grit, toughness, and respect, while my maternal relatives rooted their survival in love, togetherness, and forgiveness.

I don't remember any arguments or disputes between maternal family members. Close-knit, they are happy and forgiving and kind to others. Their house in the Garfield Projects was known as the Greens's house. The door was always wide open. The residence smelled like Pine-Sol since somebody was always mopping the floor. Pine-Sol, grease, cigarettes, and beer, those are the smells I remember. While my grandma Flo served meals to flip a profit, my grandma Peewee cooked for anybody who was hungry. Everybody was welcome at the Greens's house. Everybody came to the Greens's house. Everybody loved the Greens. Grandma Peewee would have music playing, mostly the R&B music that she loved: Luther Vandross, Marvin Gaye, the Temptations, Minnie Riperton, Stevie Wonder, and Aretha Franklin. And she would be trying to get people to dance. She loved to dance.

These are the two worlds that I come from, the Fords and the Greens.

2

MY PARENTS' CODE

From a young age, my parents taught me to live by a code. A means of survival that still lives inside me today.

When I wanted to stay with my mom, I stayed with her, and when I wanted to stay with my dad, I stayed with him. My dad's house was a place of adventure with a huge saltwater aquarium flashing bright fish, baby alligators swimming in the backyard pond, an inground swimming pool, a park, and four cars in the garage. We would feed the alligators white mice that we purchased from a pet store. My dad had a treehouse built that we would climb. Sometimes I would be brave, climb to the top and jump off. We would play video games or try to play pool on my dad's huge pool table. Green chalk would be all over our fingertips from rubbing the square block on the top of the pool sticks. My father was a year-round Santa who showered my two siblings and me with presents. We got brand-new sneakers every weekend; I loved to show off every new pair of Jordans. He bought us yo-yos and Pokémon cards. His house was packed with mini motor scooters, dirt bikes, and go-carts. Anything we wanted. Everything we wanted.

I would ask my dad to let my cousins Luv, Robbie, and Raymon come over to the house. Sometimes my brothers Reese and Dale would be there too, my dad's children from another relationship. My cousins and brothers were all five to seven years older than me. They would play Super Mario 64, 007, and other console games. I would love to watch them play and enjoy their company, but I also didn't like the way they treated me because I was younger than them. They wouldn't let me play or would make me wait to play after they had, even though it was my game.

My dad stayed on one side of the enormous house, while I stayed with my brothers and cousins on the other side. We'd run through the massive halls finding spots—inside the Jacuzzi, or under the pool table stacked with money counters, or between one of the two different living rooms.

But being the youngest was rough: once they caught me, they would make me eat fish food or try to put me in the oven. I would scream and cry, but I couldn't tell my dad. My dad never respected a snitch, even if it was his own son. He would beat all of them for bullying me, then beat me for snitching.

Still, I liked hanging with my brothers and cousins and giving them hell. I always tried my best to hold my own with the "big boys." They would punch me in the chest. Since I was smaller and weaker, I knew punching them back would do little to no damage. So I went for their nuts, strategically leveling the playing field. Luv was six years older than me and was tighter with my cousins Robbie and Ray, who were closer in age. He lived directly behind my grandma Flo and was always around. I'd punch Luv in his jewels when he least expected it and run off laughing. He could be talking to someone, then *boop*, I would hit him and roll out. He'd double over. "Yo, come on, bro." He wouldn't even try to chase me because he'd be in too much pain. "Yo, what the fuck's wrong with this little dude?" I'd rather hit Luv because Robbie, Raymon, or my brothers would hit me back. Luv would just laugh the pain away.

I was used to having my older cousins around, and I spent as much time as I could with them in the Garfield Projects. Once, when I was about six years old, I was hanging with Luv, Robbie, and Raymon, and some other kids, throwing rocks at a beehive. The hive was inside a sneaker hanging from a telephone line right behind my grandma Flo's house. The older guys were throwing bricks at the beehive, trying to knock it down, while I threw rocks. Every time we hit it, bees would swarm out. So we just kept throwing, big fun. For some reason, I ran under the hive, and somebody threw a brick and cracked me right in the back of the head.

At first, I didn't know what had happened, only that it hurt like hell. Then I saw the blood snaking down my torso. My whole scalp had split wide open. I was overcome by pain and anger, but I was also thrilled. In the projects you had to be rough, and even at six years old I knew having stitches would serve me up some bragging rights.

My brothers Reese and Dale jumped on the dude who threw the brick, their first reaction. Not that the dude meant to hit me. But we were taught, if somebody hurt you or your brothers, hurt them worse.

I never shed a tear. I was Little Bit's son.

My father molded me and my male cousins to be aggressive. We weren't allowed to cry, snitch, or do anything that would go against our legacy, which was to become "thoroughbreds." In his eyes, he would have failed as a father if we were soft, because the world was unforgiving. In his mind, he needed to prepare us for the hard truth: when you're a Black man in America, life isn't fair. To survive, you had to be tough. No exceptions.

We would have big cookouts behind my grandma Flo's house and boxing matches. My dad would get the boxing gloves, and we would fight while he looked on.

By the time I was seven years old, I gained a reputation as a fighter, for being good with my fists. I was always getting into tussles. I was one of those dudes that nobody wanted to mess with. Although I enjoyed winning fights, I never really enjoyed fighting.

I was not the type to start something, but once provoked, I would fuck up my opponent while my older cousins cheered me on.

At school, during Miss Gray's class, I got into my first real fight, when another dude called Rihanna a bitch. Miss Gray pulled us apart.

I received a suspension. It was a serious matter. I feared that my father would be upset. Instead, he asked me, "Did you win?" I nodded. He smiled, relishing the fact that his namesake could handle himself. From that moment on, I knew being a fighter would make my dad proud, even if it meant that the dominant society of law-abiding, working people didn't approve.

My father ran with several women. I knew all of them; I even played with their kids. He would say, "Don't tell your mom my business. Make sure of that. If she asks you anything, tell her, ask your dad." I never told my mom about my dad's side pieces. He would brag to his friends that I was "a thorough lil nigga," an affirmation that meant the world to me. I was my dad's confidant and running buddy. I grew up loving my sisters and my mother but distrusting women overall. That was what my father taught me.

My mother never turned my siblings and me against my dad no matter what they went through. For the most part, their fights were grown-ups' business and we stayed out of it. Later, I would learn that she became attracted to him because, as an older man, she saw him as a father figure. Her father had never been in her life. I also wonder if she saw someone else under the surface—the lost boy who needed someone to love him unconditionally. A healer with a forgiving heart, my mom can see the good in others, whatever their shortcomings. People would always compliment my mom about her smile and good energy. She would say, "It doesn't cost anything to be a good person."

She always had words of love, support, and encouragement for all of us. If I came home from school and told her I wanted to be a fireman, she would buy me a helmet. If my older sister Shalaia said she wanted to be a doctor, Mom would buy her a toy stethoscope. To this day, she has the warmest smile. Patient and kind, she encouraged me and my sisters to chase our dreams no matter how big or small. She would listen to us in a way that made us feel heard. She was thoughtful, giving gifts she knew we wanted even if she did not have the kind of money my dad had at his disposal. In every action, she made us feel loved, valued, and appreciated.

As unlike as they were as people, my parents shared a common worldview. They were both honest with me and my siblings. They saw the importance of protecting me with truth, instead of sheltering me. When I asked them questions, my parents answered to the best of their abilities with the truth. They found innovative means to express reality in a way that I could understand, and I think that really helped me evolve as a person, as a man.

I had friends whose mothers and fathers sugarcoated things, and those are my same friends who are getting in trouble now. Shelly, one of my dad's childhood friends, was addicted to heroin. Her mom had also been addicted to heroin, a fact I knew because my dad had been honest with me and told me. I remember him saying to me, "Yeah, Shelly used to be fine as hell. We all wanted her, but she gave it up to some older dude. The nigga turned her out and before we knew it, she was getting high." The harsh realities of the hood.

I remember feeling sad for Shelly. Before I learned her story, I looked at her and other crackheads like animals. I remember making jokes about them with my cousins and even sometimes throwing rocks at them. Crackheads were dirty and they smelled bad. But my dad's words sank into my head: "Everyone has a story." My mom would simply say, "Be nice to people, you never know what they're going through." She practiced what she preached and set a good example. She was kind to everybody, no matter who they were or what they did for a living. She would have long conversations with women like Shelly or any of the crackheads in the neighborhood. She would say, "Don't call them crackheads. They're just sick right now." She

didn't have to share stories. My dad's truth was vivid enough for a
six-year-old.

Thinking back, I believe my dad tried to create a bubble around me
to insulate me from all the things he had to suffer and endure growing up in segregated Pittsburgh. My dad had it rough from the day he
was born in 1966 in Larimer, one of the city's worst neighborhoods.

Now, people did not play with my father, and they did not play
with his family. He had friends who weren't tough, but off of his
strength, they were protected. Nobody messed with them. Sometimes his enemies showed him more respect and loyalty than his
friends.

Although he was a man who some feared, he had a loving side.
He did his best to make sure those he cared about were comfortable
and safe. He provided substantial financial support for the Little
League football team that I started playing for when I was five years
old. He helped save people's homes from foreclosure. He helped pay
for funerals and helped deter young men from the streets by putting
money in their pockets and keeping it real about the harsh realities
of the criminal lifestyle. I remember being in the backseat of his car
once and hearing him tell a young guy standing on the corner, "Stay
in school, dawg. This shit ain't for you. The only way out of this game
is a cell or a casket. Ain't nothing good going to come out of the
street life."

He raised me to be myself. I never heard him say, "You got to
work one hundred times harder than white people." Instead, he
would tell me, "Man, be yourself. You're already great."

I watched him build relationships. He taught me to see others
as they are. He didn't trust many people, but still had the ability to
go into any space and make friends, a quality I admired. I learned
much—how to be loyal, honest, authentic—just from watching

him. He never told me, "Hey, Leon, you do this like this." He let his life be an example. He would always say, "Even a bad example is a good example for what not to be."

One morning, my dad and I came out of the shop with my donuts and chocolate milk, only to find some guy leaning up against the passenger door of my dad's car. I had never seen a man so tall and skinny. He was all angles like a praying mantis.

"Oh, if it ain't Lil Bit," the man said. He sucked his teeth.

My dad said, "I know one thing. You better get yo ass off my car."

"Nigga, you think I'm scared of you? I don't give a fuck who you are. I'll kick yo muthafuckin ass."

Fear moved through my body.

"I know one thing for sure, ain't no nigga going to disrespect me, especially in front of my son." My dad looked at me and smiled. "Watch this, dawg."

My dad grabbed the dude by the throat, swung behind him and placed him in a chokehold, then choked the guy unconscious and let him fall to the sidewalk. My dad kicked him in the head, went in his pockets, took his money, and gave it to a homeless person sitting on an orange milk crate. The homeless man smiled.

The man that my dad choked got up and said, "Damn, Bit. I was just playing." Then ran off.

My father told me, "Never let anyone play with you. They'll try you and act like they're joking. They're just trying to see if they can get out on you. I've been wanting to beat this nigga's ass for a long time. He's the neighborhood bully. I watched him disrespect all the project dudes and waited for him to try me. He finally grew some balls to try me. He got the right one today." He smiled. "Yo, dawg, never be a bully. They always meet their match. Come on, Lee Dawg. Let's get out of here."

My fear turned into excitement. My dad seemed invincible.

3

LOCKED UP

On January 30, 1999, less than two months before my sixth birthday, my father was ambushed by some guys in his car and shot in the stomach. I don't know who the guys were, but I assumed that they were either trying to rob him or had shot him in retaliation. I remembered that in *Menace II Society* the main character, Caine, was murdered by a guy he had beat up. I figured maybe the guy my dad choked out had come back to kill him. Because he and I were always together, many people thought that I'd been in the car with him when he was shot. He was supposed to pick me up from my grandma Flo's house but never came. I would dial the number to his pager all night until he called back.

"Dada, are you coming to get me"?

"Lee Dawg, I'll get you after I bust this move."

By this time, I was used to this phrase "bust a move." I didn't really know what he was doing when he was busting moves, but I knew he was busy. I sat at my grandma's all night, waiting for my dad to arrive. Her house reeked of cigarette smoke. Erykah Badu played in the background, her voice plaintive and echoing, like a forgotten warning. I remember thinking, *Is she talking about my cousin Tyrone in this song?*

The next morning my grandma was on the phone. I couldn't hear what she was saying but I could feel that something was wrong. I looked out of the window to see my aunt Nicky parking her purple Dodge Durango, Robbie and Raymon jumping out of the backseat. Seeing them was like erasing the chalkboard. I got a burst of energy. Maybe we would play football. I ran downstairs, tripping over the shoes that my grandma had neatly placed on the steps, sending them tumbling. I didn't stop, racing toward my cousins who'd save me from the stench of Grandma's cigarettes.

I got outside to the front yard, and that's when I saw the confusion on their faces. They didn't seem like the happy cousins who'd normally welcome me. Lines twisted up Robbie's naturally goofy face, his jaw hanging like it weighed five pounds. Raymon's face seemed even more angular, his chin sharp enough to chop ice. They were worried, they were afraid. My grandma's row in the projects was normally loud, neighbors outside chatting, spending their days gossiping about who was sleeping with who on the downlow, or who just came home from prison, or about some "stupid bitch" or "trifling nigga." Their high laughs and declarations of "Ain't that the truth" were the soundtrack to my childhood. But today, suddenly, it was quiet as a tomb.

Raymon's eyes were watering. "Your dad was shot last night, but we aren't supposed to tell you."

My heart broke with fear. Was my dad dead?

On the way to visit him in the hospital, all I could think about was my cousin Darnell laid up inside that box. Would my dad suffer the same fate? Trepidation moved through my body. My dad was always surging with life and laughter. I couldn't imagine him lifeless in a casket. Plus, I'd seen his muscle; I knew he could fight. As the road sped by, a weight started to lift. How could a bullet penetrate his muscles? Impossible. He would survive. One thing I knew for sure, no matter what happened, I would not cry.

The last thing I expected to see when I entered the room was my dad laid up in bed looking comfortable, perfectly relaxed. A colostomy bag extended from his abdomen, but he was as calm as ever.

At the sight of visitors, he lit up. "Yeah, man," he said. "Those niggas were out to get me. I ain't sweating it." He smiled, flashing his gold front tooth. He started cracking jokes, his way of letting us know that he was okay.

———

Once again, I learned from his example. I had to be a big boy, no crying, no exceptions.

The surgery left my dad with a zipper scar running down his torso, breaking his tattoo in half under his sternum. Now, it read: Me Against . . . The World, with a faint white line running through it. As a kid, I wished I could have a similar scar. To me, it symbolized that he was a survivor. I would ask him if it hurt. He would smile and say, "It ain't nothin to a soldier." He was at war, like all of us.

After he was released from the hospital, his recovery required that he keep a colostomy bag attached to his abdomen. He would wear what he called his "shitbag" for several months. The bag attached to his belly under his shirt and every so often filled up with poop. It was disgusting and made me want to throw up anytime he would have to change the bag. When my brother Reese and I were in the car with him and we'd start our habitual arguing and roughhousing over who could sit in the front seat, he'd now found a wicked way of punishing us. He would roll up the windows then unhook the colostomy bag and let the odor fill the car. We pinched our noses, coughing furiously as we begged for fresh air.

My dad's booming laugh echoed through the car, a hard lesson learned. "Y'all keep fighting, y'all gonna smell this bag. I can do this all day."

I knew in those moments that my dad would recover, that he was strong.

On the morning of April 19, 2000, shortly after I turned seven years old, I was at my mother's house sleeping in my bright red car bed when a loud noise jolted me awake. *Boom!* It sounded like a bomb had exploded inside of our house. Shaking, I ran toward my mom's room for her protection.

I was shocked to see several officers with huge guns, helmets, and vests storming the house. One of the officers snatched me up and sat me on the couch next to my mom. They had put her hands behind her back and handcuffed them. Her face was soaked with tears. My sisters were at my aunt's house, which I later learned got raided along with the many other homes my dad would frequent. My dad wasn't at home with us, but the officers still took the liberty of searching the house, top to bottom. They violently flipped beds, threw drawers across our rooms, emptied closets, and even cut couches. I was terrified. Although they looked more like soldiers I'd seen in movies, I knew they were feds, DEA and FBI agents, their initials in big, bright letters on their bulletproof vests.

They kept screaming at my mom, "Where the fuck are the drugs? Where are the guns? We know this is his stash house."

My mother's lips were sealed with fear and confusion.

"If you don't tell us something, we're going to take you to jail and put your kids in the system."

As hard as I squeezed, I couldn't stop the tears from slipping out. I knew big boys weren't supposed to cry, but I didn't feel big or tough. I wasn't a soldier. I was helpless. I didn't want my mom to be hurt. I didn't want her to go to jail. I didn't want to be in the system, to have to live in one of those foster homes or juvenile facilities that I'd heard people talk about.

Finally, they stopped their yelling and took the handcuffs off her wrists, leaving our house ransacked.

My grandma Peewee came to help her clean up. "Wow, Tawn, they really cut up these nice couches. We'll replace them. Don't worry," she said, in a soft, consoling tone. Any time my mom was in trouble, my grandma was by her side. She was our safe haven.

Soon after, Uncle Rocky told me my father was arrested and indicted in federal court on several counts of drug trafficking. The story was all over the news. This was the first time I had heard someone describe my father as a "kingpin." I remember my uncle Wolf, my father's older brother, telling me, "It's over for your dad. He'll probably never get out."

I could not wrap my head around the idea that my father had been arrested. What man was strong enough to place my dad in handcuffs? What handcuffs were strong enough to hold him? The television news said that he was dangerous, but I couldn't see it. He was just my dad. The guy who gave football coaches stacks of cash to pay for uniforms. The one who took care of my mom, aunts, uncles, grandparents, his friends, my cousins, my siblings, everyone he loved. He was my provider and protector. Who would protect me now? Worry, anger, and confusion flowed through me. Everyone smiled when he came around, everyone loved my dad. I could not understand why anyone would want to shoot him or why the police wanted to arrest him. I couldn't understand why people wanted to take my dad away from me.

My teachers were all white, and after my dad's indictment, they started to treat me differently. I went from being the teacher's pet to a criminal-in-training. Nothing changed about my behavior. I was always talkative, fun, and sometimes rambunctious. But before this, the teachers would laugh at my jokes and treat me nicely. Once my dad was arrested, I would get reprimanded for the smallest infraction. Before my dad was indicted, I was never given lunch detention for talking. I guess my teacher thought she had to be a little harder on me to keep me out of trouble. In the halls of the school, I would chance upon them staring at me and talking among themselves about how my father was a drug dealer. It made me feel like a disgrace. And for any small infraction, a teacher would chastise me in the harshest language.

"Leon, stop doing that. Do you want to end up like your dad?"

This made me boil inside. I would think, *My dad has way more money than this stupid teacher.*

I moved through life with a sense of pride and dignity, so I couldn't understand why these teachers treated me as an inferior. On the streets of my neighborhood, things were different. I would be at football games and older guys from many different neighborhoods would come up to me and say, "Yo, ain't you Bit's son"? I could feel their deep reverence for my dad. This made me proud.

I would reply with confidence, "Yeah, that's my dad."

They'd say, "He's a real nigga, a solid nigga. He held it down."

I soon realized that on top of his reputation in the streets, he was respected because he didn't rat anyone out when he was busted. The guys would give me and my siblings money whenever they would see us. It felt good to be Bit's son. In the neighborhood, my dad's name held weight, and as his namesake, mine did, too.

I realized that I lived in two worlds. In one, Black people created their own culture as a means of survival, while in the other white people condemned that culture—even though their dark history played a key role in creating the world where we were forced to struggle to survive.

When I was nine years old, I watched *Rosewood* with my grandma. As the story unfolded, I felt rage and hatred building inside me for white people. An entire town was destroyed because a white woman lied about being raped by a Black guy. Watching Black people cower in fear from the whites in the town tightened my chest and hardened my resolve. I vowed not to allow anyone to disrespect me, especially white people.

White people were mysterious to me. There weren't any in my neighborhood. I didn't have any white friends. Pittsburgh is a very Black and white city. If you're Black, you grow up around Black people. If you're white, you grow up around white people. My only interactions with white people were at school with teachers that didn't support me anymore, the police officers who had ransacked our house, and the white woman from *Rosewood* who cried rape. But at this point in my life, despite these experiences, I honestly didn't know how I should feel about white people. I watched cartoons with many white characters and enjoyed them. I loved Mr. Rogers because he helped me think about my feelings. I was all mixed up.

The next time I had an encounter with the cops, I was nervous. I couldn't help but to replay the sounds of them bursting into my house in my head. I could still feel the fear of them taking me away from my mom, sending me to the system. I still blamed them for snatching my dad from my life. I was angry and didn't have a desire to engage with them.

My school participated in a drug abuse resistance education (DARE) program where police officers would come talk to me and my classmates about the dangers of drugs, then give us candy and shake our hands. I took the candy and thought maybe they weren't so bad after all. The officers were good spirited and even gave us mini badges. At the presentation, I felt conflicted. I walked out of class with my dad on my mind and tossed the badge and candy in the trash. Although these officers were cool, I told myself that I hated police officers. My loyalty to my family wouldn't allow me to view them any other way. They were bad people, end of story. The pain of losing my father overshadowed any goodness that could come from a badge.

The next summer, my ideas about the police would crystallize.

My cousins and I were playing at the park, having a battle with water balloons and water guns, laughing and having a good time. I was seven years old, enjoying the thick of summer. The sun shining bright on my skin. The cool breeze blowing air through my netted basketball shorts as I ran through the park to the water fountain to fill my balloons with water. I threw a balloon at Rob. He ducked, and the balloon burst open against the windshield of the car behind him. Splash, a balloon quickly burst on my head. I looked over and Luv was laughing while Rob screamed, "Yooooo, Luv got aim."

Luv smiled with confidence. We all were soaked and wet. Balloon fights were my favorite part of summer. The next thing I knew, some older Black woman started yelling at us from her porch. We paid her no attention as we were blissfully enjoying our summer vacation.

"You little bastards. I'm calling the cops."

We didn't think to flee the scene, only kept throwing balloons.

When the cops came, they detained us, put us in handcuffs. One cop told his partner, "Make sure you put them on nice and tight."

I was confused and wanted to cry. But I didn't want my older cousins to clown me by calling me a crybaby. So, I tried my best to keep my cool. We all were afraid, puppy eyes hidden behind this idea of being "big boys." Even though we were kids, we must have graduated to being big boys for the police to arrest us. I wondered if my dad was afraid when he was in handcuffs. Thinking about my dad, I became more worried. Would I be taken away from my family just as he was? I regretted ever throwing that balloon. I regretted having this balloon fight.

They made us sit on the ground, lined up like birds on a telephone line, then they started peppering us with angry questions.

"Do you live around here? Where do you live? Why the fuck are you out here throwing water?"

People stood and watched. We felt humiliated.

"The next time you want to take a shit, go shit where you live. Stay the fuck out of neighborhoods where you don't belong." I wanted to say this is my neighborhood and I do belong here. However, fear struck me and snatched my words out of my throat.

I remember going home and telling my mom how the cops had treated us.

She asked me, "What did y'all do?"

"Nothing," I said.

"You must have done something."

She was convinced. We had been socially conditioned to accept such inhumane treatment. I grew up among many Black people who often believed the police were always right. If they stopped you, you must have done something wrong. I remember the DARE officers saying that police officers only arrested people who broke the law. I guessed that a balloon fight was a crime.

My cousin Corey chimed in with a perspective different from my mom's. He said, "Them boys ain't do a damn thing wrong but be kids. Having a balloon fight ain't a crime unless you're Black."

I didn't quite understand what he was saying, but he had my back and that was good enough for me.

———

A few months later, on September 14, my uncle Rocky came to my school, got me an early dismissal, and drove me downtown to the federal courthouse for the start of my dad's trial. I remember being nervous. I had overheard my mom's frequent phone calls about the potential outcomes. However, I was also excited to see my dad. He entered the courtroom in an orange jumpsuit with his hands cuffed behind his back. Right away, he started looking at me and other family members, smiling his gold-toothed smile and making funny faces. Living up to his credo: "Never let them see you sweat."

He took a plea and was sentenced to one hundred and sixty-nine months in federal prison. When the judge gave my dad his sentence, my mom began to cry. But my dad didn't budge. He just said, "I love y'all," then walked out of the courtroom.

He would end up serving more than thirteen years.

He would write me many letters from prison, the first dated October 1, 2000:

> Hey, little Leon, what's up partner? Not too much this way, just missing my best friend in the whole wide world. Man, I'm truly sorry for leaving you with such short notice, but believe me I never wanted to leave none of you at all.

*When you came to visit me on Sunday, I seen all
the pain in your face, and that made me hurt even more
than when your dad got shot. I would give anything just
to watch you play one more game of football or even ride
around hollering at you.*

*Man, we had so much fun together. I never want to
be away from you again in life. Guess what, when I come
home, I'm still going to be your best friend. Man, time won't
change our closeness. It will just make us more tighter.*

*I don't want you to even come visit me down here
again, but once I get moved, you can come see me so I can
hug my other part of me, and hopefully you'll grow up to
be my best part.*

*Leon, life was so hard for me coming up, and I really
didn't want to be here, but you and the rest of my kids
made me strong when I was weak, and I'm still around.
I know as you get older you'll run into situations where
you might feel the same way, but be strong for your dad,
it's in our blood to never ever give up, so be a soldier to
the fullest.*

*I love you, son, so from here on out, no more tears,
just laugh and smile at all the fun and jokes we had, and
that should brighten your day. Stay busy, and before you
know it, we'll be kicking it again. Well, I'm going to end
this letter, but never my love. Your nigga, your partner,
your best friend, Daddy.*

In March 2001, a few days after my eighth birthday, he sent me the
following letter:

*What's up, Mini-Me? You finally hit eight years old now.
I hope you had a nice surprise hotel party. We have all
the footage from that party, too.*

Well, Lee Dog, this is the hardest letter I ever wrote you, but I have always been straight up with you. Now I want you to hear the truth.

You are really my best friend and you never let me down. I am in prison because I broke the law. Your mother is not to blame for me being in here, and you and the rest of my kids neither. It is my own fault. I broke the law, and now I must pay a penalty.

Because I am away from you does not mean that I do not love you. There is nothing you could have done to change what has happened to me. Listen to your mother. You might think that she is being too hard on you when she tell you what to do. The reason we have rules is so you will know that some things you do can get you in trouble with other people.

Rules are just like laws. They help us all keep peace in our family and in our neighborhoods. Rules and laws are good for everyone, not just for you. It would be a messed up world if everyone made up their own rules and laws.

Just because you don't like a law is no reason to break it. Some laws may seem unfair, but until they are changed, you will have no choice but to obey them. Otherwise, when you get older, you could end up like me in prison.

It would break my heart if you ever ended up like me in a place like this. Prison is an ugly place. I don't have the freedom to be with you and your sisters and mom. I can't take you to McDonald's like I used to when I was out. When I talk to you like this, it's because I love you, and I don't want you to make the same mistakes I did.

Leon, you have a very good life ahead of you. Don't waste any parts of it getting in trouble. Learn from my mistakes and stay on the right track. I hurt your mom more than enough, so don't you be hard-headed and do the same.

I'm going to end this letter, but never my love. Your pops, partner, nigga 4life, but most importantly, your dad.

Each letter touched me, moved me to my core. I loved my father for being himself, especially because he didn't lie to me. While the neighborhood made up stories that glorified him, from a prison cell he extended a hand of guidance. He imparted truth and honesty. Although I'd heard him call prison a "gladiator school," he never celebrated the fact that he was incarcerated, even if many people in the projects did. Many of us view jail as the place to be, like a rite of passage. Where I grew up, people see incarceration as an achievement worthy of reward. For example, my cousin Corey was celebrated after he was released from prison. All his friends gave him money, lots of it. I remember the chatter through the neighborhood, "Corey is home." Everyone was excited to see him.

On the flip side, when my cousin Wayne graduated from MIT with a doctorate in computer science, he barely got a dinner. Here is a man that did everything right. Countless sacrifices. Sleepless nights. Thousands of dollars of debt. And all he received was a head nod and a congratulations. No stacks of money, no reverence. It made me feel that being in the streets was the thing to do. Everyone I knew who engaged the streets were celebrated and respected while other people were looked at as squares. The dealers even had better-looking girlfriends and many of them.

Even while locked up, my father was resourceful. He would have his friends bring me money; each time a stack of twenty-five twenty-dollar bills wrapped in a brown rubber band. This started almost immediately after sentencing. The dollar amount grew with age. My other siblings received things as well. However, we weren't allowed to tell anyone what we received, not even my mom. My dad would say, "Never tell anyone how much money you have. It's not their business. If you tell them, they'll start asking for shit."

He was still feared on the streets, and his name held weight. This reality was made apparent to me on numerous occasions. Once, when I was nine years old, a football coach "schooned" me, giving my helmet a hard slap at practice after I fumbled a pass. I cried—not because it hurt, but because I was embarrassed to be hit in public. My parents never put their hands on me.

After the coach schooned me, I quit the football team and went home, told my grandma Peewee, my mom, and my cousins. I also told a couple dudes in the neighborhood who were shooting dice. They said, "Oh shit, he done fucked up. Bit gone fuck that nigga up."

I didn't understand that in striking me, the coach had made a mistake that could have cost him his life. My dad called home from prison. I told him what happened, and I could tell from the sound he made on the phone that he was pissed. A few days later, the coach apologized. Another coach told me, "Man, Leon, listen. If there's any problems you have up here with the coaches, you let me know first. Don't tell your dad. We don't want any problems up here." I felt his concern.

Around this time, my mom had a new boyfriend. He was a cool dude, a bit square, but he treated us well. My dad called home. He asked me if I liked the guy.

"No," I said. "I don't like that nigga." Naturally, I wanted to be loyal to my dad.

"Yo, is that nigga there? Put him on the phone."

I put him on the phone. His face widened in fear, all his features distorted.

Next thing, he and my mom started packing up their stuff, then we all ran out of the house. My mom's boyfriend drove us to the FBI building and contemplated alerting the authorities. Although it was clear that my mom and her partner feared for their lives, I knew my father would never hurt me. I started to imagine what I could do with that power.

4

THE BIRTH OF BIG LEON

After my father went to prison, my mother, my two sisters, and I moved to Wilkinsburg, a municipality bordering Pittsburgh. We lived in a nice house in a decent neighborhood, and we each had our own bedrooms. I would ride my bicycle from there into the city and through some of Pittsburgh's worst neighborhoods. Everybody supported me and looked out for me. I was Little Bit and Tawn's son. Random people would give me a dollar, and "uncles" and men who knew my dad would give me even more, ten or twenty dollars each, so that by the time I arrived at my grandma Peewee's house in Garfield, I would have between fifty and one hundred bucks in my pockets, which I would spend on anything from candy to football gear.

Quickly I would think of ways to flip my money. I aspired to have stacks of money just like the hustlers. I learned early on the significance of having a bankroll. The more money someone had, the more they were respected. I wanted to be revered just like my dad. The path to that success was to make money. I would turn my twenties into ones so that my stack could look bigger. I would feel affirmed: "You a little hustler," Dollar, one of my father's friends, told me as I whizzed by. My chest puffed a little bigger every time. A little moneymaker; that's what I wanted to be.

My mom would come pick me up from Garfield at my grand-mother's to take me home to Wilkinsburg. She would call me her little black butterfly, flying all over Pittsburgh.

My wings flapped in social circles, too. I learned to nurture re-lationships early on. If I went to a cookout and met some friends or cousins, I would keep contact with them myself. Although I didn't have a cell phone, I would write down phone numbers and even memorize others. I would beg my mom to take me places. I would ask if friends could stay over. I always wanted to be connected to people. I wanted to have fun, to know everyone just like my father did. I remembered the way my dad and I would drive through neigh-borhoods, stopping at cookouts where everyone knew him. Shalaia and Leona, my sisters, would always get annoyed and ask to leave because my dad talked with everyone for a long time. I was different, I was like him. I had watched his words and had a natural love of connecting with people.

Like my father, I understood the power of meaningful relation-ships. I could safely go into any neighborhood. I felt lorded over, blessed. A child who could achieve anything, without limits. People in my community told me that I was special and affirmed me. If I played football, they told me how amazing I was on the field. If I had money in my pocket, they called me a hustler. If I made a mistake, they wouldn't scream at me. Instead, they'd encourage me to do bet-ter. And like my father, I knew how to turn a profit. Every time my mom would give clothes away, I would tell her, "No, Mom. Don't give them away. We could have a yard sale." She supported the idea. I sold candy and snow cones. Hustling came naturally to me. Hustling was *in* me.

———

Once in the third grade, I sold candy bars for a school fundraiser. The student who raised the most money would win two free tickets to Kennywood, an amusement park in Pittsburgh. At that time tickets to the park were around twenty dollars. Trained by my father to understand when I was being hustled, I could not see myself fundraising hundreds of dollars just to win forty. So, I convinced my mom to find out where the school purchased the boxes of candy, then I began to sell candy on my own, for profit. I hired my friends, and we started touring the neighborhood, telling customers that we were selling candy for the school. Sometimes, we went so far as to say we were fundraising for our football team. We carried our helmets to make it look good. As my father taught me, you either hustle or get hustled. I embraced the mentality. That meant being charming, good with words, and always making sure my numbers added up. I deeply desired to be a hustler. I wanted the influence, love, respect, and power.

One of my mom's friends made a prediction: "Leon's going to either be a big-time drug dealer or a politician when he grows up."

She had no idea what each of those fates would cost me.

———

I'll never forget my last carefree summers.

Wilkinsburg took some getting used to. More than anything, I missed having my older cousins around each day. I was nine years old and in third grade by then, and it was at Turner Elementary School where I met Little Steve and Jules, my first true friends outside my cousins. My other close friends included my brothers Laquan and Devon. Each day, the four of us played football, baseball, release the den, and hide and seek. As time went on, we became more mischievous, getting into fights with rivals and throwing rocks at cars.

Staying home could be a drag because I hated being the only male in a house with three females. I was never materialistic, but my mom always wanted me to look good. I always had the fresh Jordans, and my sisters had nice clothes and jewelry and their hair was always done up. One thing about my mom: she kept us fly. But going to the mall with them was hell. Men usually make shopping a simple matter. We arrive at the store knowing that we want a pair of sneakers, a shirt, a hat. We purchase it, then we're done. With women it's different. Nothing is decided in advance. Even if my mom had a list, they would spend hours trying on clothes. We would walk past a window and my mom would say, "Look, Boo, that's cute."

Before I knew it, I was in a store while they tried on clothes. I would be strung along from one store to the next while they tried on an assortment of clothes. My mom would select a dress, Shalaia a skirt, and Leona some third item of clothing. Then they would go to another store and another one after that, a process that went on for hours. They were in their element shopping, but it was torture for me. If I could have walked home, I would have.

We would have wars after we went food shopping. Leona would sneak a whole box of Fruit Roll-Ups to her room, and I would confiscate a box of cookies. Before you knew it, someone would ask "Where's the Fruit Roll-Ups? Where's the cookies? Are they all gone?" Then we would all start arguing over who ate what.

You could never win an argument with Leona because she had a smart mouth, a wicked tongue, and would cuss you out. She was just like my grandma Flo that way. In fact, people called her Little Flo. A little princess with a big personality—and a bigger attitude.

Still, Leona and I were close, like twins, Leon and Leona. She was three years younger than me and looked up to me, trying to imitate everything I did or just be around me as much as she could. We liked to watch scary movies together. Once it was time to go to bed, I would be scared to sleep by myself. I would frighten Leona—"Yo, they going to get you"—so she'd want to sleep in my room. However, sometimes she'd go sleep in my mom's room, meaning I had to sleep in my room by myself since my dad instructed my mom that I was not to sleep in her bed. I would be pissed. The entire night, I stayed awake in my room with all the lights on, scared to death. I would tuck my head under the covers and close my eyes as tight as possible.

I'd been so happy when Leona was born in the summer of 1996. With her arrival I would get to be a big brother. I remember holding her in my arms in the hospital and telling myself, *She is my baby sister, and I will always protect her.* Since that moment I made a vow to be her caretaker. Even when she annoyed me, I made sure she was safe.

———

With my father being incarcerated, I assumed the responsibility as the man of the house. This meant I would protect my mom and sisters. In the fifth grade, a kid made fun of Leona while we walked home from school. I didn't hear what he said, but I remember Leona crying her eyes out. I didn't say nothing to the boy, I just punched him in the face. His nose immediately began to bleed. I felt powerful. A rush of excitement flooded through my body. The boy ran home and within twenty minutes his parents were at my front door. My mom scolded me about my behavior. A nonconfrontational woman, she would say, "Keep your hands to yourself." My mother grew concerned about my behavior. To provide some male guidance, she decided to send me to spend the summer with my fraternal grandfather Big Leon in rural Massachusetts. I would end up going to Massachusetts every summer until I was fourteen years old. Each time I flew alone.

My mother left it to me to pack my own suitcase. On the day of my trip, we made the drive to the airport. TSA allowed my mom to go with me through security into the terminal, then she waited with me at the gate until my flight began boarding. I was excited to see my grandfather but nervous to fly alone.

My mom told me she couldn't show me how to be a man, that's

why she was sending me to my grandfather for the summer. I always loved my grandfather, so it didn't feel like a punishment. She told me to have a nice trip, kissed me on the cheek. Speechless, I stood there looking up at her, clutching the straps of my backpack. Not until that moment did I truly believe that I would have to make the flight alone. I had never been so afraid.

The flight attendant escorted me onto the plane. She must have sensed my nervousness since she asked me if I wanted to see the cockpit.

I told her that I would, and she escorted me into the cockpit, where the pilots greeted me with smiles and pats on the back. I wondered at the constellation of machines, the lights, switches, buttons, and gauges. The pilots spent a few minutes identifying equipment and explaining various functions.

The flight attendant placed me in a front-row seat and waited until I had secured my seat belt before placing my bag in the compartment over my head. Then she gave me pretzels and a water. The kindness of the flight crew had done much to calm my nerves. Still, I wondered, what would happen if no one was in Boston to receive me? What would I do then?

An hour or so later I left the plane and entered the terminal with that question at the front of my mind. A guy who worked for the airport escorted me through this huge building, my anxiety building. Luckily, my grandfather was waiting for me in the baggage area. I smiled. I knew that I was safe, that everything would be all okay.

In more ways than one, my grandfather looks like my dad, only taller and slimmer. My grandfather is calm with a warm presence, a kind, thoughtful, and soft-spoken man. Once inside his car, an Infiniti Q45, we had much to talk about during the long drive from the airport to the rural town where he still lives.

He said, "You're looking more like your dad each day." I could feel how happy he was to have me in his world and his words made me feel proud, knowing he saw my father in me.

"Really?"

"Yes," he said. "But tell me, why are you giving your mother a hard time? She's such a good woman."

"Grandpa, it's hard living in a house with three women."

He laughed. "I imagine it is."

———

After some time, we reached a small gravel road leading to his property. We went on for a few minutes, the sound of gravel crunching under the tires, then we started to climb a steep hill until we reached his house on top. From up there I saw only forest in every direction, curtains of trees. My grandfather's property covered a few acres. His closest neighbor lived a half mile away. We walked past the garden and entered the house. The dwelling seemed simple to me, especially compared to the house where my dad had lived. However, the ceilings were high.

Once inside the house, he introduced me to his wife, Betsy, a simple woman with a big heart. The first thing I noticed was that she was white. I had never seen a Black man with a white woman before. I had never considered anyone white to be family. She was welcoming and friendly. "This is your home," she said.

Carrying my suitcase, my grandpa took me up to the second-story loft where I would be staying. I wasted no time in unpacking. My grandfather started laughing when he saw that I had brought along eight pairs of sneakers.

"This is the country," he said. "Pick one pair that you're going to wear. That's the pair that you want to get dirty and that you're going to wear the whole time you're here."

It proved to be a great summer.

Betsy is a good woman. We would do a bunch of fun stuff together. She taught me how to garden. That was a big part, getting dirty. Getting out there and working in the yard. I had never worked in a yard before. Because I was a city kid, I felt no connection to the natural world. But that changed at my grandfather's house. One summer Leona joined me for the trip, and we planted lilies. Sometimes we would go visit the neighbor to check out his dairy farm. There, we would let baby cows suck on my fingers. Leona would smile with excitement. Before then I had no idea that country life has so much to offer, so many wonderful experiences. Plenty of culture.

My grandfather would take me to an outdoor range and teach me how to shoot, both rifles and pistols. We would do projects in the yard like build firepits, paint yard decorations, and wash his dogs. We would drive up to Maine to explore the army bases up there and make excursions to visit the Dr. Seuss Museum and Basketball Hall of Fame.

Once, we went to a circus a few towns over. Hundreds of people sat under the big top eating popcorn and watching clowns entertain. At one point, while motorcyclists jumped through fiery hoops, I realized that my grandfather and I were the only Black people present. To my surprise, nobody singled us out or treated us as less than the way white people often did in Pittsburgh. Too often in our country, rural people are stereotyped as provincial and racist. That was not my experience during the summers at my grandfather's home.

My aunt Koko, my grandfather's youngest daughter, lived about an hour away from my grandfather in a bigger town in an apartment building that she owned with her mom. My grandfather lived in Germany for many years while serving in the military, where he met Aunt Koko's mother. Grandpa and my aunt Koko would converse with each other in German. Aunt Koko, being worldly, lived for culture and loved to travel. She always talked about her many times traveling throughout Europe as a biracial teenager, visiting relatives on her mother's side of her family. I was fascinated by her experiences. I knew people who traveled, but not to different countries. It blew my mind to watch her and my grandfather speak German. I had never heard Black people speak a different language. My aunt

Koko would always say, "Life is much bigger than Pittsburgh." She encouraged me to travel the world and gifted me an atlas. Together we would look at the maps, and she would point at places where her family was from and where she had traveled to. Her lessons made me more curious about the world, made me hope that I too would one day get to travel overseas. She even taught me a few words of German. I learned that her mom was my *oma*: grandmother. Big Leon was my *opa*: grandfather. These words made me curious about other lands, other cultures.

My grandpa and I often listened to music on the CD player inside his car, songs like Bob Marley's "Three Little Birds." I woke up early one morning to discover that he was already inside his car. He told me to hop in, so I did, and we started out on a drive. He'd bought me two CDs, one by the singer Mario and the other by Big Tymers. I loved these artists and was happy to have my own CDs. Once back home, I was sure that Shalaia would take my Mario CD as her own and Reese would gladly take advantage of my Big Tymers album. My grandfather slid the Big Tymers CD into the player. He frowned when he heard that the songs glamorized drugs, sex, and killing.

He looked at me in the rearview mirror. "What the hell is this?" He ejected the CD from the player, then took it and threw it out the window. That done, he started to give me a talking to.

"Leon," he said, "that music will rot your brain. And it will rot your heart. Listen to me. Life may not be God's promise, but it is God's gift. A gift that you must take care of. The city life is fast. You don't have to let it suck you in."

And then he said something that has stayed with me ever since. "Each day that we are alive offers us the opportunity to give something positive to the world."

I vowed that I would be a positive person and make my grandfather proud.

5
TRAGEDY STRIKES TWICE
NOVEMBER 26, 2004

I had never seen a kid in a coffin before. My friend, Little Steve, thirteen years old, lying before me, resplendent in his Big Ben jersey. His face powdered. His arms crossed on his chest, his hands pale and ashy. A line of mourners—friends, aunts, uncles, cousins, and other relatives—behind me. All I could do was stare, wide-eyed, wondering if Steve was looking down at me from heaven.

My mind started to drift, awash in memory. We would play release the den in the street. I could still hear his mother, Miss Keisha, loving and protective, yell at us: "Y'all better stay out the goddamn street." I remembered how we use to steal her Black & Mild cigars and smoke them in the alley.

Then I started to picture myself in a casket. I visualized my face instead of his, skin darkened with makeup. What clothing would I wear? Standing there rooted in the question, I looked around the room and imagined everyone crying out for me.

For the first time, I realized that I could die, too. Death wasn't just for the eighteen-, nineteen-, or twenty-five-year-olds I knew who'd been gunned down, teddy bears and candles placed in commemoration. Death could find me, too, although I was only eleven years old. Death had no preferred age, and bullets had no name. You didn't even have to be violent to die, you didn't have to be a drug dealer. Little Steve was thirteen. The worst thing I saw him do to anyone was crack "yo' momma" jokes. Sadness and confusion overtook me. I couldn't understand how a life so precious could be taken.

I prayed for death not to find me. I didn't want my mother and father to cry, to grieve, for my grandmother Peewee to sit at her dining room table planning my funeral arrangements as she had done for so many of my aunts, uncles, and cousins. So, I prayed: *Death, spare them from such suffering. Stay far away from me and my family.*

From that day on, I started to believe that someone would try to kill me.

Some young Black men murder each other simply as an act of survival. These are not hard dudes or thugs. They are men who have lost their fathers, mothers, brothers, sisters, aunts, uncles, and cousins to homicide. Where I come from, we are not strangers to death. Most of us have buried friends and relatives—and some of us even have loved ones serving life sentences for murder. At least we can still communicate with those behind the wall. Many people I know live by the old saying, "I'd rather be judged by twelve than carried by six." They find themselves in situations where they are forced to take a life before their life gets taken. From experience, I have come to learn that severe trauma can lead a good person to kill.

Although I lived in Wilkinsburg, I still missed Garfield. I still played football for the Garfield Gators, still claimed Garfield, and told anyone who asked that I was from Garfield. Some weekends, I went back to my old neighborhood to visit family. But these visits were not enough for me. I told my mom that I wanted to go to school in Garfield, so at the end of my fifth-grade year, she transferred me to Friendship Elementary School. My cousin Eric also attended the school, and it was through him that I became cool with his crew, including Rashee and Mal-Mal, two guys who became good friends and, later, enemies.

After I graduated from Friendship, I started attending middle school at Arsenal. It was there that I met my two best childhood friends, Poppa and Bernie. Poppa was a short, brown-skinned dude with a big head and a laid-back vibe. Because we were the two smartest kids in our grade, we had the good fortune to be in the same class from sixth grade until tenth. He loved to rap and was always spitting rhymes, but he feared performing before others.

A little butterball turkey, Bernie was fat and funny. Because he was so chill and was always making people laugh, few knew that he was dealing with a lot of drama at home with his mom and his stepfather, a man he had a hard time accepting even though he did his best to raise Bernie and his siblings. They were often at odds for one thing or another, causing Bernie to act out.

Sometimes the three of us, me, Poppa, and Bernie, would hang out together, but usually I would spend time with them separately. Papa and I had our own thing going on, while Bernie and I ran a little crew. In addition, me, Mal-Mal, and Rashee were always looking to see what we could get into, mostly chasing girls.

———

Not long after my twelfth birthday, my mom met a guy named Jeff and fell in love. My dad had scared her previous boyfriend away. After our trip to the FBI building, we saw less of him. I learned quickly that it would take a lot of courage for a man to date my mom being that my dad still had a presence in our lives. They decided to host their wedding in Saint Lucia. They invited only a few friends and family members, but they still held a large and colorful reception, with plenty of food and drink, no expense spared. My loyalty to my father inspired me to make a visual statement, a bold expression of my love for him. I wore a T-shirt with a picture of me and my father sitting on a motorcycle, the fabric bearing the legend "Ride or Die." Although Jeff was a nice guy and made my mom happy, I felt that letting him into my life would be a betrayal to my dad.

After the wedding, my mom, my two sisters, and I went to live with her new husband in a house in a nice neighborhood. But after only a few months, it was clear their relationship wasn't going to work out. They would argue over little things. I remember them fighting about dinner one night. My mom wanted to fry some chicken, but he said he couldn't stomach fried food. When my mom offered to cook something else, he said he'd rather eat out, then he left the house. More and more, things would get heated. He would curse, and even put his finger in my mom's face, but he never abused her the way my dad had. Ironically, had he put his hands on my mother, he would have felt the wrath of my father—and he knew it.

After the divorce, we moved back in with my grandma Peewee in Garfield. By then, she was living in an apartment one floor up from a corner store, in a building just down the hill from the projects. Our new quarters were cramped. Not long before, my aunt Diane had passed away, so my three cousins were also living there. Altogether, eight people crammed into a two-bedroom apartment. Somehow, we made it work. I was happy. In the afternoons, I would ride my bicycle with Leona on the backseat. She was ten years old, three years younger than me. Despite the age difference, we were still close. Leon and Leona against the world.

Four years older than me, Shalaia always vied to be the center of attention. I remember my grandma Peewee putting on some music one evening, the oldies that she loved. I moved to the center of the living room and started dancing.

My mom said, "Go ahead, Leon, bust a move." She turned on her video camera and started recording me.

Not ten seconds had passed before Shalaia ran over, pushed

me to the floor, and swayed her hips, throwing her arms in the air. My mom directed the camera at Shalaia, while I sat on the floor watching.

"What about me?" Leona yelled. We were both used to Shalaia swallowing attention.

Shalaia had to be the star in the room. A diva. Still today, no matter what I accomplish, I will always be her little brother. She won't heed advice from me. But for Leona, I was the center of attention, the center of her world.

In Garfield, we used to help our grandma Flo sell snow cones. Grandma Flo would set up her ice ball machine right on the corner by her house and Leona and I would sit there all day selling them. Grandma Flo would easily make $150 in sales, but she would only give me and Leona $10 apiece plus tips.

I would say to Leona, "Grandma's hustling us, man. We ain't doing this shit no more." But we would always help her because we wanted the money. I would always save my money, but Leona would spend hers at Martha's, the Chinese corner store under my grandma's apartment, buying Hot Cheetos and a bunch of other different snacks. She loved Hot Cheetos.

She would say, "As long as I can get some snacks from Martha's, I don't care."

———

I'll never forget one crisp day in late September 2006 when I was in eighth grade. I can still see Leona sitting in the backseat of my mom's black Yukon Denali on her way to cheerleading practice. She was her usual self, bright and happy in her orange and blue cheerleader's uniform. As my mom was heading off, I walked alongside the car with Kerrese, one of my closest childhood friends and partner to my candy business. My mom offered us a ride.

"No," I said. "We're going to walk."

They sped away. Kerrese and I continued to football practice.

After practice, we went to a house party inside a tiny basement in the projects. Several older guys from the neighborhood were there smoking weed. That night I got high for the first time. I hit the blunt and before I knew it, I was on cloud nine. All in all, I had a great time: dancing, smoking weed, laughing, talking shit.

Once the party was over, Kerrese and I walked to my grandma Flo's house and went to sleep.

Sometime later, my brother Dale shook me awake. I'd lost any sense of time. It felt like a dream, and I sensed something was wrong by the way he woke me up.

He said, "Bro, we got to go."

I remember seeing my grandma Flo seated at the table in the kitchen crying. I asked myself, *What the heck is going on?*

Kerrese and I got inside Dale's car, and we drove to my brother's house in Stanton Heights about five minutes away. I could see Dale working out the anxiety he had about sharing his news. Inside the house, Kerrese and I flopped down on the couch and started dozing off, trying to go back to sleep.

Then Dale broke the news. "Hey, Leona was hit by a truck."

"What?" I said, jolting awake again. "Is she all right?"

He started crying. I could tell it was bad. My stomach turned in fear.

He said, "Come on, bro, we gotta go."

Kerrese and I walked behind him and got into the car. My legs felt heavy, anxiety filled my chest.

From there, he drove us to my grandmother Peewee's house. By this time there were many cars parked outside. I could hear my mom screaming inside the house, the worst sound I've ever heard in my life. She kept repeating the same phrases, "Not my baby. My baby's gone. Not my baby." She kept screaming out my sister's name:

Leona, Leona, Leona.

Drained and empty, I did not want to walk up those stairs to my grandmother's apartment. I felt hollowed out, and I took each step as slow as I could. It felt like the longest walk I'd ever taken.

I found my mom lying in my grandma's bed. I'd never seen her cry that hard. What could I do? I held her, as did my older sister Shalaia, and the three of us cried together, while my grandma rubbed my mom's back. Someone was saying "It's going to be all right." Deep down I knew no matter how much I prayed, things would never be the same again. At her birth, I had promised to always protect Leona. I had failed.

I learned the details about what happened. Leona had been hit by a tractor trailer. She and the twelve other girls of her cheerleading team had been walking down a dark, winding road. The woman who had arranged their transportation got into an argument with her boyfriend and he refused to come pick them up. Instead of calling the parents, she decided that they were going to walk to the bus stop half a mile away. The three adults responsible for supervising my sister and the other girls would be arrested and charged, but they would receive suspended sentences.

The next day, my dad called from prison. He asked to speak to me. He said, "Yo, dawg, what is happening?" And then he just broke down crying. It was the first time I'd heard my dad cry. It came as a revelation. In that moment I realized that even my father could feel pain. The sound coming from him was a gut-wrenching howl, the same sound that had emerged from my mom, as if their souls were being slowly wrenched away. Neither of them has been the same since the death of my sister. No matter how bright a smile, funny a joke, or positive a conversation, there is an emptiness that only one who has lost a child can understand. Despite that pain, they've tried their hardest to push through life without breaking.

My grandma planned Leona's funeral as she had for Darnell and as she would do for other family members. She's the one that everybody else leans on. She did her best to be her usual kind and happy self. We all needed her. The love of family would help get us through.

Leona's injuries were so severe that she had to be cremated, an urn in place of a casket at her funeral. Because I never saw her body, her death never felt real to me. Even today my sister's death feels like a dream or hallucination. Perhaps I'm still high from my first puff of marijuana and will soon wake up to Leona's warm embrace.

I never felt any closure or received any counseling. I just went back to school the day after the funeral. Silence surrounded Leona's absence. At home we didn't talk about it. Everyone tried to live life as normally as possible. Still, you could feel the heaviness. You could feel the grief, the sadness, the pain, even though my mom was always smiling, even though my grandma smiled, even though my sister and cousins went on as if nothing had happened. My mom worked, my grandma worked, and my sister went to school. For me, school became an escape.

My mom felt tormented. Two weeks before the accident, she'd had a dream that a white man abducted and killed Leona. How had she missed the warning? She blamed herself. She cried all the time but kept it hidden from others. She'd be cooking in the kitchen, and all of sudden she'd run to the bathroom, as if struck by a sudden pain. I didn't think she would ever bounce back.

Later I would discover that my mom felt she had neglected me and Shalaia during this time. Her grief was so heavy that she didn't want to be a mother anymore.

One day, we were sitting together on the couch in the living room. She seemed unable to look me in the face. Something prompted me to say to her, "Mom, but you still got us." My mother says that my words awakened her from her depression.

At fourteen, I felt the need to remind my mom that she had something to live for, her other two children. I loved my mom and missed her joy. She still smiled and had a loving presence. However, her joy had departed with Leona's loss.

I told her, "Mom, I miss your smile. You should laugh more and be happy." Regurgitating what I heard so many adults say, I added:

"Leona may not be here with us in the body, but she's here with us in spirit. We have to continue to live for her."

I looked my mom in the eyes, but she didn't say a word back. Instead, she squeezed me tightly and let out a loud gasp. I could feel wetness on my shoulder from her many tears. Soon enough, my own tears started spilling, blending with hers. I felt so relieved giving myself permission to cry. I didn't know this was just the beginning.

6
HUSTLING

At the time of Leona's death, I was in eighth grade and had been an A student, always on the honor roll. But now that I was heavy with grief, I could no longer focus on my studies. I would go to school to have fun, to forget. Much of the time I spent goofing off in class, hanging out in the halls with my friends, or talking game to girls. Somehow, I managed to graduate from middle school. Graduating meant a lot to me. I was glad to somehow have made it through.

I was always a great salesman. Since the fourth grade, I always found a way to sell Milky Ways, selling more candy bars than Kerrese. In seventh grade, I stopped selling candy bars and started selling knockoff sneakers with the help of my "uncle" Travis, Robbie and Raymon's stepdad. Travis would buy the sneakers in New York and then sell them to me, so I could turn a profit by moving them on the street. I made good money, usually between $200 and $300 profit from eight pairs of shoes. My dad knew that I could do even better.

He instructed me to buy a whole case of sneakers from Travis. I did, and I immediately noticed the invoice was inside the box. Now I had a direct connection to the folks in New York, meaning I could buy at the wholesale price and turn a bigger profit. Ever the hustler, my father missed no opportunity to pass on his knowledge to me.

That said, selling sneakers was a grind. Every day, I had to spend a lot of time trying to convince people to buy from me and haggling over prices. My cousin Money was selling marijuana. Everyone knew Money, he kept a bankroll of cash in his pockets, had a nice red Mustang, and plenty of women.

He told me, "Cuz, you gotta sell some shit that people need every day. That's how you make it happen. Your clientele want sneakers, but it's not a necessity. My clients, they come through daily. Smoking bud is a way of life and, shit, it'll probably be legal in a few years, so it's not too bad."

I trusted Money and listened to his advice. I knew I could master the art of selling weed and make thousands of dollars more. Out of respect, I went to my grandma Peewee and told her, "Grandma, I want to sell weed." Her face flashed with shock and fear.

She said, "Grandson, I don't think that's the best idea. I never wanted you in those streets. It's a dangerous game."

I understood her concern. However, in my heart I had already made up my mind that I would become a dealer. As I expected, she tried to discourage me. She gave me a pep talk, hoping I would do the right thing.

"Leon, you know you can get into a lot of trouble."

"Grandma, don't worry. I will be careful."

She must have seen the determination in my eyes.

"Look, grandson, if you do it, don't do it behind my back. You can trust me. Always feel free to come to me for anything."

She made me promise not to let any of my friends know that I was dealing or to sell to them. With that promise made, she picked up the phone and started calling her friends who smoked marijuana, saying, "Hey, Leon got the good stuff." I was in business.

Her friends would buy from me every Friday after they got paid. It was easy money. Then I upped my game. By the time I started high school that fall, my sister Shalaia had a Jamaican boyfriend, an industrious dude who bought and flipped properties. I started working for him, gutting out homes.

Then one day I saw a big plastic bag in the back of his car. I knew it was weed. He fronted me a pound, which I sold to my cousin Money, making $300 in the process. Within hours, I called the Jamaican guy for more. He was both surprised and impressed.

"Damn," he said. "That was fast."

This time he gave me three pounds, which I sold to Money and two other cousins. Soon, he was giving me five pounds a week to move. Although I had more money than I could spend, I was always looking for a leg up. I was good at leveraging relationships, and in time, I found another connection. I was now in a position to supply the Jamaican dude. That was until he got jammed up and was deported.

While working on his properties, I built a good relationship with his friend T, from Trinidad. He took a liking to me because I was young and fly. What T didn't know was that I would soon change his life. My new plug pulled up to my garage, not saying much but "I'll see you next week with the same thing. Just make sure the paper is right." I was excited, even though I didn't know what I would receive. I figured five or ten pounds. He rolled over a huge bag. I could barely lift it.

"Thanks, Unc," even though he was a friend of the family.

"No doubt." He got into his car and drove off.

I closed the garage door and opened the bag to see five huge blocks the size of pillows, wrapped in green Saran Wrap, smelling like Vaseline and oil. I was confused. I had never seen anything like this before. Written on the blocks were numbers: 28, 36, 45, 15, and 30. I grabbed a razor and began to cut the plastic. To my surprise, it was weed, lots of it. Luckily, I had heavy-duty garbage bags in the garage and began cutting each block open and dumped the weed in them. As the weed found its place inside the new bags it expanded, and I realized I had more than I could imagine. After weighing the weed and placing 16 zips, or one pound, one by one into a Ziploc bag, shake included, I found I was fronted about 163 pounds of weed. I would only have to pay $900 a pound and would sell them for $1,000, which meant I was going to make $100 off each pound. This was much better than the sneaker and candy business. I immediately called T.

He answered, "Yo, my boy."

"Come see me, bro."

"What's wrong with you? Are you okay?"

"Yeah, just meet me at my garage."

When he arrived, I opened the door.

"Damnnnnnn, my nigga," he said in his Trinidadian accent. "What the fuck! You just a little boss nigga, huh." He smiled. "Nigga, you show me bitches, you drive and don't even have a license, nigga. You is prime nigga." He laughed.

His excitement made me ten feet tall.

"Yo T, I need help getting rid of these."

"I, I got you, my nigga," he stuttered.

"You can trust me with your life, nigga."

I did trust T, and within three days he moved over one hundred pounds for me. The rest went to my cousins. Within that week I was sold out and ready for my next shipment. It felt good counting up $163,000, even though my profit was only around sixteen thousand dollars. Not bad for a high schooler.

Looking back, I remember my drug deals more clearly than I remember prom, basketball and football games, and any other high school experience. To me, school was a joke. One deal and I could make my teacher's whole salary.

My sister's death had shaken me to the core, and my entry into high school had awakened an identity crisis. Once I started making good money from selling weed, I realized who I wanted to be: a major-league hustler. School couldn't offer me anything. Or so I believed. My interest in classes didn't extend beyond the teachers who shared with me what they knew about philosophy and real estate. I seemed to be following in my father's footsteps, learning how to make money, acquire capital. In my eyes, he was still a king.

Those who hustle are often portrayed as bad or violent people. Most aren't. The reality is that if you don't have access to resources and are facing poverty or otherwise struggling, you might be more inclined to carry a gun, to rob, to shoot, and to kill. All those people are like anyone else. They are all surviving. People learn different ways to get by based on what they are exposed to. Me, I was exposed to the hustle; it was in my heart and soul. When it comes to survival on the streets, you have to recognize the difference between hustlers and gangsters. A drug dealer only knows how to sell drugs, while a hustler can sell anything. A hustler is a person who capitalizes from any opportunity, whether it be tech, real estate, or drug dealing. The streets are simply a market. As long as there are users, there will be a business.

A hustler combines the qualities of a politician and an entrepreneur. He possesses the gift of gab, knows how to make people feel comfortable, knows how to be beloved, respected, and earn a deep reverence from others. A hustler is always solving problems, trying to figure out: *How do I make a buck?* I learned this from growing up in the hood: people will respect you if you're good at what you do. Everybody wants to talk to you or be around you. However, if you don't have any money, they're going to treat you like a dog. If you get busted and go to prison, they're going to say, "He was stupid. He should've done this, should've done that." However, while you're making money, everybody's your friend.

Given who my father was, early on, I learned more about how to make money than I did about Black history or religion. From my dad's perspective, cash is king. You can't be broke. You got to do something. Earn. He ran several successful businesses, including a record store called G Town Records and a clothing store, My Brother's Closet. His credo was "sell to turn a profit."

Be that as it may, he got word from the streets about my efforts to follow in his footsteps. He was not happy. When we talked on the phone, he told me, "Dawg, you know what comes with it, and you end up where I'm at. I ain't sending you money, because you've made a conscious decision to live your life like that."

He hoped that my older brothers Reese and Dale would serve as role models, that they would be able to advise and guide me, although they had been raised apart from me. When I started high school, Reese was twenty-one and Dale was eighteen, both living on their own. Dale was always on the straight and narrow, a positive dude who tried to live by the principles of his religious upbringing as a Jehovah's Witness and who tried to encourage me to do the right thing—stay in school, stay out of gangs—and be an upstanding person. He married his high school sweetheart then joined the construction workers' union, becoming a foreman.

One day, I was hanging out with him, helping him with his Icee ball stand, a side hustle that earned him some extra dollars. We needed to make a run, so I got into his car. But instead of turning the ignition, he started sniffing.

He said, "It smells like weed in here, bro."

I had weed hidden inside my backpack, but I tried to play it cool. "I don't know. What are you talking about?"

"You got weed on you?"

He checked me, dug his hand into my backpack, and found my stash, then he just launched it out the window. He didn't care who it came from, who had fronted me, how much money it would cost me. He always wanted what he thought was best for me.

He asked, "So you're dealing now?"

"Ain't you the pot calling the kettle black," I said.

Dale was selling a bit on the side, but he didn't know that I knew since he'd always tried to keep his activities hidden from me. I have no recollection of him ever talking to me about it or flashing what he had.

Because I was the golden child, everybody thought that I could be anything in the world. Now Dale realized that I could be snatched away by the snares of the streets. That was a revelation for him. He decided he would put dealing behind him and try to lead me by example, rather than by what he said.

Despite Dale's positive influence, I was drawn to Reese. Wild, aggressive, and hot-tempered, he was always in trouble. He saw me as the perfect sidekick. I could fight. I had heart. I was down for whatever. He could influence me, sway me, lead me in—and out—of hot water regardless of the consequences. My grandma Flo often warned me about hanging out with Reese, saying he would get me killed. However, he was my big brother, and I loved him dearly.

My admiration for him would have consequences.

7
LEARNING ABOUT LOVE

When I was in the ninth grade, I started dating a girl named Medina, my first serious crush. I would see her going about the halls of the school and in the cafeteria, a slim light-skinned beauty with long, pretty hair. I really liked her style and the way she carried herself, more confidently than the other girls in our school or those I knew in Pittsburgh. She always wore bright-colored clothes that matched the color of her socks. Somehow, she made it work. She would say, "This is that DC swag." She was very proud to have spent her early teen years in the Washington area because that made her different, special, not just another around-the-way girl. I decided I had to get to know her although she was two grades above me. As a ninth grader, dating an eleventh grader was not likely. However, I took my shot.

After school one day I started flirting with her, complimenting her smooth skin and her beautiful hair. I said, "Your swag is different."

She said, "I like your swag too."

She gave me her number. For two weeks straight, we talked on the phone every night. I learned that she had been born and raised in Pittsburgh, but she and her family had spent the past few years in Washington, DC. They had just moved back.

"That explains why your swag is different."

"No. My swag is just me."

I got to know her mom and some other members of her family. We used to skip school and hang out at my house. And she would skip dance practice to come to my house.

Somehow her mom figured out what was going on. She popped up at my house one afternoon. My cell phone rang. I heard her mom on the other end. "Hey, Lee. I'm outside of your house. Is Medina in there?"

Medina, lying in bed with me, began shaking her head. "Say no," she said. Instead, I did the opposite.

I really liked her mom and could not lie to her. "Yeah, she's in here."

Her mom gasped. "Thanks for being honest with me. Can you ask her to come outside?"

"I will."

My honesty had gained her mom's trust.

Medina and I had a solid relationship for about a year, the longest I had ever dated someone. We would go to the movies, go out to eat, and when we were not together, we would spend hours talking on the phone.

One Saturday night, we had plans to hook up, only for her to call and cancel. She told me she wasn't feeling well, that it felt like the flu. I was disappointed that I would not be seeing her.

Then her mom called me a few hours later, around midnight.

"Is Medina there?"

Her question surprised me. "No, she ain't here. I thought she was home sick."

"No, I thought she was with you. Well, if you hear from her, tell her to call me."

"I will."

I hung up, confused. I started calling Medina's cell phone. She didn't answer.

An hour later, her mom called me again. "Is she there? Did you hear from her?"

"No."

Now I was worried. Maybe something had happened to her, something bad.

I called her cousin, named Chrissy. "You know where she at?"

"I don't know."

I found her answer strange because she and Chrissy were tight and knew each other's business.

"When did you last hear from her?"

"Well, I'm not sure."

I could hear something in Chrissy's voice. She was holding back on me. And I could tell that she felt bad doing so because we were on good terms. She felt some loyalty to me. At the same time, she wasn't going to throw Medina under the bus. She was in a tough spot.

"Chrissy, where the hell is she at? Why you lying to me?"

"Don't be getting all loud. I told you I don't know."

"You lying."

"I got to go." She hung up.

Now I was pissed. Where the fuck was Medina?

Her mom continued to call me through the night until around ten the next morning when Medina finally came home.

Later on that day, I hooked up with Mal-Mal and we was doing our thing. He said, "Yo, I saw Medina yesterday with my old head from Homewood."

"What?"

"Yeah. She was in this car at the gas station with that dude Mizy."

"You sure it was her?"

"I kid you not, my nigga."

"Whoa." I was thinking. "Oh, all right." Mal-Mal had no reason to lie, so I believed him.

After I left Mal-Mal, I called Medina and arranged to meet her. We met up at our favorite pizza joint. The moment she saw me, she pulled me in for a hug and kissed me on the lips. I tried to be my usual self and not let her know that I was upset. Maybe Mal-Mal had lied to me. Maybe there was a good reason why she had been out all night. I ordered us a slice each and paid, then we sat down at a table, me on one side, she on the other.

I let her take a few bites of her slice before I asked her, "Where were you last night?"

"Oh, I was hanging with my girl."

"I thought you was sick?"

"I was. But I decided to go to my girl's house."

"You know your mom kept blowing up my phone last night?"

Medina took a bite of her slice then wiped her mouth with a napkin.

I said, "I already know you was with this dude. I already know you was with Mizy."

"What?"

"My boy saw you with him."

"He told you that? He lyin' on me. Nigga's always lying."

But I could tell by the look on her face that what Mal-Mal had told me was true. She couldn't even make eye contact with me.

I got up and left the pizza joint and called Chrissy.

"Yo Chrissy, how long has Medina been messing with Mizy?"

Shocked that I knew this detail, she quietly responded, "For a couple months. My bad, bro."

What Medina did hurt, ripping my heart out of me. For the first time, I knew what it was like to lose in love.

In my mind, Medina's betrayal confirmed everything my father had once taught me to believe about women. Up until then, the women in my life had always been loving, but I now started to share my father's skepticism. The women you dated were not to be trusted. Medina's cheating on me also made me want to step up my game. I figured she was with the dude Mizy because he had a car, and I didn't.

I decided that I would buy my first car. But I had no idea what it would cost me.

8

THE MAN I SHOT

At age fourteen, I lacked the self-awareness to see Reese for who he was—like me, a young man in search of identity and a father figure. I looked up to him, I wanted to be like him. He was charismatic, could fight, and carried a legal firearm. Trying to emulate him, I began doing stupid things like carrying guns. True, I sold weed, but I never felt that my life was in danger, meaning I had no need of a weapon for protection. I bought a pistol for $80 off a white junkie who called and reported the gun stolen in front of me to ensure it was a clean, licensed gun that had not been used in a crime. I caught my first gun charge walking down an alleyway with Reese and a friend. The police cruiser pulled up in front of us, blocking us in. I threw the gun into some bushes, but the cops found it.

To avoid a felony conviction, I pled to a misdemeanor and was placed under house arrest with an ankle monitor and ordered to complete the Community Intensive Supervision Program (CISP), a six-month anti-drug and -alcohol rehabilitation program aimed at young offenders. By that time, my mom and I were living in Stanton Heights, but the CISP facility was right across the street from my grandma Peewee's apartment in Garfield. I would go to school during the day, then go straight to the program, and from there walk right across the street to my grandma's place for dinner. That said, I hated those five hours I had to spend each day at the CISP facility. You had to keep your shirt tucked in, an uncool look for a teenager. And you had to sit through anti-addiction classes and group sessions, activities that felt like a big waste of time.

A week before my fifteenth birthday, Reese called me one morning and asked me to help him move some things from a storage unit to his apartment that he would share with his girlfriend Lei. We packed up the back of the U-Haul and completed the task in one trip. Noticing the U-Haul, Lei's sister Jazz asked if we could move some things for her as well. Lei interrupted, "No, that's doing too much. Plus, you don't know if he's there."

Reese responded "Who?"

"My ex-boy."

Lei cut her off. "Her abusive-ass ex."

Reese's ego kicked in. "He ain't gone do shit. We'll do it." He smiled.

I had a bad feeling in my stomach that I shouldn't go, that I shouldn't leave the house. However, I was loyal to Reese and I trusted him, so I voiced no reservation. It was snowing that day; the streets were slick and slippery. At one point, we started down a hill, then lost control of the truck and slid all the way to the bottom, almost crashing.

I was rattled but tried not to show it, did my best to control my breathing and impress my older brother.

Reese asked, "Y'all think we should go back?"

I said, "Yeah, yeah, yeah." I didn't want to do the move in the snow, especially after what had just happened. And I still had that gut feeling.

Reese said, "Nah, fuck it. We already out here."

Jazz had filed a protective order against her boyfriend, Charles. However, when we arrived, we found Charles and his friend in the apartment, sitting on the couch playing Madden on the PlayStation.

Reese and I tried to be friendly to him. "Hey, what's up, bro? What's going on?"

And he was friendly in return. However, I felt uncomfortable, unnerved. Something wasn't right.

Reese went into a back bedroom and started to take apart the baby's crib.

"Yo, this dude," I said. "We should leave."

Reese grew arrogant. "Fuck that dude."

I figured Charles didn't know us, and we didn't know him. He was probably thinking, *Does Jazz mess with one of these dudes or something?*

It was a super-bad situation to be in for a bunch of young people. Reese was twenty-one years old. The two other men might have been a year younger. And Jazz was only eighteen. All of us were on edge: a group of scared, young people.

Reese and I moved some things out of the apartment. Once back inside, I kept my eyes on Charles. I watched him go inside the bedroom and pull a pistol from a nightstand.

I told my brother, "Yo, this dude just picked up a gun, bro."

Reese said, "He ain't going to do shit."

I was agitated, every nerve alert, thinking, *This is crazy*.

We continued to move things in and out of the apartment. At one point, I was standing in the kitchen when Charles grabbed Jazz with his arm wrapped around her neck. He put the pistol to her head, then pointed the gun at me, before pointing it at Reese on his left.

He started shouting. "You think I'm scared of these niggas? I'll kill you! I'll kill them!"

The front door was through the living room on my left, Charles was directly in front of me, and Reese was to my right in the hallway, meaning that I was literally stuck in the kitchen, trapped.

Reese started walking toward Charles, and the latter aimed the gun at him. "Yo," Reese said. "Just chill, man. Chill. What's going on?"

Charles said, "We'll all meet our maker."

The standoff continued, Charles in turns aiming the gun at Reese, aiming it at me, then at Jazz, at me again, and so on. I was terrified, afraid to die. My sister had died, Little Steve had died, Darnell had died, and I knew that death is indiscriminate.

Then I heard a gunshot. My mind and body physically shut down. Had Charles shot Jazz? Had he shot my brother? Or me?

Once I came back to my senses, I realized that Charles was lying on the floor. My brother had pulled his own gun and shot Charles in the leg. Now that Charles was down, Reese ran out of the apartment, Jazz behind him, leaving me alone with these two dudes.

I tried to run out the door, but Charles's friend came toward me, tried to stop me, so I punched him in the face, knocking him unconscious. That was when I saw Charles reaching for his pistol on the floor. Thinking fast, not really thinking at all, I picked up the gun before Charles could. My fear was overtaken by a strange feeling of power. I'd beat him to the gun! I was safe! I would live! To be sure, I squeezed the trigger with force and could feel the explosion from the barrel of the gun. I shot him twice, the sound so loud I could feel the impact in my body, resonations jumping. I let the gun drop to the floor and ran out of the apartment.

All this had transpired in a moment. When I pulled that trigger, I felt so powerful, like I was back in control. As much as I was afraid, I also experienced a simultaneous sense of excitement and safety.

Once I was inside the U-Haul truck, Reese started freaking out. "What the fuck happened? Yo, what did you do? What did you do?"

I said, "Y'all left me in there! Why would y'all leave me in there?"

I was shouting, but my voice sounded like a whisper in the aftermath of the gunshots. Our voices sounded far away as if we were inside a bubble.

"Sorry," Reese said. "My gun jammed."

"What?"

"My gun—"

"Shit! Fuck!" I tried to slow my breathing.

Reese drove off.

"Bro, no!" I said. "No, call the police! You have your license to carry. Don't shoot and leave."

Jazz started crying. I knew what she was feeling. Charles was abusive, but he was also the father of her child. In that moment, I started hoping that Charles wouldn't die. I understood the significance of having a father.

We knew that we didn't break the law and that Reese was licensed to carry. Therefore, the responsible thing would be to call the police. Fleeing the scene could turn out to be a criminal act, or at least this is what we thought with our limited understanding of the law. We called the police, then turned the truck around and waited for them outside the building. I didn't want any of us to catch charges over shooting Charles. Best to get the police involved. The shooting was justified, self-defense.

The cops escorted us to the precinct to take our statements. I told them what had happened step by step, and they wrote my words down on a form. Then they asked me to tell it again, so I did. They asked me there was anything else I wanted to add.

"No," I said.

They asked me to sign my statement. I did.

To my surprise, one detective said to me, "You should have killed his ass. Would have saved us some paperwork." He smiled.

Reese and I looked at one another with confused faces.

Reese muttered under his breath, "We should've killed that nigga."

We stayed at the police station for about two hours, unsure of what would happen next.

After a while the Black detective said, "All of your stories match up, plus this asshole had a warrant, and Jazz filed a protection from abuse order against him a month ago. He wasn't even supposed to be in that house. He deserved everything he got."

His words blew me away. Charles's life meant nothing to him beyond a few hours of paperwork. To make matters worse, he was a Black detective. Here was another experience that made me dislike cops and hate the system. The policing system is such that anyone inside of it, white or Black, will have the same negative attitude toward Black men.

For days, Charles was in the ICU. It seemed as if Reese went about his life, unconcerned. In contrast, Dale would take me into his confidence, trying to talk sense to me, quoting scriptures aimed to impart a sense of moral responsibility. He would say things like, "Deuteronomy 5:17 says, 'You shall not murder.'" He would say I was "feeling myself." Then one day he asked me, "Yo, how are you going to feel if this man dies?"

His question frightened me. I never considered having a body weighing on my conscience. How would it feel to be a murderer? How would God judge me? I remembered one scripture Dale had quoted, "Whoever strikes a man so that he dies shall be put to death." If Charles died, would I also die? For days such thoughts tormented me. I even started to have trouble sleeping, my sleep riddled with nightmares. In one, I was alone in a funeral parlor standing a few feet away from a casket. I approached the casket, expecting to find Little Steve's body inside. When I looked down, I saw Charles lying there pillowed in white satin, his body bleeding with bullet holes.

But I was trapped between two worlds. One of my older cousins praised me for shooting Charles. "Congratulations nigga," he said. "You finally popped your cherry."

And many of the older guys I knew from the streets had similar attitudes. They would say to me, "Man, fuck that nigga!" In the streets, besides taking a life, shooting someone is the most "gangster" thing you can do. I was still in the ninth grade. I didn't feel tough, or hard, or a gangster. I was just confused, afraid, and traumatized. I was afraid before the shooting. I was afraid afterward. In that way, nothing had changed. But, in shooting Charles, I had earned a new level of respect and was now able to mask my fear with fearless-ness. It was easier to lean on respect than to accept the hard truths Dale tried to impart to me.

———

Almost a year after the shooting, Charles was scheduled to go to trial. The prosecution expected me to testify in court. Even though Charles had done wrong, I couldn't imagine taking the stand. Snitching would be a violation of my code. A few years earlier, my father's own brother Wolf had testified against him in a murder case to earn a reduced sentence. Although my father was acquitted, my uncle's betrayal had caused an irreparable rift in our family. Wolf had nothing to do with us, and we had nothing to do with Wolf or any of his children, my cousins.

The trial was to start on a Monday. The Friday before, several cops came to our apartment in Garfield looking for me.

I told my grandma Peewee, "I ain't no snitch. I ain't testifying." I hid in the closet.

I heard them tell my grandmother that they had a warrant for my arrest on a gun charge. It seemed that the gun charge would be dropped in exchange for my testimony against Charles.

"He ain't here," she said.

After they left, I slipped out the back door, determined to make my way to my other grandmother, Flo. What I didn't know was that the police were watching the house. They began to chase me. I ran past vacant lots overflowing with weeds and garbage until I found an opportunity to slip inside an abandoned building. I breathed in complete darkness to the sound of rats running across the floor and along the window ledges.

My mom ended up getting in the police car to help the officers search for me. By that point she was almost beyond herself with fear, fear that the cops would shoot me.

One officer told her, "Nothing's going to happen to him."

She said, "Please, I will get him to turn himself in. Just let me be there."

Once I thought it was safe, I exited the building and ran, block after block, doing my best to stay undetected. I cut through alleyways until I made it to the home of my childhood best friend, Bernie. Exhausted and out of breath, I stopped to rest in Bernie's backyard. I let my back rest against a tree. Within a minute, both of my grandmothers were there, too. Then the police vehicle pulled up with my mom in the backseat.

"Run!" Grandma Flo yelled.

"No, Leon," Grandma Peewee said.

Then I heard my mom crying through the window of the police vehicle. "Leon, stop running."

Grandma Peewee said, "Just turn yourself in."

Then Flo: "Fuck it, keep running." She told my mom and grandma that they were nothing more than a bunch of "stupid snitches."

My mom pleaded, "Don't run. They're going to shoot you."

I did not want to be shot. I did not want to die. I could only concede. I came from behind the tree and out of the yard with my hands up, and they cuffed me and placed me under arrest.

———

At the police station, the cops wanted to question me. Since an adult had to be present, my uncle Rocky rushed to the station from his house in Larimer. My mom had asked him to come since he was used to dealing with law enforcement. The very sight of him was a comfort to me: he looked the part of a pimp, flashy with necklaces and diamond rings. He sat down next to me.

Several detectives came into the room. One asked me my name. I told him.

A second detective said, "Leon Ford. Are you Little Bit's son?"

I said, "Yeah."

The detective said, "Y'all might as well take his ass to Shuman Detention Center. He ain't going to talk."

They took me to the juvenile detention facility where I would be held that weekend until the start of the trial on Monday. I felt proud that they had acknowledged my way of thinking. In my mind, I had achieved an important rite of passage, my first lockup. All my friends had talked about going to Shuman, had bragged about the brawls and beefs there and told colorful stories about playing basketball and fighting, making it sound like an exciting place to spend time. I'd always wanted to go. I entered the processing room with a smile on my face.

They put me in a cell and told me, "Take your clothes off."

I took off my T-shirt, then my pants. Immediately the chill hit me, and I started to shiver. The room was cold because the air conditioning was going full blast.

"All your clothes."

My entire body became rigid. Had I heard correctly? "What?"

"Take off all your clothes."

I had never been nude in front of another man. Moving as slowly as I could, I removed one sock, then the other sock. Even more slowly, I slipped off my boxers. I covered my genitals with my hands.

"Raise your hands, squat, and cough."

I did.

"Lift up your nuts and cough."

I did. None of my friends had told me about being strip-searched. I felt violated, felt like I had been molested. Here was a rite of passage I could do without.

During the trial, I took the stand and simply said "I don't remember." I had abided by the code. Little Bit's son.

Because I refused to testify, Charles was acquitted.

That day, more than anything else, I was proud of abiding by the code of no snitching that my father and Uncle Rocky had taught me.

Years have passed, but I still believe I made the right decision. Every person has a story. We all go through things. I could have simply written Charles off as a bad person, a threat to others, a man unworthy of grace and compassion. I try my best to remember that we are all human beings, capable of the worst but also capable of the best.

This experience also showed me that the law had little regard for my life. They wanted to use me to convict Charles, but they never considered the consequences I would face in my community, such as the possibility that I might be killed for being a snitch. All that mattered was convicting Charles. To put him behind bars, they would do anything, including locking me up, stripping me naked, humiliating me.

———

I had a fateful encounter with Charles less than a year after his trial. One morning, I was on my way to school when a car pulled up beside me. Four men were inside, including Charles in the rear passenger seat. He rolled his window down. *This was it,* I thought. He was going to shoot me.

Instead, he spoke to me. "Man, I really respect you. How old are you?"

I told him I was fifteen years old.

"You're that young? I really respect you, bro."

I stood there at the corner, feeling good hearing him say that. At that age, it felt good to command the admiration of a full-grown man. I felt like an adult.

The car pulled away, and I continued to school.

Because of the way he abused Jazz, Charles lost the right to see his child. I'm sure he suffers this loss. He was wrong to mistreat Jazz and to draw down on us with a gun. Still, to this day, I respect Charles, and he respects me. Make no mistake, we're not friends, but we've reached a level of mutual understanding and acceptance. Neither of us harbors resentments. In fact, we reach out to one another for advice and support.

Two countries go to war. Lives get taken. Despite the losses, despite the devastation, at some point, life resumes a type of normalcy. Reconciliation is possible.

In a Twitter post, someone calling himself Stef Starkgaryen after a World of Warcraft character writes, "You can't truly call yourself peaceful unless you're capable of great violence. If you are not capable of violence, you're not peaceful. You're harmless. Important distinction."

I never imagined how deeply my desire for reconciliation would be tested.

9

THE BIG TIME

I would catch one more gun charge before I turned eighteen.

By 2011 when I was in my senior year of high school, I was attending Career Connections, a charter academy in Lawrenceville. The classes were kept small. It was a good environment for me since I liked being around kids from backgrounds unlike mine.

That said, I often hung out with Mal-Mal and Rashee, from my previous school, Peabody, in East Liberty. We had an ongoing situation with some guys we'd been fighting since middle school, petty, dumb stuff.

One afternoon while I was in class, I received a call from Jamal. He said, "Yo, bro, we gone beat those niggas up after school." And so on.

"Bet," I said. "I'm on my way." I agreed to meet them, although I had a gut feeling that I shouldn't go, a sense that we would be met by something more than the usual posturing, banter, and harmless drama. But I didn't want to let my friends down. I would show up. I took my time getting there. I left school, then stopped at my grandma Peewee's house to change my shoes and my clothes. My grandmother had some music playing, Rufus and Chaka Khan's "Tell Me Something Good." She tried to get me to dance with her.

"Not now, Grandma. I gotta make a run."

"Where you rushing off to?"

"I'm going to meet some of my friends."

"You want to eat before you go?"

"I'll eat when I get back."

"Well, be safe."

"I will, Grandma."

I was about to get inside a car outside her house when I saw somebody I knew from Peabody.

He asked me, "You hear what happened?"

I told him I had not.

"Mal-Mal, Rashee, and his little brother got shot." My stomach turned with fear. I had already lost friends to gun violence and could sense death in the air.

Luckily, my three friends survived the shooting, although they suffered life-changing injuries. Mal-Mal still has a bullet in his head. Rashee bears scars in an arm and one leg, and his little brother is forever traumatized by the shooting.

Eight months after the shooting, I was hanging out one Thursday night in the studio with my cousin Big Stacks, rapper-producer French Montana, Montana's close rapper friend Chinx, and a dozen other people. Stacks was Darnell's younger brother, my uncle Teddy's second son, and he had a formidable reputation for moving large quantities of drugs. I looked up to him and aspired to be like him. He had a white Caddy, with white rims, and sounds that you could hear from a block away. With his big smile, charm, and gentle soul, everybody loved him. I admired everything about him.

Somehow, he and French Montana had become good friends. French Montana had traveled from New York to Pittsburgh with a large entourage. Also present were a bunch of hustlers from Pittsburgh who simply wanted to be in the mix. And there was a group of chicks, and other artists in a studio. At the time, I had some aspirations to be a producer like RZA, Kanye West, or DJ Khaled. I'd dropped a few thousand dollars on recording equipment that Poppa kept at his home, and Poppa and I often recorded tracks that we posted on social media.

Excited to be hanging out with the big dudes and doing big things, I recorded a song called "Cocaine" featuring French Montana and produced by my boy Rick P, of Taylor Gang, a track that I never released. I had released music before but didn't see myself as a rapper. I saw myself as a producer, executive, or manager. I had the money for studio time, and Poppa was like a brother, so I had no problem making an investment in his career. The plan was for Poppa to do a song with Montana, but he got shy and froze up. I was pissed.

"Yo, bro, I already paid this nigga five bands for the feature."

"I'm good, bro. I don't really got nothing to rap today."

I saw the nervousness on his face. He had never asked to come to the studio. He didn't even ask for me to pay for the feature. It was all my idea, being ambitious.

"Fuck it," I said. "I'll jump on the song."

French Montana and I hit the booth, and the rest was history.

As we were leaving the studio, we noticed the feds taking pictures of the vehicles parked outside of the studio, a nervous sight. We learned that the law had it in for Big Stacks and some of the other men there. The following week, Stacks and his crew were indicted on drug charges. Since I was moving cocaine, I decided to bury the song to avoid incriminating myself. Four years later, Chinx would be shot and killed in Jamaica, Queens. My cousin Big Stacks would serve almost ten years in prison. Ironically, nine months after he was released, he died in a fatal car accident. My uncle Teddy would bury another son.

The night after the studio session, I got to hang out in a club with Montana, Chinx, and Big Stacks. Underage, I had only been allowed into the club because of Stacks. We were having a joyful time. French Montana and Chinx were poppin' bottles, and everybody was imbibing. We were all seated in the roped-off VIP section, the music loud and the lights dim, heavy weed smoke in the air. The two rappers flashed bling so heavily that I wondered how they were able to move. Big Stacks and his right-hand man Belvy also flashed their jewelry. I got a call on my phone from Mal-Mal. The music was so loud that I could barely hear what he was saying on the phone. He was outside the club and wanted to come in. I started to plead his case to Big Stacks, although by that point I was a bit tipsy. Mal-Mal joined us.

When it was time to go, Mal-Mal didn't have a ride home. He asked, "Hey, can I ride with you?"

Again, that gut feeling. I really didn't want him to ride with me. It felt like I was on a roller coaster on a steep drop going sixty miles an hour. I just felt it. Almost like indigestion. Still, I agreed to give him a ride. "All right, cool, I can drop you off." What could happen?

We made it to his house, but were locked out and couldn't get in.

He asked, "Can you take me to my girl's crib?"

I agreed.

On our way there, the cops came up behind us with their siren blaring. We pulled over. I didn't know that Mal-Mal had a pistol on him. As quickly as he could, he placed it inside the glove box. I keyed the lock after.

Once the cop was outside my door, I let the window down.

"What's the problem, officer?"

"You ran a stop sign."

"You're going to write me a ticket?"

"Yes, but I also need to search the car."

Strategizing, I told the officers that we were minors and asked them if it would be okay to allow me to drive two blocks to my aunt's house. They agreed.

Mal-Mal and I got out of the car and went inside my aunt's house.

I saw both officers get inside my car and start searching. A minute or two later, they came into the house and grabbed my keys off the table to unlock the glove box.

Jamal started pleading with me. "Man," he said. "I can't go down. I just got shot."

"Okay, fine," I said. "I'll say the gun is mine."

Jamal was like a little brother to me, so I had no problem protecting him. Truth to tell, I wasn't worried. I knew enough about the law to know that this would be ruled an illegal search. Still, I caught a gun charge. Awaiting trial, I was placed on house arrest. To avoid repeating the CISP program, I decided to go on house arrest at my sister's home in Carnegie. Each day, I attended school and had to participate in a program called Phase 4, where I simply completed work on a computer for a couple hours.

I wasn't convicted, and I was released from house arrest. Beating the case emboldened me. I felt that I could do anything. No risk was too great. Elevating my game, I began making a name for myself in the streets, selling weed and anything else I could get my hands on, including cocaine and heroin. I did it with a clear conscience, never once considering the negative impact it was having on the community. To me, nothing seemed dirty about my operation since I moved weight, only supplying dealers, not addicts. In addition, I never feared going to prison because I wasn't running the streets. I would make a move or two a week and earn tens of thousands.

Today, I attribute my lack of remorse or regret to cultural conditioning. We're socially conditioned to do things or not do things based on how we grew up. Some people grew up in households where their parents or grandparents smoked cigarettes, so they also started smoking. Even though they know there's a risk of cancer, bronchitis, and other ailments, they've been brought up to think that smoking is normal. The nicotine you get from smoking is so immediate and visceral, the threat that you might get cancer disappears in the moment. Fast money works the same way. The thrill, power, and freedom that drug dealing provides is so enticing that it erases the fear of being incarcerated. I didn't grow up around people who used drugs, but I was surrounded by individuals who sold them. I knew that you could go to prison or get robbed or shot, but I also knew you could live a good life off the fast money.

After I started hustling a lot of weight, I decided to move out of my grandmother Peewee's apartment in Garfield and get my own place. It didn't make sense to be sleeping on my grandmother's couch when I had my own money. I also felt it was time to leave the hood for a more low-key environment, the best way to both stay off the radar and secure my investment, or at least that's what I thought would happen.

Once, my great-uncle Rocky and I decided we would go pay my father a visit in prison. We enjoyed each other's company, and we often did business. Our drive up to the prison was uneventful. I mostly listened to him tell stories about the old days, how hard he, his sister Flo, and their nine other siblings had it growing up in Larimer. Life had dealt them a bad hand. Survival became an existential exigency.

"Our mother had her own church," he said.

"Really?"

"Yeah. It was just a little storefront. You could barely get fifty people inside there. And the congregation were some raggedy stingy motherfuckers. Mom did all that preaching, but she was lucky to collect five dollars each Sunday. That church shit was a weak hustle."

Laughing at old stories the whole way, we had had a good time. The hours passed quickly.

Following the protocols, we made our way inside the prison. We prepared ourselves for inspection. Rocky pulled a folded bundle of hundred-dollar bills from his pocket and placed it inside the bin. Then a second bundle. Eventually, fifteen bundles in all filled the bin.

Several weeks later, my Uncle Rocky and I did a deal for $16,000. He paid me in one-hundred-dollar bills, laid out in sixteen stacks, a thousand dollars per stack. He asked me if I wanted to count the money.

"No," I said. "It's cool."

"All right," he said. "That's fine."

I didn't count the money until I arrived home. To my surprise, each stack was short by $100.

I gave him a call. "Yo, Unc, this is short."

He said, "How do I know it's short?"

"What do you mean? I just got it from you, and I didn't take no money out."

"Well, you learned a valuable lesson. No matter who you're doing business with, you got to make sure the money is right. Always count the money in front of them." Then he told me, "And if you got to take a gun or any protection to do a business deal, don't do the deal. Look, if you can't sit there, and count the money, and feel safe and comfortable, and hang out for a minute, then don't do the deal."

He hung up the phone. I was pissed, but he was right. He *had* taught me a valuable lesson.

In his book *Visions for Black Men*, Na'im Akbar writes the following: "The most effective way to gain proper orientation is to be thrown into the center of the arena of life. Learning about oneself comes from the confrontation of problems and the development of solutions for those problems. As you face real problems, you are forced to either sink or swim. If you sink, then you fail to make the transformation or you must be rescued by someone who can swim. If you swim, then the first lesson has passed."

My uncle didn't save me. He created an arena of life for me and threw me in to see if I would sink or swim.

From that day on, I always made sure the money was right before I left the scene of a drug deal. I would count the money twice. I only did business with people who I knew wouldn't try to rob or kill me. Learning such hard lessons helped me discover how to solve problems in life. They helped mold me, helped give me a strong sense of self. Too often we can't look past the flaws of parents and elders and are quick to dismiss them. Instead, we should take knowledge from anywhere, be it a book, a situation, or a person. Far from perfect, my uncle Rocky nevertheless imparted wisdom to me through his example.

As an adult, I look back and think, *Dang, I was selling drugs to Uncle Rocky. My own uncle was making money off of me.* I was his plug, the one who supplied his business. Uncle Rocky knew he could get drugs from me for a good price. That made his life easier. Here was this seventy-year-old-man buying drugs from a sixteen-year-old nephew, taking advantage of a kid who admired him. The relationship sounds really twisted. But I'm not sure it was that simple.

I believed Uncle Rocky thought it was better for him to do business with me than for me to do business with somebody who might rob me or who would snitch on me if they got busted. In that sense, Uncle Rocky was trying to protect me. We had a complicated relationship. He made money with me, but he also tried to look out for me, especially after my father went to prison. I remember going to his house in Larimer one day when I was thirteen or fourteen years old and saying to him, "Yo, Uncle Rocky, teach me how to be a pimp."

He just looked at me for a moment. Then he said, "Boy, you ain't no pimp. You don't know nothing about being no pimp. You don't want that life."

Despite his admonition, had I become a pimp, I believe he would have taught me everything I needed to know. In my father's absence, he wanted to serve as a role model for me. He was not the type of man to put drugs in my hand, but once he knew I was selling drugs, he decided to make me wiser about the game. "All right. Let me give him the game, let me tell him what comes with it, let me tell him about prison, let me tell him about robbers, let me tell him that you don't want to carry a gun on you."

He taught me many things. Simple rules like, "Don't use drugs. Have self-control. If you want to sell it, sell it, but don't ever use it." He would point out certain people on the streets of Larimer. "You see him? Back in the day, he was big time. He used to make forty thousand dollars a day, now look at him."

At that age, when I was sixteen and seventeen years old, I felt conflicted. A part of me simply wanted to be a normal teenager, but older men in the neighborhood were grooming me to become a criminal mastermind. I did love money, but I also wanted to box, fix cars, and chase girls. Instead, my plug would bring me heavy weight and I had to figure out how to get it gone. Although I admired my father and wanted to be like him, he didn't want that life for me. He wanted me to be tough, but he never wanted me to be working in the streets. After my gun charges, he had harsh words over the phone for me. "So, you're doing the dumb shit now? Don't go out like a sucker. Those streets are real."

Never proud of anything he'd done, he always said, "I just survived. I grew up hard." However, knowing that I wanted to be like my father, older men in the hood put him up on a pedestal and glorified him. They exploited me so that they could make money off me.

When it came to dealing drugs, I thought I was a king, but I did not understand that others were manipulating me. I had not yet learned how to lead. True leaders are kings. I was a pawn. And I was about to learn what it meant to be expendable.

10
TROUBLE IN PARADISE

If some men wanted me to be their pawn, Reese wanted me to be his knight. Reese saw an opportunity in me. Although he had been raised as a Jehovah's Witness, he aspired to be a hustler. I decided to use his aspirations to my advantage. Smooth talker that I was, I convinced him that I had strong relationships with people who could afford weight. He needed me because he didn't travel among the kinds of people I knew, those who could dole out $50,000 or more on a deal. Be that as it may, he made it known to me that he wanted to get his hand on some kilos. I told him I knew someone who could help.

I reached out to my friend Bernie's father and arranged a buy-and-sell. Reese and I drove over to Bernie's house, and we made the deal. What I remember most about that day is counting out $80,000 in cash, all crisp one-hundred-dollar bills. I was sixteen years old.

As we were headed home to my place in East Liberty, Reese told me, "Don't mess with them. We ain't going to mess with them no more. I think they're snitching."

That was fine by me. I'd made my cut.

Then I ran across Bernie's father a few weeks later. I was

surprised when he told me, "Your brother was just at my crib yes-terday."

Reese had cut me out of the deal. I was betrayed by my own brother. Or so I thought.

Recently I learned that Reese had started studying again with the Jehovah's Witnesses and that he was trying to leave the drug-dealing life. He had gone to Bernie's dad to explain this to him. As it turned out, Reese ended up saving my life because, six months later, Bernie's father got indicted. At the time, I had no idea that Reese's "be-trayal" had saved me from getting arrested.

His arrest hit home. Perhaps the writing was on the wall. People I knew were going to jail, but I foolishly believed I would not get caught. For one thing, I ran a smooth operation. I would pick up the drugs, then within a few hours, I would either drop them off to someone or someone would pick them up from me. There wasn't a lot of back-and-forth, and I didn't carry any weapons.

Others like Bernie's dad might have faced problems, but all seemed to be going well for me. I was independent. I had my own place and a car. Back then, I did not understand that in the drug life, you always live encased in the fog of war. You never know who might have their eyes on you at any given time.

Several times a week, I did deals with two of my cousins. They'd have $50,000 for me one day, then a few days later there'd be an-other $50,000 or $60,000. Things went well with them for over a year and a half, until they ended up getting busted by the feds.

In the weeks before their arrest, they kept calling me for pick-ups, but I would tell them to call me the following week. I was doing my best to stall because I was facing a drought on my end. Under the surface, I was already starting to feel that dealing wasn't for me. My heart wasn't in it.

They ended up doing business with somebody else, and they got busted. That was my final sign, my wake-up call. I thought, *That could have been me.* I knew that I had to do something different, but

I didn't know how to extricate myself from this world I'd become caught up in.

In the summer of 2011, I lost three of my childhood friends: all murdered. I remember going to their funerals. I was torn apart by grief but also consumed by the idea that I didn't want to end up in a box myself. Few people knew how worried I was inside. Externally, all appeared well. I had money. I had cars. I had women. I had respect. Still, nothing could ease the constant fear I felt. I was afraid of dying, of going to prison, and of not getting out of this life. I wanted more from my life, but I felt trapped.

From prison, my father would advise me, time and time again, that I needed to stay in school and stay out of trouble.

The old heads from the streets of Larimer and Garfield told me the opposite. They would tell me outrageous stories about him, glamorizing his most negative behavior. How he had submerged a dude headfirst into an aquarium until he drowned. How he'd shot all five fingers off some other dude's hand. How he'd killed this person or that person in some gruesome manner. My father never talked about his life in the streets, so I had no idea whether these stories were true or not. But my dilemma was this: if I was not to be a man like my father, who was I to be?

I recognized that I was intelligent, driven, and ambitious, but I had nobody in my life who could show me how to use my talents and energy in positive ways. Back then, the older men I looked up to needed me to stay in the game and move weight to make money off me. The more product I could get, the more money they would make. Their interactions with me took on a form of deceit, where they encouraged me to sell drugs while pretending to impart wisdom, a fact that I recognized only once I became an adult.

Looking back, I now understand that I longed for guidance. I looked up to several teachers at my high school, but their words had little impact on me when I had my uncle Rocky and my cousins to feed. Studying for school didn't work when I had to supply this dealer and that dealer. Not to mention the fact that at age eighteen, I had $130,000 in cash in a shoebox under my bed.

———

Poppa was my running buddy. When I started selling weed at age fourteen, he started selling weed, too. Once I went up in weight, I went to him and asked if he wanted to partner up.

Then he began selling for me. I trusted him. Often, I kept my weed or my money at his crib rather than at my grandma's house. I would leave thirty, forty, or fifty pounds of weed and not a gram ever went missing. I would leave ten or twenty grand and never a missing dollar. In return, I treated him like my little brother and treated him to gifts like clothing and jewelry.

I would pay studio time for Poppa to rap. I'd take him shopping and drop a few thousand dollars on clothes. He was more into clothes than I was. Taking after my uncle Rocky, I liked to spend my money on vintage cars. And we would take trips out of town. We would skip school on a Friday, drive to Atlanta, and stay with my sister Jamilla, my father's oldest daughter. We would spend the weekend just having fun, going to car shows, eating chicken and waffles, trying to pick up girls.

Spending time with Rashee and Mal-Mal was different. We would sneak girls into the basement of Rashee's house because his mom was never home, and his grandma was bedridden. When we weren't doing stuff like that, we were trying to find ways to make money. Rashee was a great basketball player and played on the school team. Mal-Mal was also a pretty good player, although not as good as Rashee. We would go over to the Hill District and play some of my older cousins for money. We would always win. Once we won five grand, serious loot.

That was the foundation of our friendship: money. We would plot and scheme trying to figure out how to get another buck, how to get rich.

It wasn't like with Bernie or Poppa. We had a real connection. With Rashee and Mal-Mal, everything was about money.

Mal-Mal was a friendly hustler who was very entertaining, a talented poet, and MC. Rashee was a hooper, one of the best basketball players I've ever seen. I loved to watch him dominate on the court. The three of us together was a mixture of ego, raw talent, and ambition. Three fatherless children searching for identity all while trying to impress one another. Our union came with the potential for violence. One moment we'd be kicking it and having a good time. The next, we'd be fighting one another or whooping ass in the neighborhood.

———

Bernie and I never got into it. For one thing, he didn't want smoke with anybody. He was a peacekeeper, always leading with his heart. Although he knew how to front and act tough, the last thing he wanted was to make a fist or to square off against one. Knowing this about him, I often had to step in and fight for him. However, I had no qualms about doing so. He was my guy. Poppa had good instincts that warned him not to deal with certain people. As we got older, I became closest to him. I knew he was a person I could trust.

When we were in eleventh grade, Mal-Mal started running with this older dude from Homewood and started selling dope for him, heroin. He really changed after that, started treating Rashee funny, boasting about how much money he was making. Rashee wanted to start selling dope, too, but Mal-Mal wouldn't introduce him to his dude from Homewood. They started bumping heads, getting into fights. I sensed some jealousy from Mal-Mal over Rashee. He always seemed to feel some type of way about me and Rashee being close and would try to turn us against each other. Be it using girls or tongue wagging. "Leon said you fucked that stank bitch." Petty lies like that caused me and Rashee to get into it more times than I can count. Although Rashee was the older of the two, Mal-Mal was a master manipulator and knew how to work him.

Although I ran with Mal-Mal and Rashee, I tried to keep Poppa away from them because I knew how they rolled, knew that they could both bring trouble.

I began distancing myself from them. Whenever one or the other called me to try and hang out, I would make up some excuse. Eventually they took offense.

"Nigga, you act like you too good to hang with us."

"Nawl," I said. "I'm just doing me."

In time, I would have some serious beef with them, the kind that leads to bodies left dead on the street.

———

Fast money brought envy, and envy brought danger. Many of my peers were jealous because I hung out with older guys and had earned their respect. My peers would see me looking fly coming through the hood in vintage cars. They knew I was traveling out of town, but they didn't know the details about what I was doing since I didn't share my business with them. They didn't even know where I lived. I never brought anyone to my place. While other dudes would abuse and insult women, I was always respectful. Out of sheer jealousy, some of my friends would bad-mouth me to girls I was talking to and tell them, "Yo, we're going to beat up Leon. We're going to rob him and fuck him up." And so on.

Through a woman I knew, I heard that Rashee and Mal-Mal had said they were going to smoke me. I believed her. I knew I had to watch my back.

One day while I was driving, I spotted their crew standing around a car near Peabody High School in East Liberty. I pulled up nice and loud in a beautiful black vintage Monte Carlo with custom rims. Once outside my vehicle, I walked past the crew, all of them watching me and grinning at me. They outnumbered me seven to one. Other people lingered about, no telling who might jump into the mix.

I saw a kid holding a basketball and asked if he would pass it to me. Right away, I started dribbling the rock in a casual manner, nonchalant, talking to the kid while looking at the crew, waiting for them to make a move.

Rashee challenged me. "What's up?"

I answered his challenge. "What's up?"

"No, what's up with you?"

I threw the ball into his face. Angered and insulted, he ran up to me, and we teed off. I punched him again and again, and he couldn't get a blow on me. Hoping to escape the pummeling, he flung his body into mine and tried to wrap his arms around me and slam me to the ground. But I was much stronger than he was and managed to throw him off. Then somebody I didn't know got in between us and started fighting him. I was trying to catch my breath when Jamal and I got into it. Although I was winded, I quickly got the better of him and started stomping him out.

I heard one of their crew say, "Go get the gun. Go get the gun."

Everybody started running. Full of adrenalin, I jumped in my car and sped off.

In the days that followed I heard from one person after the next that Rashee and Mal-Mal were planning to gun me down. Although they were grimy and jealous, haters, we'd all been through a lot together. We were boys for life. I loved them, and I still love them to this day. With that said, I couldn't simply let them kill me. I decided to take them out first.

For several days in a row, I sat inside my car outside of Rashee's house, with a gun on my lap, waiting for him to appear. He never did. I'm grateful that he didn't. If he had, I'd be in prison now. I also staked out Mal-Mal's residence, looking to ambush him. He lived on a dark, winding road, meaning it would have been easy for me to corner him and kill him. I wondered what it would feel like to pull the trigger. Killing a man would be different than shooting guns with Big Leon on an outdoor range. Different from shooting Charles out of fear.

On the third night of my stakeout, Mal-Mal finally appeared, exited through the front door, and walked down the stairs to the street. Right away, I pulled up on him in my Monte Carlo, challenged him. "What's up?"

He looked at me with fear in his eyes but said nothing. Because he was wearing a T-shirt and shorts, I knew he wasn't strapped. All I had to do was aim the gun and pull the trigger. At that moment, some feeling came over me, a relaxation in my body that brought a change of heart. I told myself that I didn't want to kill him or anyone else. With that thought, I put the car in drive and drove off.

I was a good kid, but I never fully understood that I was caught up in a losing game. The drug-dealing lifestyle is alluring, but nobody wins. Nobody. You make a bunch of money, then you end up going to prison, burdening your people with the responsibility of taking care of you. You miss birthdays, holidays, and funerals. If you don't end up in prison, you end up in a box, leaving your family to suffer.

———

In hindsight, I also understand that I was full of greed. I was subject to manipulation because I was manipulating people myself. In the same way that older hustlers were encouraging me to be on the streets, I was encouraging some of my friends to be on the streets. I now realize that I was putting Poppa in harm's way. Although I loved

Poppa, my right-hand man, his room was my stash spot. Had the cops raided my house, they would have found nothing. Had they raided his, he would have gone to prison. When you're in the streets caught up with daily survival, you don't always realize how your actions can negatively impact others.

People often ask me if I would go back and change the way I lived as a teenager, but I honestly don't know if I would have done anything differently. In those days, I felt lost, confused, and afraid. I lacked a sense of self and direction. I had no control over my thoughts or actions. However, all that would change in a matter of months.

TWO

RISE

11
PREMONITIONS

Although she has never been one to attend church, my mother takes it upon herself to read the Bible whenever she is looking for understanding or inspiration. For her, reading the good book is a way to take reprieve from life's many daily challenges and gain important spiritual guidance, practical knowledge that she can use in her dealings with the world. Sometime in late October 2012, she came upon a story that she found of particular interest, the account of the paralyzed man in John 5:8. The verse offers a simple, stark account of Jesus's healing of the crippled believer: "Rise, take up thy bed, and walk." The passage is meant to be uplifting, but my mother did not take it this way. Instead, for some reason, she found it unnerving, although she could not say why.

She read the passage at a strange time in her life. I was a year or two out of high school and starting my life, and for months, she'd been haunted by a gut feeling that something bad was going to happen to me. She couldn't put her finger on it, and she never expressed her fears to me. But whenever I saw her, she would tell me she wanted me to leave Pittsburgh and seek greener pastures outside the city. Convinced that I needed to get out, she took it upon herself to fill out an application on my behalf for the Art Institute of Atlanta.

Like many young Black men, I aspired to be a rapper, filmmaker, and producer. Once I heard she'd sent in the application, I was hoping I could enroll there or at another institution to take next steps in my career.

It was only natural that she worried about me. I was still dealing drugs, although by this time I had scaled back my business to one or two deals a week. But I imagined I'd stop dealing eventually. At that point, I had found a new passion, auto detailing. I now spent most of my time working for money on the books at a shop owned by one of my "uncles." But these developments didn't comfort my mother. Her foreboding went beyond my involvement with drugs, even if she could not put her finger on the source of her anxiety.

Try as she might, she could not convince me to leave Pittsburgh. I had my reasons for wanting to stay. Foremost among them, my father was about to come home from prison. I needed to be there for him. While incarcerated, he had to endure the deaths of loved ones like Leona and his mother, Flo, who had passed away in 2009, alone. He had not been allowed to attend their funerals or to properly grieve and say his good-byes. In addition, although he was a strong, muscular man, his years in prison had come with harsh physical consequences. He had spent long periods in solitary confinement and had suffered a severe stroke, losing function of the left side of his body for a time. He'd also undergone bypass surgery.

I wanted to be available for my father. After all the years of separation, I also needed him to be there for me. I feared experiencing what so many of my friends had. While their fathers were locked up, they patiently waited. They dreamed about being reunited and what their future lives would look like together. Then, when their fathers were released, they didn't spend adequate time together. Before you knew it, they were just as distant as ever. I'd been waiting for thirteen years for my father to come home. We had a lot of catching up to do.

On February 10, 2012, my father was released from federal

prison. He was greeted by a welcome party outside the gates. All my siblings and a few of my cousins, including Luv, Raymon, and Shianne. I stood with them and waited expectantly, ready to take him home for the first time in thirteen years. We stood bundled up in winter coats against the cold. Although I wore gloves, my fingers became stiff and frigid, forcing me to stuff my hands inside my pockets. Then I heard the tall gates clang open and saw my father step out dressed in an orange prison jumpsuit and with a skullcap snug on his head. He wore no coat, only carried a brown paper bag containing his few belongings under his arm. His lips parted into a gold-toothed grin, releasing a puff of winter breath.

He came to live with me in a two-bedroom house that I was renting in Forest Hills, a small, racially diverse suburb of working-class people just east of Pittsburgh. I thought the area would be good for both of us since it was outside our usual stomping grounds and people kept to themselves. No one had heard of Bit or Little Leon. Folks spent their evenings quietly barbecuing with family instead of beefing over turf. I knew there would be no loud arguments, no drug dealing, no shootings. When you walked down the streets there, it was quiet. I knew we wouldn't face any of the usual drama. I'd worked hard to get my own place and to save five thousand dollars that I gifted my father. When I handed him an envelope after dinner, he looked impressed.

"What the hell? My son is giving me some money."

He spent about three months looking for jobs but kept getting turned down. Then my brother Dale helped get him into the construction union. During this time, I continued to hustle, although I tried to keep it from my dad as best I could. He knew of course, even if he didn't ask any questions. He probably didn't want to know the details.

Still, he would find opportunities to make his point. "Man," he would say, "the streets ain't what everybody think. I don't know why people want to get caught up in the life. I lost so much."

He was talking about other people, but I knew he was trying to drop some wisdom on me.

I heard him and took everything to heart. Trying to lessen his worries, I started to hustle even less and put more time into working at the auto-body shop. Also, giving serious consideration to a career as a truck driver, I signed up for school to get a commercial driver's license.

On March sixteenth, my mom and I went out to dinner to celebrate my nineteenth birthday. We savored fried snapper, sipped tropical cocktails, and enjoyed listening to each other's stories about Leona.

Over ice cream, she asked if I had thought about going to college outside of the city.

"Dang, Mom. I don't want to leave Pittsburgh."

"This isn't the only city in the world, you know. Maybe you could try doing music in Atlanta?"

"Of course, I know that. But why do you want me to leave so bad?"

"I just think it might be good for you."

I didn't respond.

"Mmmm . . . hum. It's all those girls. You need to stop messing with them."

"I'm just trying to find the right one."

At the time, I was dating four women: Avery, Bree, Neek, and Shany. The image of masculinity I'd learned from my father and Uncle Rocky involved dating as many women as possible. In fact, every man I looked up to had more than one woman. I was young and popular and being a player felt like what I was supposed to do. But my involvement with these women started to get complicated.

Avery and I had been dating since my last year of high school. Many of my friends were surprised that I went for her because she wasn't part of the in-crowd. I usually dated popular girls like cheerleaders and fashion queens. Avery and her friends were considered weirdos because they had no swag. Ordinary clothes and sneakers. Nothing fancy or name-brand. Once I got to know her, I discovered that she was just quiet, someone who liked to do her own thing. She preferred to spend her Friday nights training for track meets then hanging out with her girls. That was what I found attractive about her, her independence. Light-skinned and ordinary looking, she was athletic and excelled at sports, including wrestling and track and field. Things were good between us until she started to suspect that I was seeing other girls. She never said it, but I'm pretty sure that my cheating broke her heart.

In May, she called me one day and told me that we needed to meet. She had something important to tell me. I suggested that she swing by my crib. By that point we had pretty much stopped seeing each other. And when we did get together, we argued a lot.

She arrived about an hour later and sat down on my couch. When I sat down next to her, she got up and moved to the armchair on the other side of the room, keeping her distance from me.

"I'm pregnant," she said.

I sat there, mute. I honestly had no idea what to say.

"What do you want to do?" she finally asked me.

"I don't know," I sputtered. They were only words I could think of in the moment.

"What do you mean you don't know?" she pressed. I was getting more nervous by the second, but I couldn't be the one to make the call.

"I don't know," I repeated.

"You want me to have this baby?" she asked, this time locking eyes with me.

"Are we even still together?" I quipped back.

"I don't care about that. I'm having the baby." She got up and walked out of my apartment.

I could not believe what she'd just told me. You always hear men in the hood say, "I got her pregnant when I was done with her." A dude would get a woman pregnant right before he was about to break up with her. Now I was about to become a father. I felt like a mark. My father had always said you couldn't trust women. In that moment I believed him.

My mom was the first person I told about the pregnancy. When I called her to tell her, she screamed in excitement. "That's great, Leon." She had been wanting me or my sister Shalaia to have a child since Leona passed away. "Now you need to leave all those other girls alone and be with Avery."

"But I'm not sure if I want to be with her."

"She's going to have your baby."

My father had a different perspective. "Dawg, she gon be a problem." To this day, I don't know why he thought she was trying to sucker me. In time I would learn that those were not her plans.

His pessimism only increased my uncertainty. Honestly, I was not excited about becoming a father. I was more nervous than anything. I didn't know what to expect. I didn't know if I was ready. The whole situation was scary.

I went to a few doctor's appointments with Avery, but for the most part I did not involve myself with her pregnancy. Instead, I continued to do my own thing and date as many women as I could.

Despite the looming responsibility of fatherhood, that summer was super fun for me. I spent my days boxing at the gym, detailing cars at the shop, and buying different cars for myself, and my nights going to a lot of parties. I got an old-school 1971 Cutlass, all black with yellow stripes down the middle. I was planning to put on custom rims, at $2,500 each. That was my hot summer, doing my thing. Coming into myself.

I had a love for boxing going back to my childhood. When I was a boy, my dad used to take me and my cousin Raymon to Weightmaster's Gym, a kind of run-down, back-alley place that produced some serious fighters. Everything about the place fascinated me. Then I started boxing again at age fourteen after I caught the first gun charge. Shalaia had a friend named Matt who, hoping to keep me out of trouble, took me to a gym. There I started to train under my uncle Darren, who was married to Uncle Rocky's daughter. I continued to box on and off up until that summer of 2012. I was straining at 3rd Avenue Gym and hoped to become a top-level amateur fighter, possibly even go professional. The one amateur fight I'd had, I'd won by decision after really beating up the other boxer.

—————

By that fall, my father and I had enjoyed many months of bonding. Living together came easy, a small blessing. We cracked jokes, enjoying every opportunity to make each other laugh. Still, he wanted a place of his own. He made good money working construction, but time and again his rental applications were denied because he had a criminal record. Although he'd paid his dues, when it came to housing policies the stigma that came with incarceration seemed substantial if not insurmountable. We decided we would face this challenge as father and son.

We would put our minds together and find a solution.

In November of that year, I received word that Uncle Rocky was in the hospital. Luv came into the shop while I was working on a Mercedes jeep, a silver S550, a 2010 model. The front driver's side had been bashed in during an accident. I was so proud of myself for making such good progress on restoring the car that I decided to take a few photos on my phone, the same photos I would show to a police officer a few nights later.

Luv said, "Yo, Cuz. I got some bad news."

"What's up?"

"Uncle Rocky's in the hospital."

"What happened?"

"Yo, Cuz. It don't sound good."

Later we learned that Uncle Rocky had been admitted to the

hospital the previous week. Against doctor's orders, he'd checked himself out after only a couple of days. Someone owed him money and he needed to collect. He became even more ill. When he went back to the hospital, doctors told him he had terminal cancer, but he didn't let anyone from the family know.

Luv and I went to see him the next day. He laid in bed, eyes closed with tubes trailing from his nose and mouth and an IV snaking out of each arm. I knew he was suffering. I said to Luv, "He don't want to live like this."

"Cuz."

Uncle Rocky was a go-getter. He didn't want anybody taking care of him, so to see him in the hospital bed like that really crushed me. What I did not know was that, a few days after that visit, I too would be in a hospital bed fighting for my life.

Uncle Rocky passed away a few months later, on January 1, 2013, the same day that my son, LJ, was born.

By that time, I had lost so many people to death that Uncle Rocky dying at age seventy-five felt like a blessing. Where I come from, you feel almost grateful when someone gets to live that long.

I miss my uncle Rocky and think about him every day. He's the reason why I have all these old-school cars in my garage. Each time I buy one, I think of him. I also think of the fact that the lives that both of us knew ended at roughly the same time.

12
SUNDAY TRAFFIC STOP

The Sunday I was shot, a surge of dread flooded my stomach from the moment I awakened that morning. An overwhelming feeling told me I shouldn't leave the house. The feeling was so overpowering that I stayed home all day. For hours, I worked on editing a music video I'd filmed a few days earlier. That evening, I was still editing the video, in my boxers, when I got a call from one of my cousins, who owed me about $2,500. He told me to come pick it up.

I told him I would, and that I was on my way. But I still couldn't bring myself to get dressed and leave the house. I just kept working on the video.

––––––

Another cousin called me. He also owed me money. I promised to see him soon. Again, after the conversation, I resumed work on the video. Then I received a third call, this time from my stepsister. Like the other callers, she owed me money. So, finally, I got dressed and prepared to leave the house. I figured I'd pick up my money before heading to my grandma's house for a late Sunday dinner.

When I came downstairs, I found my father in the kitchen cooking.

He asked, "Yo dawg, what time you coming back?"

"I'll be back in the morning. What time are we working out?"

"The same time."

We had fallen into a routine. Each morning, we spotted one another lifting weights at a nearby gym.

I left my house and started up my car, heading for my grandma's place in Garfield where I always had Sunday dinner with my grandma, mother, and Aunt Terri. When I reached Homewood, I spotted Lil Trill, a hotheaded sixteen-year-old, who was in and out of Shuman. We wore the same size, so I used to give him all my old clothes. I would try to look out for him, doing what I could to guide him and keep him out of trouble.

I yelled at him from the window of the car, then pulled over to the curb.

"Bro," I said, "you need to chill. You got to be focused. You got to get back in school. The streets ain't for you."

He said, "Yo, you right, bro. I hear you."

He asked me for a ride to Larimer.

I dropped him off then drove down to Auburn, a housing project that we called "AU." After that, I drove to my uncle's house, also in Larimer. I started up the steps. To my surprise, I could smell weed wafting from inside the house. My cousin Butters and I, we had a pact: never smoke weed. We were both athletic, worked out and boxed. Neither of us wanted to be the stereotypical hustler who sat around drinking and smoking weed. We were better than that.

I went into the house and found Butters chilling on the couch with a woman I didn't know. He passed me the money he owed me.

"Damn, Cuz, you high?" I asked.

"Yeah, bro. I'm high as hell." He started laughing.

"Damn, you a sucker, bro. You're smoking weed. We don't do that."

"Ain't nothing to it," he said. "Just this one time."

I studied him, thinking. After a few moments, I asked him, "I got to go run and pick up this change. You want to ride with me?"

"Yeah, I'll ride."

He told the woman that he would be back soon.

We left the house and walked to the car. I opened my door, and he did the same. However, before he could get in, I changed my mind about bringing him along for the run.

"Nah, bro," I said. "Never mind. You smell like weed. You ain't riding with me."

"Damn, bro, for real?"

"Yeah, for real."

"All right, Cuz. Fuck it. I'll chill here."

Later I would ask myself, *Would the night have gone differently had Butters been in the car with me? Would they have still shot me? Would they have shot him, too?* I can only speculate.

I might not have been shot had I said to the officers, "I'm uncomfortable. Please have your supervisor come here to the scene." These are words all young Black men should know.

What I do know: I got in the car. I drove off, made a left turn onto Shetland. That was when I saw the police cruiser driving up the one-way street, the wrong way.

Over the course of that twenty-minute traffic stop on November 11, 2012, all the social conditioning I had meticulously followed up to that point failed. Never drive in a car with your hoodie on. Check. Don't drive with anybody in the backseat. Done.

The one rule I hadn't followed came down to the tinted windows. I couldn't help myself and I got them, and sure enough, they would get me pulled over often. In fact, I had just been pulled over four days earlier. Butters was beside me in the passenger seat around one in the morning when a cruiser came up behind us, flashing lights and sirens. I sped up, made a left turn, and parked. We exited the vehicle. That's the thing, if you park and exit, they can't search your ride.

I still wonder if the cops who stopped me on the night of November 11 were those same cops who'd stopped me four days earlier. I can't say. What I do know is that I took every other precaution that night.

Be polite. Done. Use respectful language. Always.

And yet.

During my criminal trial, my attorneys asked the officers if they ever felt threatened. No, they said. They had not.

And yet.

I got shot anyway.

———

The first thing I remember, afterward, were bright lights glaring down at me. My chest and arms burning. My legs, hurting. My whole body, in so much pain. My chest felt like it had been ripped open. And a foreign object snaked down my throat, plastic tubing. An IV ran from my right arm to a white cocoon of clear fluid. Some time passed before I realized I was lying in a hospital bed, before I recognized that I was surrounded by police officers and that my feet were shackled to the bed. How long had I been in the hospital? How long had I been unconscious? Before I could even ponder those questions, my mind went black, out again.

At some point, I came to, opened my eyes, and saw a white-coated doctor standing near my bed. I heard him say, "We have some good news, and we have some bad news. The good news is you're going to survive. The bad news is you will never walk again."

Honestly, I didn't feel anything when I heard those words. I was in too much physical pain. It was as if my whole body were boiling in a vat of hot liquid. Woozy, I felt I might pass out. I was probably high from all the medication. I had lost all sense of time. Blinking in and out of consciousness. I wondered: *Did my family know I was here, or know what had happened to me?* The possibility that they might not know seared me inside.

A cop told me that I was under arrest. I would be arraigned there in the hospital.

Later I would find out that my family had no idea what had happened to me. To this day, they believe that my whereabouts and my condition were being kept hidden, in hopes that I would die in the hospital, the damaging truths dying with me. The worst witness is the one who survives. He can sink you.

———

As my dad recalls, on the night of the shooting, my iMac kept receiving calls; the computer was ringing and ringing. He thought it was strange that I never answered. He unplugged the computer to silence it so he could sleep. The next morning, he got up at 5:00 a.m., as he always does, but he was surprised to discover that I still wasn't home. He decided to text me. No response. Then he sent a second text. Then a third. Still no response. Where was I, he wondered. Rather than go to the gym and work out without me, he tried calling me. No answer. He tried again and again. An hour passed, then two hours.

He called my mom. "Hey, is Leon there?"

"No."

"Well, he was supposed to meet me. I keep telling him if he is going to stay out, he needs to call me. Too much stuff is happening."

My mom wasn't concerned. "He probably just fell asleep somewhere," she said.

Ever since I was young, I had the bad habit of going to someone's house and falling asleep. She figured I'd done so again. She told my father she would check with my grandma Peewee.

Next, my dad called a few of my female friends. "Hey, is Leon there? Have you seen him? Have you talked to him?" No one had. Worried now, he started riding to all my spots. Nobody had seen me. Nobody could find me. My dad called the county jail. Around the same time, he saw a TV news report about a police shooting involving a car similar in make to mine. He didn't think much of it until he received a hysterical call from my mom. She told him that my car was in the pound and was being held under investigation. Connecting the dots, he said, "Them motherfuckers shot my son."

Independent of one another, my parents started driving around Pittsburgh, checking all the hospitals, but none had a patient named Leon Ford, leaving my parents to believe that I was already dead. They met outside Presbyterian Hospital. They were devastated. My mother started crying, and my father took her in his arms and sought to comfort her. My mother repeated my name again and again.

As luck would have it, inside the corridors of Presbyterian Hospital, my father chanced upon a guy he'd gone to high school with who now worked at the hospital. He pulled my dad aside. "Your son, he's here. The cops shot him. He's still alive. He's in the ICU."

My father breathed deep. He and my mom rushed up to the ICU desk. They asked after me. The nurse manning the station checked her computer. She seemed to become agitated at what she saw on the screen. She told my parents to wait, then left the desk and disappeared through a door. A short time later, several police came before my parents, a blue wall of force.

One officer said, "I understand that you are asking about Leon Ford?"

"Yes," my mother said. "We want to see him."

"That won't be possible."

"Why not?"

"Look, we're going to keep this short. What I can tell you is that your son, Leon Ford, resisted arrest and was shot because of his actions. He is still under arrest and is not allowed any visitors at this time."

"Is he there in ICU?"

"That's all the information I have for you."

"Where the fuck is my son?" my father said. "What the fuck did you do to my son?"

"It's time for you to leave unless you also want to get arrested."

"What the fuck did you do to my son?"

"You want to go to jail?"

My mother pulled my father away from the officers. They looked at each other, lost, wondering what they could do next.

Two days later, my brother Dale organized an impromptu press conference in Garfield. He delivered a message: "You shot the wrong kid. The Pittsburgh Police made a mistake. This is not something that will be swept under a rug."

Soon thereafter, my parents hired an attorney to file a motion for them to be allowed to see me. After two weeks, my mom was granted permission to see me in the hospital for a short visit, only fifteen minutes. When she arrived at Presbyterian, she found ten officers standing outside my room, a terrifying sight. She didn't know what to think. Was I in danger? Was she? Should she still try to go in to see me? Yes, she had to.

When she entered the room, she saw me prone in the bed, a spidery creature webbed up in tubes and gauze. She broke down crying. Then she tried to kiss me, but the female police officer guarding me screamed at her, "Don't touch him. Don't kiss him." Immediately, I became furious, but in my condition, what could I say, what could I do?

I kept pointing at the tubes in my throat, kept tapping my legs.

My mother asked, "Are you in pain?"

I was, but I shook my head. While my mother watched, I continued trying to motion, trying to get through to her. However, she didn't know what I was trying to communicate.

She said, "I'm going to get the doctor."

I shook my head and I kept shaking it because I didn't want her to find out I was paralyzed. Against my wishes, the female officer went to get the doctor. When he came into the room, he repeated the words he'd spoken to me two weeks earlier: "We have some good news, and we have some bad news. . . ."

Now the meaning of John 5:8 was made clear to my mother. Good Lord: it had been a premonition. She started praying.

———

One day Dale and my dad came for a visit. I was ecstatic to see them, but the tubes in my throat prevented me from sharing my fear, my desperation, and my need to connect. Nor did I have the strength to sit up in bed. Staples held my chest together. I gestured toward my legs, although I don't remember what I was attempting to tell them. By that time, I could no longer feel anything below my waist.

I started making other gestures, frantic movements with the arm that didn't have the IV. Dale came up with an idea. Perhaps I could spell out some words. They started reciting the letters of the alphabet, A-B-C-D. When they reached the correct letter, I would nod. Eventually, I spelled out the words: apple pear. I wanted an apple pear. My brother and dad started laughing. All that effort over a piece of fruit. How would I be able to eat it?

I'll never forget the moment when the tubes were removed from my throat, and I was finally able to talk. My mom told me about the quiet prayer she'd uttered during that first visit with me. She had prayed to God, thanking him that I was still alive. She told Him that she was willing to take anything else as long as I lived.

"Dang, Mom," I said. "You could have prayed for my legs, too."

We both laughed.

Those early weeks in the hospital are hazy, a blur, but I remember bits of my first conversation with my dad. A few people owed me money. I wrote down their names so that he could collect it for me.

The overhead light glinted off his bald head. He gritted his teeth and said, "Man, I don't care about that."

I never ate hospital food. Each day, my father would bring me breakfast at six in the morning, home-cooked meals, hash browns with peppers and onions, eggs and omelets, turkey sausage, and French toast. Every day. For lunch he would bring me turkey sandwiches, salmon, and chicken and shrimp. Then some other fresh meal for dinner. He would say, "Man, you ain't eating this bullshit down here." My mom would stay with me all day, sleeping on a chair in my room, rarely leaving the hospital. She was at my bedside for months. Her concern for me was so deep and strong that she even lost her job.

That type of support and love was so profound. I could feel it, the doctors could feel it, and the nurses could feel it. I was hurting, physically and mentally. However, the love was stronger than the pain.

Thinking back on that time, my mom remembers how I would just look out in space dazed from all the medications, zoned out. I also remained in an unstable condition, going in and out of the ICU.

When my grandma Peewee came to visit me, I just looked at her and started crying. She said, "Aw, Leon." I don't think she'd ever seen me cry before.

A group of family members came to see me, everyone crying. I started laughing and joking as I had seen my father do in such situations. "Hey, everyone," I said. "No, don't cry. I'm cool. I'm all right." That became my mind-set from that moment until I started undergoing therapy seven years later. Hold it all in. Big boys don't cry.

Sometimes I would feel embarrassed for my visitors. I had a wound VAC, and it smelled awful. Still, the family members who mattered most came and sat with me. Poppa and Bernie also came to see me on the regular. The biggest shock came from those who never visited, people I thought I was close to like some of my friends from Garfield and Larimer. I never knew that certain folks would write you off once they'd discovered you're paralyzed. Even my brother Reese never bothered to show up. I was crushed.

Avery came by once. She sat in the chair by my bed, but I don't recall her saying a word. She was really showing by then, and she kept her hands on either side of her belly. Because it seemed like she didn't really want to be there, I also didn't want her to be there.

My father told me, "Man, only people you can depend on is me, your mom, and yourself. Don't worry about anyone else." He said, "It is what it is, dawg. They ain't in this pain, you are. So, you got to rise up."

My cousin Luv had a hard time accepting that the cop had shot me for no reason. I remember him sitting in the chair next to the bed and asking me, "Man, what the fuck did you do?"

I said, "Cuz, I'm serious. I really didn't do anything wrong. Those cops were just on some weird shit."

I sensed that "weird shit" was eating up my father, and he was wrestling with his ego. A man had shot his son five times and paralyzed him, and my father had yet to retaliate. He had a code to abide by. I felt for him, and I feared for him. Things were volatile, uncertain. However, my father is systematic in his thinking and always weighs the pros and cons of any decision or action. Given his personality, I took comfort in knowing that he would do nothing that would return him to prison or take him away from me. I needed him more than ever.

It frustrated my father that local news outlets continually painted me as a bad guy, implying that I deserved to be shot. He called it "niggermania." This stereotyping of me he could not tolerate. If he could not stand up to the cops, he could to the media. Whenever a reporter tried to interview him, he'd say, "Man, get the fuck out of my face."

13

WHO WILL DEFEND ME?

With felony charges of resisting arrest and felony assault I was facing twenty years in prison. I was in a tremendous amount of physical pain and in a dark place psychologically, unable to even think about the criminal matter. Shalaia bought me a set of Beats headphones, and I spent most of my time listening to music, trying not to think about what had happened to me, trying to escape the pain in mind and body. I remember listening to a lot of 2Pac and Erykah Badu, getting lost in the beats and the words. If nothing else, the music helped the time pass and offered a bit of relief.

My father took it upon himself to find me legal representation. However, deciding on an attorney would not be easy since every lawyer in Pittsburgh wanted my case. Thinking it over, my father sought advice from some savvy buddies in California who were familiar with the system. They recommended a firm. Wasting no time, my father spoke to a lawyer there about my case.

The attorney told my father that I had strong grounds for a civil suit. He would send my father a contract to review.

My father says that he read the contract three times. He told himself, *Wow, this is crazy.*

The firm wanted 48 percent of the judgment if they won my case and half the money if the judgment was $10 million or more.

My father called the lawyer.

"Hey, Leon," the man said. "How are you doing today? Did you get the contract?"

My father said, "Yeah, I got the contract, absolutely."

"I know, it's kind of hard to understand."

My father said, "I read it a couple times. It's not hard to understand, it's just the way you put it." He continued, "Let me ask you a question."

The lawyer said, "Oh, sure."

"How many times did you get shot?"

"I don't follow. What do you mean?"

"How many of those bullets did you take?"

"Excuse me."

"That's exactly what I'm saying." My father fought to control his anger. "You ain't take a bullet, but you want half the money."

The lawyer said nothing in reply.

"Man, y'all got me fucked up." He hung up the phone. He told himself, *These lawyers don't give a fuck about us.*

My father had been in the system, and he had seen guys get screwed over. He wasn't going to let that happen to me. He had to assume the role of my protector. In the months and years to come, he would let the cameras stay on me and my mom, while he laid back in the cut observing all the activists—the movers and shakers—and figuring them out. Then he would tell me, "I don't trust this motherfucker right here. This person's a creep. That person's a creep. We're not working with them anymore." We were a perfect team.

We did hire the firm, but only after my father had negotiated fair terms and made sure that they were committed to my case. With so much on my mind, I left it to him to handle most of the dealings with the attorneys. I would have been lost without him.

Unfortunately, the social justice movement in our country today is as much a business as it is anything else with lawyers, activists, politicians, and other prominent players earning top dollar from legal fees, speaking engagements, and lucrative book deals. I always encourage the families of those victimized by cops to see these players for who they are. No matter how significant their voices and actions, at the end of the day, they aren't taking any bullets.

———

One day, Bree came to visit me in the hospital. Her visit was unexpected since she'd been one of my side chicks. We'd had a lot of fun together, often hanging out with her cousins in the East Hills Projects.

I could tell by the look on her face that she was shocked to see the condition I was in. I'd been muscular before from working out and boxing; now I was rail-thin, weighing only about ninety pounds. She hesitated at the door as if unsure if she should come.

"Bree," I said.

"Leon," she said.

She walked over and sat down in the chair next to my bed.

"I'm surprised to see you," I said.

"You know I had to come see my dude."

She stayed for an hour, trying to make conversation. I didn't have much to say, to her or to anyone. My self-esteem was low. I was skinny and worthless, my body slowly disappearing from the world.

Before she left, she said, "You know you got to get well so we can do our thing." She gave me a lascivious smile. I smiled back at her, unsure that I would ever be anything like what she remembered.

She started to visit me on the regular, at least once a week. Spending time with her always lifted my spirits some. At least one woman in the world besides a family member cared about me. Whenever she came, she always made sure to bring me some of my favorite foods even if it was nothing more than an apple or a can of ginger ale. And she always told corny jokes, trying to cheer me up. Despite all I was going through, she was a welcome presence. She would help me out of the bed into my wheelchair.

Then, somehow, she found out that Avery was having my child.

She confronted me during one of her visits. "You was messing with that bitch while we was together?"

"I didn't know we was supposed to be serious. I thought we was just kicking it."

"Oh, so that's what you thought." She sucked her teeth. "Now look at you. Ain't nobody ever going to date no dude in a wheel-chair."

With that, she left.

To my surprise, she continued to come to the hospital, always bearing a food treat. She would hold my hand or rub my shoulders. Somehow, she saw herself as replacing Avery as my girlfriend. But in my condition, how could I be a boyfriend to her? To anyone? What did she see in me? I grew suspicious, figuring that she had some ulterior motive. Still, her presence was a comfort. I welcomed any person or any little thing that would help me get through a day.

14
STUDYING THE ART OF DYING

Each day in the hospital pushed me to extreme heights of suffering: physical and emotional pain that I did not think I could bear. In the morning and in the evening, I endured painful sessions in the physical therapy unit, with additional exercise midday in my room. While hospital staff saw to my body, no one saw to my mind. I didn't get a single visit from either a social worker or a psychologist. Mentally, I was in a dark place. That I would never walk again was a reality I could not accept, torment that caused me to experience feelings of worthlessness and abandonment. Avery, expecting our child, never came to see me after that one visit. Whatever had happened between us, she was to be the mother of my child. I figured that she should count for something, that she should regard me as a person of importance in her life. So why didn't she? Was I less of a man in her eyes?

Even though I hadn't been the best partner, I was hoping we could have rebuilt something together, that she could have proven to me that she was trustworthy, even if I wasn't.

My confidence plummeted. I no longer felt like a golden child. I was more like a weakling, a nothing. This sense of worthlessness made me bottle up. I refused to talk to my lawyers, my parents, or other family members.

My brother Dale would say to me, "Yo, this is your life. You have a voice. You have to speak up." He would say, "Look, you're not dead. You need to fight for yourself. You need to open up your mouth. You need to speak up for what you feel you need to do." But I didn't have it in me.

Though I told no one, I was consumed by thoughts of revenge against a system that had paralyzed me and that wanted to put me behind bars for twenty years. I knew what I would do. Once I was released from the hospital, I would get my hands on an assault rifle, wheel my way into a police station, and kill as many cops as I could. And then, they would kill me in return. So be it.

I had ordered books by George Jackson, *Blood in My Eye* and *Soledad Brother*, and I read the pages voraciously. When I was not reading, I watched videos of Malcolm X, Huey Newton, Louis Farrakhan, and Khalid Muhammad on YouTube. Because he was the rawest in his hatred for white people, Khalid Muhammad was my favorite. Watching him, I would think, *This man here, this is going to be me.* In Jackson, Malcolm, and Muhammad I saw an anger that reflected the hate I felt.

Fixated on the idea of revolutionary suicide, I spent every available moment studying the art of death. Certain words from a 1993 Khalid Muhammad speech would repeat a silent chant inside my head: "We kill the women. We kill the babies. We kill the blind. We kill the cripples. We kill them all . . . When you get through killing them all, go to the goddamn graveyard and kill them again because they didn't die hard enough."

My parents seemed to sense what I was feeling. My mom would say to me, "Leon, this ain't it for you. You're going to be all right. You're going to give testimony. One day you will be speaking and reaching millions of people."

I would simply stare at her in disbelief. My only hope was to walk again. I would be nothing unless I could walk again. That was my only reason to live: to see if I might one day walk again. Walking was life.

One day I was trying to transfer from the bed to my wheelchair, and I fell on the floor. My dad stood looking down at me. "Leon, get up," he said.

I drew myself upright. "I can't," I said. I was thin, frail, and weak. "Nigga, pick yoself up off the floor."

I did not move. There was no way I could do what he asked. I didn't have it in me. After a time, he gave in, bent down, lifted me up, and placed me in the bed. It would be his last time doing so.

My time in the hospital taught me some valuable lessons about parenting. Often, we strive to better ourselves because our parents drive us to do so. If I could not dress myself, my mother would dress me. If I could not comb my hair, she would comb it. If I could not feed myself, she would put food in my mouth. No matter how bad I felt, how down I was on myself, my mother would show me that I was deserving of her attention, that my life was worth something even if I was incapable of seeing the worth.

A nurturer, my mother would do anything to bring me comfort, while my father would push me, using discomfort as a motivator to encourage me to change my circumstances. A mother's love is the engine, the foundation. A father's guidance is the steering wheel, direction.

15

LESSONS IN FATHERHOOD

Avery's delivery date approached. She was scheduled to give birth at West Penn Hospital, the same hospital where I was born. West Penn was far from Mercy, the hospital where I was recovering. Given my daily medical regimen, the distance might make it difficult for me to be present at the birth of the baby. Strategizing, my mom reached out to Avery, begged her to forgive my past wrongs, and asked that she deliver the baby at Mercy. My mother also helped Avery arrive at a name for our child. He would bear my name, another Leon Ford.

On New Year's Eve, Avery arrived at Mercy preparing to go into labor. Hospital staff escorted me to the delivery room. However, the surgeon determined that she needed to be moved to another room for a C-section. We made our way there. To my dismay, I discovered my motorized wheelchair was too large for the room. I would not be able to witness the birth of my son all because of a few inches of doorframe. Truthfully, I did not feel disappointment, sadness, frustration, or anger—only numbness. I was empty.

A nurse escorted me back to my room.

Time passed. I do not know how long I waited, only that the doctors wheeled my son into my room inside a clear plastic cradle, the baby wearing a little cap and wrapped in swaddling blankets. I could only look at him. Because I had the staples in my chest from the surgeries and was on sternum precautions, I could not hold him. Even if I could have, I would have been afraid to do so, for I was still in physical pain and weak. I still weighed only about 90 pounds. In addition, my mind was running too hard to see what was in front of me.

I noticed that the baby had Avery's complexion, but little else registered. The baby had been born, and I had seen it. Now I could either listen to some music or simply go asleep. I wasn't able to be present for my son or love him as overwhelmingly as I do now. I was disconnected from my emotions because I was in so much pain and because I felt torn up inside by the darkest thoughts.

————

I was released from the hospital the following month, in February of 2013. My discharge papers provided detailed follow-up instructions for my physical care. Most important, I had to remember that I was on sternum precautions. Every four hours I also had to insert a catheter into my penis to drain urine from my bladder. I had to check my body each day for bedsores. A nurse would visit me every day to check my wound VAC and attend to other matters. However, I still received no instructions regarding my mental health. Discharge papers usually instruct patients to follow up with their primary care physician. At the same time, no one ever tells gunshot victims to see a mental health professional. I was sorely in need of therapy.

My father took me back to the house that he and I shared before I was shot. By that time, I had gained enough body weight and strength to use a manual wheelchair, although the effort strained every muscle in my arms. A walkway had been installed in the back of the house. I remember rolling up the ramp and then rolling through the back door. I recall guiding myself into the living room where I found a large hospital bed. This would now be my living space. The room seemed larger than I remembered. And I felt small inside it. Still, I was home.

My father is Mr. Make It Happen. Because I was now in a wheelchair, he decided to sell his car and purchase a van. To figure out how large a van we would need to accommodate me, I asked him to measure from the bottom of the wheel to the top of my head. He did. Less than a week later, he bought the van, along with a ramp that I would need to roll my way inside.

I'd been home from the hospital for maybe three or four days, but I had a follow-up appointment with my primary care physician. My father rolled me up the ramp, intent on getting me inside the van only to discover that the ceiling was too low.

He said, "Duck, duck, duck."

I ducked. The staples had been removed from my chest, so my entire torso was still sore and would be for a long time. My father pushed me into the van. I was completely bent over, my chest touching my knees. I was stuck.

He started freaking out, "Oh my God, I fucked up, dawg." He felt so bad.

I had not fully settled in at home before I received word from my attorneys that the district attorney had filed a motion to put me on house arrest. My attorneys fought back, hard. And they won. However, the hostile efforts of the DA only further embittered me, making me want to lash back through violence. I longed to gun him and some cops down.

It so happened that my return home took place around the time of the Christopher Dorner shootings in California. I remember obsessing over the Dorner situation, celebrating this man who shot down cops. My father and I watched the CNN reports as if we were watching a movie, both of us rooting for Dorner and living vicariously through him.

My father said, "I hope they don't catch that nigga. I hope he gets away."

He never really said much about the two cops who had stopped me and third cop who'd shot me, but "I sensed that 'weird shit' was eating up my father, and he was wrestling with his ego. A man had shot his son five times and paralyzed him, and my father had yet to retaliate." And here was Chris Dorner, enacting justice on our behalf and for the many others wronged, cut down.

Although no longer in the hospital, I continued to fixate on death, moving between thoughts of murder and thoughts of suicide. Some days I wanted to live. Others, I wanted to die. Some days I wanted to kill a police officer, other days I wanted to kill myself. A dance.

Most of my time each day was taken up with reading. I continued to read George Jackson, Huey Newton, and Malcolm X. For reasons I didn't understand at the time, I would also watch self-improvement videos on YouTube, things like Bob Proctor's "Do You Know Who You Are?" Self-improvement struck me as a curious concept. I could not walk. No way to improve that. I could improve the world by killing a few cops.

Somehow, my father knew what I was feeling and thinking, and he would say, "Dawg, you know what, I can't respect nobody that kill theyself. That's some sucker shit. You know what I'm saying? If somebody kill themselves, they leave their whole family to suffer. It's selfish."

He always made sure to generalize, speaking harshly but never about me. He wouldn't say, "You are a sucker if you decide to do this."

Although difficult for him, he could be gentle at times. He would tell me, "You got this." I would do my best not to cry in front of him, but I was no longer my talkative, gregarious self. I kept my feelings locked up inside, boiling as if in a pressure cooker. I was living in a shroud of so much darkness and pain. My new life of paralysis never changed who I was to my family or how they treated me. But it did change how I interacted with my family and the world. I never felt that my inner circle wouldn't love or support me. But, in quiet moments, I grappled with who I could become now as a person with a disability. Before I was shot and paralyzed, I had never paid attention to people who used wheelchairs. I had no point of reference for what this new life would be like.

———

One day, I sat despondent in my wheelchair. I stared emptily at the walls of my living room. I could feel the words pounding in my mind, over and over again. "There is nothing left for me to live for."

My father looked me in the eyes. "Man, look. You got to choose to live because if you die, I die." He almost broke down. "We need you here. You're alive for a reason, and you're my heart. I need you. I need you to be here."

At a loss about how he could help me, he had a conversation with his father, Big Leon, about what I was going through. A few days later, my grandfather called me from Massachusetts. He said, "You're experiencing the lowest moment of your life. Right now, it's pretty bad. Your life is shit right now, but you know what? You can't fall off the floor." I kept listening. "You can't get any lower in your life. And so, just get up. Get up off the floor and how high you climb depends on your willpower. Nobody can do it for you. We'll be here for you, we'll support you, but you have to get up off the floor yourself."

Many of my family members spoke similar words of encouragement. My family challenged me, supported me, and encouraged me to find my life's purpose. But it would take years for that to happen, a long and painful process. It would require dust to settle for me to rise out of the ashes.

———

Sometimes I would try to get out of the bed and stand up from my wheelchair having forgotten that I could no longer walk. Once reality hit me, I would become so angry that I wanted to break something.

I remember lying in bed one Sunday morning watching TV. Some pastor was giving a sermon about faith. He ended by saying, "If you send this money in to my church, you're going to receive a blessing." Hearing a pastor say something like that always made me feel even more cynical. Religion was about money, not God or healing from suffering. The pastor's words discouraged me and made the potential miracle of my walking again seem unlikely.

———

After I was released from the hospital, a nurse would come to our home every day to attend to my wound VAC, help me have a bowel movement, and to treat and bandage my bedsores while my parents watched. I would end up having to wear the wound VAC for three years.

The nurse always seemed to be in a rush to finish and leave as soon as possible. Minutes after he stepped out the door, my bandages would come undone. This happened one time too many.

My father said, "Oh, hell no."

My mother said, "I'll just do it." She rewrapped the bandages. From having watched my nurse attend to me for weeks, both she and my father had memorized my caretaking protocol.

From that day forward, my mom became my nurse, coming to the house every day. She would turn me on one side and treat and bandage any bedsores. Then she would attend to my bowel program.

While I felt humiliated, I was still grateful to have a mother capable of showing me such love and support. At the same time, my dependence on her dealt a blow to my self-worth and made me feel less like a man.

A typical day, I would wake up in the morning and smell my dad cooking breakfast. He would be playing Maxwell or another R&B artist, the music that he loves. I would hear a knock on the front door. At that point in my recovery, I was still unable to get out of the bed and into my wheelchair without assistance, so I would shout and tell my dad that someone was at the door. He'd answer and it was always my mom. They'd greet each other, and he'd ask her what she wanted to eat. She would tell him, and he would return to the kitchen and resume cooking.

After breakfast, my mom would attend to me. She would roll me over and do her thing, stick her finger up my butt. It became routine, but I never got used to it.

———

She and my dad took such good care of me that they motivated me to try things on my own. I did not want to disappoint them.

One day I decided to bathe myself rather than be washed up in bed. Showering was something I figured I could manage. All I had to do was sit on a chair in the bathroom. Easy peasy. So, I asked my father to let me try it on my own. He carried me into the bathroom and placed me on the chair. I started to clean my body. All was going well, and I felt so proud of myself. Then I fell off the chair. Sitting on the wet floor, I felt devastated. I was helpless, a loser. Staring at the bathroom cabinet, I felt like I was staring at a brick wall, a permanent impasse.

He ran in, picked me up, and started cracking jokes, clearly trying to make me feel better. "Man, look at you. You got your balls all out."

We both laughed.

A jokester, my father would come into the living room walking like a zombie. He would say, "When you start walking, you'll be walking like this." I would just crack up laughing.

I would not have survived but for the love and the support of my mother and father. They showed and expressed that love in different ways. My mom would do anything to make me comfortable. Every day, she was willing to come over and cook and clean for me while I remained in bed doing nothing for myself. She may have complained to her friends, but I never heard it. She never said, "I'm tired of Leon," at least to me.

On the other hand, with love, my dad would say, "Nigga, get your ass up. You ain't a fucking bum. What's wrong with you? You're a grown man. Go and get your own fucking food. I don't care if you're in a wheelchair."

These are two different types of love, but they were equally important to me. If possible, children should not be deprived of the love of either parent. The way a father pushes you is different from the way a mother nurtures you. When you admire and respect your father, you don't want to let him down. The same holds true for your mother. You need both parents to achieve the proper balance, to keep you grounded.

Of course, I was now a father myself. Avery would come by the house and drop off our son, who we called LJ. My father would help me care for him. For many months I couldn't hold my son because of precautions for my sternum. I'd been instructed not to lift anything over four pounds. My father did most of the work preparing formula and changing diapers. I would simply look on in wonder at LJ. How would I ever be a true father to him?

I did not think I was capable. Looking at his little arms and legs kicking in his crib, I tried to imagine what I could be for him. It was so hard to even think about it because there was so much that I could not do. I always had pictured playing football, wrestling, or racing with my son. None of that was possible now. In my mind, I could never live up to my ideal—to be the father I wanted to be for my son.

On the other hand, being a father changed me. It was a gradual process, but my thinking began to change. LJ was such a special child. Even before he could talk, he always reached for me. He didn't see my wheelchair or my rage. He would just drink his bottle and stare up at me with his big, curious eyes. When I looked back, I saw nothing but love. He would put his chubby legs on my face. Honestly, at first, I was in too much physical and emotional pain to love him back. Then his innocent affection for me softened what had felt hard, immovable inside. Even today I can't pinpoint when it happened. The more time I spent with him, the more I longed to be in his presence.

Many of the values that my parents and grandparents had instilled in me began to surface, and I started to look at my plight through a different lens. I knew that my decisions would have consequences for my son. If I chose to be violent, in all likelihood, my son would also be violent. How could I act in such a way as to honor my parents and grandparents but also create a legacy for my son?

I was learning that when we are at our lowest, it is easy to choose anger. Anger is the path of least resistance. Love is not easy. It's always the right path, but learning to step on it is not easy.

I told myself, *I can't change what happened to me. Now that I'm in this wheelchair, what can I do to add value to the world around me? What can I do to make my life purposeful?*

I had no clue. However, in time, the answers would start to reveal themselves.

16
BUILDING BACK CONTROL

Likely because LJ was in our life, Avery and I started spending time together again. We did simple things together, like watching movies, listening to music, playing chess, and going out to eat. Then, somehow, she found out about Bree.

She shouted at me one day while I was laid up in the bed in my living room. "You're just half a man. You're lucky I'm here with you. No other woman wants you."

The way Bree and Avery belittled my manhood made me feel like no other woman would be interested in me. So, I felt like I had to be with one of them. I would break up with Avery and go back to Bree, and then would break up with Bree and go back to Avery, a vicious cycle that went on for several months until I got tired of them making me look stupid. I started to date other women although each relationship would fizzle out only after a few weeks. In hindsight, I recognize that some of the women really liked me, more than I liked myself. I still didn't believe that I could fully be a man for them.

Ironically, I found out that Bree was doing her own thing behind my back. She was cheating on me with one my homeboys, Bizzie. One day, I asked Bree to drive me over to Bizzie's house.

When he came out to the car to help me get inside, he avoided her. I found that strange since I knew that they knew each other.

I said, "Y'all ain't going to speak to each other?"

They both ignored my question.

Once inside his house, I started bad-mouthing her, talking about the nasty things she said to me sometimes and bringing up all her other character defects.

I said, "Man, I'm just using her so she can drive me around when I need a ride."

Bizzie gave me a strange look but said nothing.

The next day she called me and said, "You're using me. You're using me."

That's when I knew he had told her everything I said. I called him.

He said, "Bro, I'm so sorry but I got to be honest with you. I'm in love with her."

His words gut-punched me. How would I ever be able to trust a woman again?

———

My father had a homie named Sticks who'd been in a wheelchair for about thirty years. He arranged for me to spend the day with Sticks, hoping that his partner could reach me in ways that he couldn't. Once a date was set, he dropped me off at Sticks's house. We sat in the living room facing one another in close proximity, me in one wheelchair, Sticks in another.

From the jump, I was struck by Sticks's disposition. He was talkative and cheerful, and he seemed to have an infinite number of jokes at his beck and call.

"Youngblood, your pops told me you been having some trouble," he said.

"I guess so," I said.

"What kind of trouble?"

I said nothing.

"It must be bitches. You should chase some money that way you won't spend your time chasing bitches."

Still, I said nothing. Uncle Rocky used to say the same thing.

Unbothered by my silence, he tried again and again to get me to open up. I didn't have it in me, so he just came out and asked me what I wanted to know, if I had any questions for him.

Unsure of how to describe the tumult I felt inside, I said, "I'm not sure."

Then he started dropping science, telling me about what life would be like for me in a wheelchair.

"People will treat you like shit if you let them. Life in that chair is hard enough without people trying to shit on you everywhere you go. They either think you sorry or they feel sorry for you. So, you can't feel sorry for yourself."

Everything he said surprised me. He touched on the most mundane matters, things I'd given no thought to such as trying to roll up a hill, which required muscle-breaking effort.

He said that he had something I needed to see. While I sat and watched, he showed me several videos of himself having sex with women.

I was stunned on a few levels. "Wow," I said. "You can still do that? I can still do that?"

He replied, "Yeah, fam. Your life ain't over." He smiled, and I returned it with one of my own.

We went out to his garage. Sticks showed me how he worked the hand controls on his car. One connected to the brake, the other to the accelerator. All you had to do was squeeze the handle you wanted for to car to go or stop. Driving was as easy as that. I could teach myself how to use the devices in no time. The first step was for me to learn how to lift myself out of my wheelchair and get behind the steering wheel.

During our few hours together, Sticks showed me that I could still have a life. Far from being "handicapped," he traveled, played basketball, dated, drove a car, and lived independently. He helped boost my confidence and in doing so forever changed how I viewed myself and my wheelchair. Before this moment, I couldn't picture myself in bed with a woman or behind the wheel of a car heading to my grandma's house for Sunday dinner.

The moment I got home, I ordered a set of hand-control devices. I started to spend time each day working on getting into the driver's seat of my father's van. After a week the hand controls had not arrived. A second week passed. I asked my father if he had any knowledge of their whereabouts. He said that he did not. It would take a third week for him to admit that he had been hiding the controls, afraid for me to drive.

His deceit was both funny and surprising.

"Dang, Dad. What do you think I'm going to do, run over somebody?"

"Nawl," he said. "I was just trying to look out for you. My bad." I was just starting to see how I could look out—and look out further—for myself.

My grandmother Peewee still lived in her Garfield apartment above a store on Penn Avenue, the place where I'd planned to have dinner the night I got shot. You had to climb about fifteen steps to reach her front door, and they brought back fond memories. These were the same steps that I used to run up and jump down when I was a kid, the ones she used to chase me down with a broom after I had accidentally busted her fish tank. She came at me swinging the broom in the air like the cadets on one of my favorite childhood movies, *Major Payne*.

Now, in my new hand-controlled van, I would park outside on

the street and honk my horn, and she would look out the window. I'd ask, "Who's all up there?"

"Nobody but me," she'd say. "I'll be down."

Then she would bring me some delicious, home-cooked food.

If someone I knew and trusted happened to pass by, I would have them carry me up the stairs to her apartment.

One day, I drove over and honked my horn. "Gram, who's all up there?"

"Nobody but me. I'll be down?"

"No," I said. "One minute."

I opened the car door, assembled my wheelchair, and lifted myself down onto the seat. I made my way into the vestibule, and once there, I lifted myself out of the chair and lowered my body onto the steps. Slowly, I started up, one stair at a time.

I heard my grandmother call down to me from the top of the staircase. "Leon, what you doing?"

I continued to use the banister to pull myself up.

She repeated her question. "Leon, what are you doing?"

"Gram, I'm tired of waiting on people to bring me up these steps."

"Aw, Leon." She walked past me to get my wheelchair and bring it up.

From that day on, every time I went to her home, I would jump out of my car into my wheelchair, then make my way up to her.

———

One night, around Easter of 2013, something strange happened at Grandma Peewee's when I wasn't there. That evening, my aunt Terri had come over for dinner. Full, relaxed, she decided to stay the night. She had just settled into bed when she heard a bang on the front door. It frightened her.

She called out, "Who is it?"

No one answered. She kept asking but received no response.

Then the person banged on the door again. Because she didn't know who it was or what might be going on, she decided to call the cops. Several minutes later, after the cops arrived, she went downstairs to let them in, and she found two officers in the vestibule, a man and a woman. The man stood a few feet away behind his partner, in the darkness, his face hidden. The woman started asking my aunt Terri questions about who was knocking on the door.

"I don't know who it was," she said.

"Do you know why that person wanted to get into your building?" the woman asked.

"No."

As she continued her interrogations, the second cop stepped forward. My aunt Terri recognized his face: Officer David Derbish, the man who'd shot me.

Could it be?

She looked at his badge. Seeing his name, she grew terrified. Her legs started shaking. She felt like she was going to fall to the floor. Panicked, she ran back upstairs and told my grandmother, "Oh my God, you'll never believe who's downstairs."

It was a shock. For one thing, because he'd shot me, she figured he'd been assigned to desk duty. Here he was still patrolling the streets.

Derbish and the female officer came upstairs and stood outside my grandmother's apartment. He started asking my aunt Terri weird questions. "Does anybody here sell drugs or anything like that?"

"No," my aunt Terri said. "Where did that come from?" She had no idea where he was going with his outlandish inquiry, but then another thought struck her: *What if Leon had been the person who opened the door?*

Hearing this story later caused heat to move through my torso and arms as if I had been injected with fire. I had to get in my car and take a drive to cool off, to calm down, all the windows lowered to let the air blow in. That wouldn't be the last time my family faced Officer Derbish.

17
THE FIRE THIS TIME

One day in November 2013, almost a year after Officer David Derbish shot me, I decided to take in a movie, figuring that a few hours in front of a big screen in a dark theater would help take my mind off my new life using a wheelchair and my dating troubles. I drove to a theater in Pittsburgh's Waterfront and purchased a ticket for *Fruitvale Station*. The choice was almost arbitrary since I'd never seen a trailer or commercial for the film. Nor was I aware of Oscar Grant's story. What drew me to the movie is that it starred a Black actor, Michael B. Jordan. I guided myself to a spot designated for wheelchairs and watched the movie. I saw Michael B. Jordan as Oscar Grant interacting with his mom, then with his daughter and the mother of his daughter. Now he's hanging out with friends. They go to an event. The scenes seemed almost random. I said to myself, *Yo, what is this about?*

Then comes the scene inside Fruitvale Station where a cop shoots Oscar Grant in the back, mortally wounding him. Triggered, all my suffering rose up and spilled out. I could actually feel my skin swell and tighten with pressure. I started crying uncontrollably; I couldn't stop myself. In a strange way, the tears seemed to start outside my body, in the floor underneath me, as if my wheelchair and my legs were conduits. The crying spell left me physically exhausted. Nothing left. An usher had to push me out of the theater and to my car.

I remember returning home and just sitting in the living room near my bed sobbing. My dad came downstairs and saw me, and his whole demeanor changed. Every muscle in his body tensed; his face tight with rage. His anger was so visceral that I could feel it. I feared that this would be the day he would finally go out and retaliate. After all that had happened, the loss of my father would be too much for me to bear, too much for all of us to handle. It became clear to me that I could no longer go on living the way I had been. I needed to do something to save the both of us. But what?

The thought struck me that I could rally others to my cause. That possibility alone energized me. I developed a routine. Each day, I took to social media for a few hours and started sharing my story with every nationally recognized activist involved in the antiracist movement, along with entertainers and other celebrities who I felt might be sympathetic to my struggle for justice. Up until then, I'd never been socially conscious and had paid only passing interest to the stories of Trayvon Martin, Eric Garner, and Michael Brown. I never felt a call that made me wake up one day and say, "I want to be an activist. I want to save the world." I became an activist because everything was on the line. My motives were purely selfish. I had to fight for my life because nobody else would.

My efforts on social media went largely unnoticed. I would post the facts about my case, along with news clips about the shooting and clips of my family speaking, photos of me emaciated and hooked up to tubes in a hospital bed. Those I reached out to usually responded with platitudes, kind words, and expressions of solidarity. Some of them started following me on Facebook or Instagram. On occasion, a person might even repost me. However, that was usually the extent of their involvement. They did just enough to show others online that they cared but never made any efforts to bring greater attention to my story. I was hoping that they would say, "Let me do everything I can to help you." Rallying support for me seemed like the best way to pressure the DA to drop the criminal charges against me.

Although I was disappointed, I was starting to discover that the more I stayed positive, the more interesting people I would meet. For example, championship boxer Eddie Gomez reached out to me and offered his support. Two men who instantly became mentors, Brothers Jason Rivers and Malcolm Thomas, called me and extended an invitation to me to attend the meeting of a men's group at Sankofa Village, a community center focused on Black heritage in Homewood. I discovered that both men were in their forties, my father's age. For two hours, twenty of us sat in a circle and talked. The conversation was mostly serious, touching on weighty subjects like men's health, the need to get out in the community, and galvanizing young people. Mostly listening, I found all of it engaging, even if I had no opinions of my own that night.

I recognized one man I saw there: Lenny McAllister, a local Pittsburgh media personality and political commentator. After the meeting, he came over to me and said, "Child of God, you're a natural leader. One day you're going to be running against me for governor or something."

I didn't know what to say, so I only smiled.

"One day you're going to lead this country."

I said, "If you say so." I welcomed the encouragement but thought he was crazy.

He said to Jason and Malcolm, "He is an international leader, and we have to give him the tools and resources that he needs to have the impact on the world that he is destined to have."

Hearing him say that surprised me, for I had never viewed myself as a leader. Was this a true possibility? I had no idea. Thinking back, I realize that he was the first person who saw me as something more than a neighborhood guy. Indeed, he would become a mentor and push me to do more.

I spent some time talking to Jason and Malcolm. They told me that I should turn my pain into purpose. They felt it would be good for me to speak at schools and inspire young people to get involved with my cause. I agreed. Following up on my commitment, they arranged for me to speak to students over the next several months.

My first speaking engagement was at Duquesne University in a spacious ballroom filled with about two hundred young Black men, the entire senior class of Pittsburgh public school students. I was so nervous waiting to take the stage. Not only would it be my first time speaking, but several powerful Black men that I respected were present and would be listening. I thought, *Why did they push me to do this? I've never done this before. What will I say?*

Brother Malcolm seemed to sense what I was feeling. He leaned down next to me and whispered in my ear, "You have a story."

I wheeled up onto the stage. What I said that evening is mostly lost to me. I started out saying, "Hello, I'm Leon Ford. I was asked to speak to you all today." Then I remember telling the audience about the traffic stop and being shot five times by a cop. "I'm having a hard time. These people are trying to put me in jail. They shot me, put me in this wheelchair, and now they're trying to put me in jail." I stuttered all the way through my speech.

The audience gave me a standing ovation. I knew that I had not spoken well, but they still seemed to connect with what I was going through. Perhaps I really did have something to say that others wanted to hear.

There were more speeches to come. With each speech I improved, little by little.

These appearances did indeed provide me with a sense of purpose. Every time I spoke to young people, I felt a little better about myself. They got me, and I got them. They laughed when I did. They thanked me for my words of wisdom. With each passing day I came more and more to believe that I had a reason for living and that I could face life in a wheelchair.

However, I was still facing twenty years in prison for assault and resisting arrest, an injustice that poisoned every waking moment. I hated the cops. I hated the system. I hated white people. I hated Black politicians and organizations like the NAACP and the National Urban League who had not rallied in my defense. Although the Black Lives Matter movement was now a thing in America, my life did not seem to matter. My story had yet to gain national attention. Angry and bitter, I told myself I would kill and be killed rather than go to jail.

Toward year's end, I received word through Brother Jason that the Pittsburgh Friends group wanted to meet me and lend their support. I knew nothing about the Quakers. Honestly, I don't think I'd even heard of the denomination. Seeking help wherever I could find it, I decided one Sunday to attend a Quaker service. The church looked like many others I'd been in before and since, but the service was unlike anything I'd encountered. No sermons. No music. People mostly sat quietly and meditated. And the church was full of white people; Jason and I were the only Black people there.

After the service, an older white woman with blue eyes introduced herself to me. She thanked me for coming, then asked me how I had enjoyed the service.

I said, "It was different."

She chuckled. "We love to see you here."

She told me that for months they'd wanted to help me, but they didn't know how to reach me. So, when they reached out to me, and I answered the call, they were happy that we'd finally connected. She said they'd always wanted to get involved with the social justice movements in Pittsburgh but didn't know how. Some Black leaders were standoffish and apparently didn't trust them.

Then she went on to give me a fascinating history of the Quakers, explaining how they had always fought for social and racial justice and were willing to rally resources and time to advocate for change. They were willing to fight the good fight. They had opposed the "peculiar institution" of slavery, working as abolitionists and stationmasters on the Underground Railroad.

She ended by saying, "Leon, we will help you."

That vow of support would prove invaluable in the months and years to come. The Quakers would show up in numbers at many of my rallies. They would appear each day at my criminal trial. Most important, they never asked for anything in return or wanted credit for their involvement. Possessing the purest hearts, they genuinely cared about me. At a time when I didn't trust white people, the Quakers performed acts of kindness that awakened me to our shared humanity. Their involvement was pivotal to my development. The Quakers are truly my Pittsburgh Friends. Though after that, it would be harder to discern who was really on my side.

18
FALSE PROPHETS

One day, to my surprise, the attorney Benjamin Crump responded to a tweet I sent him. His message did much to lift my spirits, for the Trayvon Martin case had propelled Crump into the national spotlight as one of the leading voices of the BLM movement. We struck up a friendly conversation. Then I made the bold move of asking him if he would consider joining my legal team. He said that he would. When I discussed the matter with my lawyers, they told me and my father flat out that, for several reasons, they were opposed to Crump joining the team. Foremost, he could not practice law in the state of Pennsylvania. Also, they did not feel that he had a strong trial record. What could he bring to the table other than media attention? My lawyers suggested that we simply hire a PR firm if we wanted publicity. Despite their objections, my father and I felt it would be good to have Crump in our corner.

At our invitation, Crump came to town and sat down with me and my father and my lawyers. We all seemed to be on the same page. After a few handshakes, Crump had officially joined the team. At first, I had every reason to believe that we'd made the right decision. His presence alone made a significant difference in bringing attention to my upcoming criminal trial. For the first time I received vows of support from traditional Black leaders, namely members of the local chapters of the NAACP and National Urban League. Members of these organizations swarmed around Crump like locusts. They were more interested in talking to him than they were to me.

Crump put his plans in place. He tried to get national media outlets to come to Pittsburgh and set me up with interviews. Part of his strategy appeared to be painting me as an innocent, a saint. Whatever his intentions, that cut me the wrong way. Why would he try to sanitize my image? Facts are facts. I had a juvenile record, and my dad had a reputation in the streets. Nothing I've done in my life justifies a cop shooting me five times and paralyzing me.

It seemed that many high-profile activists like Crump work hard to perpetuate the narrative of the perfect victim. They are quick to say, "He didn't deserve this" or "He did nothing wrong." Any problematic or troubling facts about the victim should be ignored. Why? We need to recognize that there are no perfect victims. We are all equal under the law. We are all deserving of respect. No person's dignity or rights should be violated. No one deserves to be beaten, choked, brutalized, or shot.

Crump did other things I found unacceptable. He coached my parents about how to deal with the media, and he prepared a script that he wanted them to recite from memory at a press conference. His script seemed designed to paint my parents as the perfect Black family, churchgoing folk. Then, the straw that broke the camel's back: once in public I felt that he cried fake tears when he spoke about my case.

My father felt the same. He looked at me and whispered, "Man, this fake-ass nigga."

My mother was willing to go along with it all, anything to support me. But my father could not.

We decided to have a face to face with Crump and express our dissatisfaction. When we did so, Crump ducked and dodged and deflected. He started saying something about my attorneys being money hungry. Although we did not let it be known to him, my dad and I both felt that we'd rather be represented by a money-hungry lawyer than one who is looking to be famous. An attorney motivated by money wants to win, while an attorney chasing fame only wants some time in the spotlight.

A few days after that confrontation with Crump, I decided to fire him. I asked my attorneys to give him the news, the first major decision I'd made since David Derbish shot me.

———

A few months later, I encountered Crump at a rally in Washington, DC, where Al Sharpton and several prominent activists were scheduled to speak along with the family members of people killed by the police. Thousands upon thousands of protestors were in attendance. As I rolled through the crowd, people started noticing me. I heard them saying, "That's Leon Ford. Get Leon up front. Get Leon up there, man." The crowd literally began to part to offer me a clear path to the stage. At last, I would be able to tell my story to a national audience.

I had reached the side of the stage and from there could see him standing near the podium, waiting for his turn to speak. I said to someone, "Yo, grab Benjamin Crump. Grab Benjamin Crump." That person caught Crump's attention. On seeing me, he seemed flabbergasted. Still, he walked over to the edge of the stage and stood looking down on me.

"Oh, wow," he said. "It's good to see you. How are you?"

"I'm good," I said. "I'm trying to get up there with the families."

"All right." A peculiar look came over his face. "Is your dad here?"

"No," I said. "I'm here by myself."

As soon as I spoke those words, he turned around and walked back over to where he'd been standing and acted like he didn't see me. I felt insulted, but what could I say or do? Comforted by the fact that I would soon be able to speak, I sat and waited patiently.

It was a raucous event. There were too many speakers and not enough time. I'll never forget when one young activist snatched the mic away from Al Sharpton. At some point, someone lifted me onto the stage. I had only been up there for a few seconds when the leaders of the rally started to leave the stage, setting out to march. So much for my plans to speak before a national audience.

I felt deflated, but all was not lost. I figured, if nothing else, I could join the leadership at the head of the march. Someone lifted me down from the stage, and I set off after them. However, no matter how quickly I rolled my wheelchair, I could not reach the front. Those leading the march were simply walking too fast. I could not help but feel that a message was being sent. Could it be that some activists were only out to benefit themselves?

Ever the mover and shaker, Crump had lined up interviews for me with media outlets like the *Steve Harvey Morning Show*, the *Rickey Smiley Morning Show*, and CNN. However, after I fired him, those interviews were canceled. When I reached out on my own, my calls and messages went unreturned. Effectively, Crump had walked away with all his connections. How would I now achieve justice?

My attorneys were filing motions, trying to get the charges against me dismissed. They wanted me to avoid doing anything that might antagonize the prosecution such as media appearances. We were at odds here. I had been shot; I had been paralyzed; my name had been besmirched. I could not sit passively in silence.

Rather than do nothing, I decided I had to build my own platform. I would start by organizing a rally. It was mid-January of 2014. I gave myself two months to put everything in place. I picked a location, Pittsburgh's Peabody High School and a time and date, March 8, and created a flyer, "Stand Up for Leon," which I posted on social media.

For the next eight weeks, I spent most of each day promoting the rally. In the mornings, I would visit high schools and speak to students. Then between three in the afternoon and eight at night, I would go to barbershops, hair salons, nail shops, and malls. Afterward, I would go to the bars. On the weekends, I would do more of the same, hit the barbershops, hair and nail salons, malls, and shopping centers, and I would also drive through the Black neighborhoods of Pittsburgh, hop out of my car, and hand flyers to people on the street. Soon, local rappers, artists, and influencers began sharing my flyer on their social media. Everybody in the city talked about coming to my event.

A few hundred people showed up for the rally. I took pride in the fact that average people from the hood turned out in numbers, ordinary Black men and women who were simply trying to survive. There were the OGs that my dad and I knew, and Black youth. These were not the kind of people usually found at protests: the church folks and politicos associated with the NAACP and like organizations. Others in attendance included professional boxer Eddie Gomez, who drove down from New York, a group of women who came in from New Jersey, and some guys from Philadelphia.

The time came for me to speak. At first, I had no idea what I should say. Although I had organized this gathering, I had not grown up around politics and for that reason was unfamiliar with the language of protest. One thing I knew, I was good at connecting with young people. It made sense then to simply share some of what I'd been saying in schools, aiming to be a positive role model. The crowd heard each word and responded, by turns shouting out in anger and yelling vows of support.

Other people also took to the podium; pretty much anybody who felt compelled to do so. That day, for the first time, I met Brother Victor, a fiery orator from the local Nation of Islam mosque. He knew how to move an audience, either to earn their applause or to piss them off. "Man," he said, "y'all older folks keep judging these young Black men for how they dress. If you raise their minds, their pants will follow."

The Nation of Islam became one of my main supporters. Even today, I can go to any city in America, and the Nation will get in contact with me and provide security for free.

After the rally, I began to gain more of a following, both locally and nationally. Invitations to speak flowed in. And certain celebrities like Teyana Taylor and Keyshia Cole started writing posts about me on social media.

My second rally took place on May 3, 2014, in several cities, including Philadelphia, Dallas, Houston, Atlanta, New York, Washington, San Francisco, and London. Raspy Rawls, an experienced activist and close friend, organized the rally. He helped me understand the importance of using my voice on social media to tell my story and to mobilize people in different locations. For my part, I brought all my hustling skills to social activism. While the families of victims often raise millions of dollars through donations, I never accepted a contribution. Instead, I raised my own money selling T-shirts and wristbands. After using my whole SSI check of $700 to buy merchandise, I would get in my car and drive to Philadelphia, Baltimore, or Atlanta and pass out flyers, talk to people, and make sales by the thousands.

In August of that year, I organized a large, spur-of-the-moment protest. I went to a basketball court in East Liberty and started speaking to the guys playing hoops. Soon, we were marching together throughout the neighborhood, picking up more and more people on every street we passed. We shut down East Liberty. It was a beautiful moment, one that made me realize the impact I could have.

Now that I was in the public eye, I found it necessary to protect those I loved. Some of my family members and close friends never came to the rallies because they wanted to take things into their own hands and retaliate against the cops. For that reason, I suppressed

my anger. Had I communicated my pain to the world with negativity and brokenness, I would have only caused more brokenness.
Lacking the facts, outsiders were quick to comment on Facebook
or Instagram about what I was or wasn't doing. They did not understand that lives hung in the balance. As I was learning, being a public
figure came with a new sense of responsibility.

———

In hindsight, I now realize that 2014 was a watershed year for me.
My organizing efforts helped shape me into a leader, as did my
love for family. I had gained supporters by the hundreds, if not the
thousands—people who admired me and who would fight for me.
These were people who would fight with me to reach the land of
milk and honey. People who would fight with me to make sure bad
cops faced consequences and that I had a chance to rebuild myself
as a man.

At the same time, I had to come to terms with a hard truth: my
demands for justice had not been met. On that front I was still at
square one. Unfazed by public scrutiny, the prosecution had decided to proceed with their criminal case against me.

19

A TRUE FRIEND

At age two, LJ reached a major milestone. He started to walk, stumbling his way through my apartment to discover everything under the sun. Our favorite father-son activity soon became me chasing him around the house in my wheelchair as he would run as fast as he could, bubbling with laughter. Nothing else in my life gave me such joy. I welcomed every hour I spent with him. But when he wasn't with me, I would fixate on my inability to walk and the criminal charges I faced, and I would quickly slide into a depressive mood. At such times I wanted to rush out and buy a gun and take my life.

A voice inside me would tell me to get in my car and drive. So I would. Before I knew it, I would be heading toward my grandma's place in Garfield almost as if some force were guiding me, trying to save me. Being around family always made me feel good. I would park at the corner across the street from where my grandma lived. Then I would just sit there in my car without the strength or will to exit it. Kendrick Lamar's song "Sing About Me, I'm Dying of Thirst" would play over and over, and I would start crying. I would sit there listening to that song for what seemed like hours, unsure if I could go on living. Death had to be better than the pain. My face would grow numb from crying, and I would start the engine and drive away and return home without visiting my grandmother as I'd planned.

Had it not been for my cousin Butters, I am not sure if I would have made it during that difficult time of my life. He would show up unexpected at my house and demand that I go for a ride with him. Whenever we'd hung out before I got shot, we would mess with a bunch of women, trying to outdo each other and get the most phone numbers. Now, Butters would drive me to a club, and find us a table, and we'd just spend the night sitting there, talking. I would ask him about his business. He was doing what he had always been doing: hustling to make a few dollars. Then Butters would start in on me. He would remind me of the "missions" we used to take to find women.

"You were the dude," he'd say. "Be that dude again."

"How am I gon be that in this wheelchair?"

"You know how to talk to women, so talk."

He would take me to clubs and encourage me to flirt with women like in days past.

"See that woman over there? She's your type. Buy her a drink. And invite her over. Do your thing."

Butters helped me regain my confidence and lessen my fears about dating. I was so thankful for his presence and support. He put great effort into lifting my spirits. Even his life seemed to illustrate the meaning of recovery. Out driving one day, he rear-ended a car. The airbag failed to open, and he was thrown headfirst into the windshield. He spent two months in a coma in the ICU. After he regained consciousness, he had to learn how to walk and talk again. The crazy thing is that, once he was back, he was back. He started to come around to take me out, helping to brighten my mood.

During this tough period of my life, I also spent a lot of time with Bernie and Poppa. I could trust them to do anything I asked them to do. Bernie often ran errands for me.

As part of my disability benefits, the state allowed to me choose anyone I wanted as a home aide. I selected Poppa. He would handle many of my daily essentials such as taking me grocery shopping and taking me to my medical appointments or to pick up prescriptions. Also, he handled less pleasant tasks that many people might not want to do like cleaning out my car, doing my laundry, and taking out the garbage. Often, he came by my house just to keep me company for a few hours. The state paid him for his services via monthly deposits on a debit card.

He told me, "Bro, I don't want the money. I'm going to be here for you regardless."

He insisted that I keep the debit card and use the money as I wished.

Had it not been for Butters, Bernie, and Poppa, I'm not sure that I would have pulled through this phase of my life. The three showed me the true meaning of friendship.

20

A DAY OF RECKONING

During the summer of 2014, I often found myself going to a house of worship several times a month to join in fellowship with the devout. I might attend a Baptist church service one week, visit the Nation of Islam mosque the next week, then a Jehovah's Witness or Quaker service another week. Where many might feel conflicted, I did not. Growing up in a nonreligious household allowed me to be open-minded and receptive toward all beliefs. My exposure to different forms of worship helped me grow as a moral and spiritual being. I am a student of all religions, but I practice love.

I wish I could say that joining in fellowship with others elevated my spirits. It did not. Though I had plenty of supporters, I was not in a good place mentally. I was often quiet; inside I felt a growing sense of dread. My trial was scheduled to start on the first of September, a fact that weighed heavy on me.

Luv and I were hanging out one day.

I told him, "Man, I need to just do something."

He said, "You know what, Cuz, don't even worry about it. You know what, let's just go, go fly off. I'll get you a ticket."

The following morning, we flew down to Atlanta. For the next few days, Luv treated me, paying for everything that would put me in another state of mind. We went to strip clubs, rooms dripping with the smell of baby oil and incense. The music was so loud at times that the metal in my wheelchair started vibrating. Luv kept the gin flowing until my mouth went numb. All the strippers told me I was so handsome, and for a few fleeting moments, I felt like the old Leon. When one stripper, the French Tickler, invited me to dance with her, I started to wheel my chair this way and that, doing my own dance.

We went to visit family. Our time together, laughing, joking, cutting up like we'd done back in the day and hadn't done in so long, felt like the hangouts I'd treasured as a teenager.

I came back renewed, and full of hope.

———

My trial had been assigned to one of the smallest courtrooms, with only about seventeen seats available for observers, which the media were quick to claim. Then the bailiffs started kicking the media out and letting supporters of the police have the seats.

The Quakers would come to my trial, not to observe but to hold seats for members of my family. A silence filled the room, no one on either side speaking to each other. Because my family came out in numbers, they had to take turns sharing the seats. We were so thankful for the Quakers for helping us take up space that day.

From the beginning, I was disappointed with the court proceedings. The arrogance, the haughtiness, the lack of remorse. The authorities viewed me as worthless. I saw it in the judge. I saw it in the police officers. I saw it in the DA and their representatives. I noticed the way the police officers and judicial system work closely with the press and the news channels. They falsified what happened in court on any given day. They would say things like "Ford ran the stoplight," and "Ford would not comply with the officer's instructions," and "Ford tried to run over the officer with his car," and "The officers saw a bulge in Leon Ford's pocket that they thought was a gun."

At first, I thought it was accidental, a poor choice of wording. Or maybe they heard something, saw something I didn't see. But I soon realized that everything was calculated, and the odds were stacked against me. As a deeply segregated city, Pittsburgh has a long history of police brutality. Cops had taken the lives of many Black people like Jerry Jackson, Jonny Gammage, Ernest T. Williams, and dozens of others, and they had also brutalized people like Thomas Phoenix, Thomas Holland, and Jordan Miles. However, these cops had almost never been held accountable.

Certainly, officers were never held to account at my trial, seemingly about anything they had done. For example, a microphone in the squad car recorded the cops saying certain vile things like "I do what the fuck I want. I'm a police." My lawyers would point out the inappropriate language, the raucous behavior, only for the DA and judge to simply ignore their statements and proceed.

Once the first week of the trial ended, we held another rally that drew the attention of local news and media channels. I'd met with Lenny McAllister for dinner a few times, and he coached me on how to talk to the media. I knew just what to say. The following Monday, the judge placed a gag order on me. I could no longer discuss my case in public. By every indication, the system was trying to railroad me.

The trial was all about trying to make the jury believe that the cops had been right to shoot me. The district attorney sought to criminalize my demeanor and behavior on the night of the traffic stop. The prosecution painted me in the most negative manner. According to them, I had attempted to drag the officer, run him over. On the stand, all three officers were claiming they believed their lives were in danger. My car was a weapon. This last statement even contradicted something they'd said earlier in court: they never feared for their lives.

My legal team raised questions about how criminal charges were brought against me since I had never been placed under arrest before being shot. The main investigator took the stand. One of my attorneys asked him, "Did you ever talk to Leon?"

He claimed he had gone to the hospital and spoken with me.

"Did you question him?"

"Well, he was in surgery."

"So, if he was in surgery, you didn't talk to him?"

The main investigator said, "No, but I was going to come back the next day."

"So how did you get the evidence to charge him with all this stuff?"

He said because other cops told him.

"So, you didn't even question Leon, but you listened to this other cop?"

"Yes," he said. "Cops don't lie."

At one point, a woman testified for the prosecution that I had told her I tried to run over Officer Derbish. Her testimony backfired. The dates she claimed this happened, I was in a medically induced coma. The district attorney simply laughed when the facts were revealed. To my surprise, none of the witnesses suffered repercussions for lying under oath.

I remember seeing the three cops in the courtroom. They looked different in suits from the night they stopped me. All three seemed to have bowl cuts, a bit of hair on top but shaved everywhere else. Officer Derbish seemed to be shorter than the other two men. They admitted that they had broken many protocols. My attorneys pointed out that no active warrant had been issued against Lamont Ford. Trying to dismiss the facts, the district attorney would say, "These officers aren't on trial. Leon Ford is on trial. We're not here to look at what the officers did wrong. We're here to look at what Leon Ford did wrong."

During his testimony, Officer Derbish claimed that he saw a bulge in my pocket that he thought was a gun.

One of the other officers said they thought I was suspicious because "we noticed an all-white T-shirt."

Even today that statement makes no sense to me.

One of my attorneys asked Derbish, "If this were to happen again, would you do anything differently?"

Derbish replied, "No."

Overwhelmed, my aunt Terri got up off the bench and left the courtroom.

One day, during a recess, my mom, Grandma Peewee, and my aunt Terri stepped onto the elevator. Packed in, they stood waiting for the doors to close. Then Derbish got on. They couldn't believe it. It seemed to us that there was no end to his arrogance.

The jury deliberated for a week and a half. My lawyers were hopeful, but I could also feel their anxiety. Then too, I felt the judge would view me in a bad light because he had overseen my dad's state trial for homicide in the early 2000s. (He was acquitted.) I told myself, If I win this trial, I'm going to be more like Dr. King. However, if I lose this trial, I'm going to be like George Jackson. Somewhere in his writing, Jackson said he could disarm a fighter plane by killing the pilot, a statement that at the time I thought was the most profound thing I'd ever heard. Should I be convicted, I would kill the pilot. I had no plans of going to jail. Even if it cost me my life.

Awaiting the verdict, I would visualize Little Steve's body in the coffin. Then I would see myself lying there. Soon, my life would be over, at only twenty-one years of age. I'm certain that I felt the way many young Black men feel, men who don't expect to make it to eighteen or twenty-one. When you plan to die early, you think a certain way, you live a certain way, and you spend money a certain way, not the way you live and act when you expect to reach a ripe old age.

Then, the verdict was read: Not guilty. I cried tears of joy. In the past couple years, I felt like I'd cried more than my younger self would have ever imagined possible. All my family members stood up and hugged and kissed and cried; there was so much energy in the air. We celebrated for a week. During that time, as happy as I was, I also came to terms with some sobering facts. Although I had beat the odds and defeated the criminal justice system, I wasn't done with them, and they weren't done with me. I was now a real problem for them, a devil in their eyes, the one person in a million who had won. I was Little Bit's son, a regular-ass Black boy who had grown up in the ghetto and who society expected to go in and out of jail selling drugs. I had somehow flipped the script.

Equally important, I had to also recognize that there were white people, the Quakers, who loved and supported me. After growing up seeing the way white people treated us, that fact was mind-blowing. Their positive example played a crucial role in my transformation, in my becoming a person who embraced light rather than darkness. Where I had been studying the art of death, which bred tremendous anger and hatred toward white people, I started studying the art of living. Among other things, I began to read authors like Eckhart Tolle (*The Power of Now*), Don Miguel Ruiz (*The Four Agreements*), Bob Lancer (*Master Yourself, Master Your Life*), Gary Zukav (*The Seat of the Soul*) and Paulo Coelho (*The Alchemist*). I was on a new path, ready for a new mission.

21
FINDING MENTORS

On November 22, 2014, I attended an event at an HBCU, Morgan State University, that featured Minister Louis Farrakhan. The gathering was by invitation only, less than one hundred people. The sole speaker, Minister Farrakhan, took to the podium for about an hour, and in his articulate, honest, and controversial way gave his thoughts about the Black Lives Matter movement, words both encouraging and critical. Once he was done, each person in attendance was afforded a brief opportunity to meet him.

He knew my story, knew that I'd been shot five times by a cop and paralyzed. Reflecting on the shooting, he told me that I had been "baptized in the fire," a powerful statement that I would ponder in the days and weeks to come. Eventually, I arrived at an interpretation. During a baptism you're submerged under water, then you return to the surface with your sins washed away. Now, you face a choice. You can go back and live your life as you had before or you can work on becoming a better person. As for fire, hot flames burn away all the impurities leaving the purest metal, a principle of alchemy. Minister Farrakhan was helping me to see that the shooting could serve as a catalyst for finding my true self.

I accepted an invitation to visit Minister Farrakhan's home in

Chicago on December 18, one month after the Morgan State University event. Once inside his stately South Side mansion, brothers from the Nation asked that we proceed to a bathroom and wash our hands and feet. There were perhaps thirty of us, a small contingent of Black Lives Matter activists from around the country. We sat and talked about the way forward with the Minister calmly listening in and, from time to time, offering his thoughts and advice.

I know that Minister Farrakhan is a controversial figure. However, talking to him, I never felt like I was having a conversation with a radical leader. Instead, the experience was akin to chatting to an older, wiser relative, such as my grandpa.

Perhaps I too could be a leader helping to elevate Black people. Such was my thinking, although I didn't know what form that leadership might take. Now that I was hopeful about my future, I started seeking opportunities for personal development. Sometime in early 2015, Brother Jason Rivers told me about an organization for Black men called BMe and suggested that I look into it. According to its founder and CEO Trabian Shorters, BMe strives to "update the narrative about black men in the United States, and to reveal them as catalysts for community building and national social change." BMe aims to connect "authentic black male leaders with key influencers across industries and sectors who share their belief in valuing all members of the human family," an approach to bettering the world that I found appealing.

I applied to their fellowship program and was accepted, a heart-gladdening achievement. On May 28, all the fellows convened at a hotel in Washington, DC, sixty people from six cities. For the next four days, I had the opportunity to interact with some amazing Black men who were doing great work all over the country. Some of the men had just come home from prison and had found ways to serve the community. Some were feeding the homeless. Others wrote books, or produced movies, developed real estate, or ran foundations. The fellowship program broadened my network of successful Black men across America.

A tall, brown-skinned man, Trabian cuts quite an appearance in a Nehru jacket over a collarless shirt, his preferred manner of dress. He's a visionary who can see the big picture. Preaching the gospel of "asset framing," he shows young Black men what excellence looks like, an invaluable type of exposure. He believes that we should look to discover a person's best qualities rather than emphasize their worst. As he puts it, "Define people by their aspirations, not their challenges."

Observing Trabian, I discovered that he is present with everyone he meets whether that person be a millionaire or homeless. During his first encounter with a stranger, he can immediately identify that person's strength. Truly concerned about others, he observes and listens in an attentive way, and he speaks with love and conviction. He carries himself with honor and dignity.

When so many people only focused on Leon Ford the activist, Trabian provided me with opportunities. He made it possible for me and ninety-nine other BMe brothers to receive commendations from President Obama. I learned so much about leadership, life, and love from Trabian, from both his words and his actions. He taught me what success could look like, on a grander scale, for me.

He reached out and said, "Do you know about the Aspen Institute? I want to nominate you to be a fellow there." I listened as he explained to me that the fellowship would teach me networking and leadership skills and that the Institute would open numerous doors for me. The idea of doing a fellowship in beautiful Colorado with a group of wealthy and powerful people intrigued me. I started to imagine myself as powerful, a leader who could have a positive impact on the lives of other people. Anytime Trabian connected me with someone, I followed up, and I showed up. I was always very intentional about calling him and keeping in touch, and he was always intentional about connecting me with people and providing opportunities.

In 2016, investor Stephen DeBerry, founder and managing partner of the Bronze Venture Fund, gave a presentation at a BMe gathering. He inspired us all with an amazing speech. I was hooked from the start. He said, "Big things start small. I have a love for adventure and travel." Sitting in the dark auditorium, I listened as he explained that he was a mountain climber. I'd never heard of a Black mountain climber. Was such a thing possible?

We also watched an inspirational video, *An American Ascent*, of him climbing Denali, the highest mountain in North America. Here was a man who had achieved much. From his bio I learned how much he was worth. I'd never met a Black man that wealthy.

Six months later, I sent him a friend request on Facebook. He added me. On his page I discovered that his wife was an assistant district attorney in San Francisco, a woman who is also involved in criminal justice reform. Hoping to connect with her, I sent Stephen a message, saying I would love to get on a phone call with him. We coordinated the call. During the conversation, he started sharing some details about him and his wife, and I shared some details about myself.

He asked, "Who are you? Where exactly do I know you from?"

And I told him, "I'm involved with BMe. We met at the event." We didn't meet, he'd only spoken to us, but I decided to take some liberties. "Are you familiar with my story?"

He said, "No."

I told him about my life, about everything that had happened.

He said, "Wow, that is crazy. I want to help you."

Slowly, over the course of a few years, we developed a relationship. If Trabian gave me a platform, Stephen helped me build on it by asking "What are you going to do with that megaphone?"

Stephen is like Batman. During the daytime, he's Bruce Wayne, a wealthy guy with privilege who makes money. However, at night, he's Batman, a superhero who goes out and fights crime by taking out bad guys and helping those in need. That's Stephen DeBerry.

He uses investments to leverage his power and influence to bring about a positive impact on the world. Through him I was starting to view the struggle for social justice through a wider lens. I learned that money can be put to work for good things. As activists, we can do more than march and protest and vote. We can also be impact players who can influence the world.

I have gleaned much from Stephen about love, loyalty, leadership, and money. To this day he calls me and presents investment opportunities. My journey in life thus far has brought me into contact with numerous mentors, from real estate developers to spiritual leaders to venture capitalists to educators to people within the foundation community to athletes and agents and attorneys, all wise individuals, each savvy in her or his own way, people whom I admire and respect. For any decision I make, I first think about them and ask myself: How can I act in such a way as to make them proud?

My mentors are not the type of people who are always in the public eye. Instead, they work quietly behind the scenes and find ways to empower others. I have come to understand that we need all types of mentors. Someone who teaches us about wisdom, another person who guides us in family issues, someone wise in spiritual matters, and still someone else versed in leadership and professional development.

Through people like Brother Malcolm Thomas, Lenny McAllister, Trabian Shorters, and Stephen DeBerry, I have also come to understand that true leadership is about solving problems. Before meeting these men, I had simply wanted my voice to be heard. Now I was starting to realize that leadership wasn't just about voice. It was about action. All these men have visions. They don't use their power to complain or simply bolster themselves. Instead, they make things happen. For example, with my own eyes I had watched Brother Malcolm break up brawls without raising his voice. He had also taught me the pledge "Give up to go up," which I in turn have taught to many others. The pledge involves learning to give up negative attitudes and behaviors that hold you back from achieving in life. Or as they say in Twelve Step programs, avoid "people, places, and things" that lead to your getting high.

Witnessing all these men in action changed my understanding of manhood. Being a man involves more than sexual prowess and physical strength. Personhood is a force for change.

Observing these men move through the world has inspired me to emulate them to reach my highest potential. I began trying to incorporate certain aspects of each man into my own life. Like Lenny, I strived to be well-spoken. Like Stephen, I sought to be adventurous and to understand the ins and outs of money and finance. Like Trabian, I began to understand the importance of leadership, narrative, and storytelling. These men taught me to think big and see myself as an asset to society rather than a burden.

22
LOSING POPPA

Even as my life seemed to be on the up, many of the people I loved continued to suffer. One day early in January 2016, Poppa's brother called me crying. He said, "Yo, Poppa was playing with his gun, and he shot himself."

"What?" I said. "Man, he's weird as hell. How the hell he do that?"

"I don't know." His brother continued to cry hard.

"Bro, he's going to be all right, bro. Don't even worry about it. He'll be cool. He'll be all right. What hospital he at?"

He told me that Poppa was at Presbyterian.

"All right, cool. I'll meet you down there."

He said nothing.

"Bro, I'm telling you, it's going to be all right. Don't even worry about it."

An hour later, he met me in the downstairs lobby of the hospital. We went upstairs to the ICU. A nurse instructed us to have a seat until a doctor came to speak to us.

Ten minutes later, a bedraggled-looking doctor came over to us. He said, "You two can go back there and see him, but there's nothing we could do."

I said, "There's nothing y'all can do? What do you mean? What the heck is going on?"

Poppa's brother began to cry again. I was still trying to process it all.

Nothing could have prepared me for what I saw inside Poppa's room. Poppa was propped up in bed with the top of his head elongated like a watermelon. They had wrapped his head in bandages all the way from the top down to his eyes because his eyes had swelled up and almost popped out of his skull. He was already brain-dead. I had never seen anything like that before in my life. There was my friend, my man Poppa. I just broke down crying.

Poppa died on January 7, 2016, leaving me many with unanswered questions. Was it an accident? Was it murder, or did he mean to shoot himself? I swore up and down that there was some foul play involved because I couldn't see him being so careless as to shoot himself. Nor could I see him intentionally shooting himself. Even today I can't bring myself to use the word "suicide." I do know that the police launched an investigation, but his family never told me what, if anything, they'd discovered. I do know that a few years earlier Poppa's father had died. The loss hit Poppa hard. He had always been upbeat, but he became quiet and withdrawn at times, possible signs of depression. But we never talked about what he was going through. He never let me in on his feelings, his struggles, his suffering. All I know is that he made himself available for me at a time when I often thought about ending my own life.

23
LJ THE KING

My son, LJ, continued to have a major impact in changing how I thought about myself and the world. He would push me and encourage me when I was incapable of pushing and encouraging myself.

Once, when LJ was three or four years old, we returned home from an outing. At that time, I drove a little Ford Focus hatchback. My wheelchair was in the trunk, disassembled. LJ sat strapped in a car seat on the passenger side behind me.

We arrived at the house. I pulled into the garage. In those days I was still living with my dad, and he was supposed to be home to help me and LJ get out of the car. He wasn't.

I called him on my phone. "Dad, where you at?"

He said, "Sorry, dawg. I'll be there in about thirty minutes. I had to stop at this place."

"Oh, snap."

LJ and I sat in the car waiting.

After a few minutes LJ said, "Dad, are we just going to wait for him to get here?"

I could tell that he was antsy in the backseat. Now I was in a bind. "He should be here soon."

"Do we have to wait?"

What to do now? I told myself, *I can either sit here and wait, or I can show my son how to make things happen for himself.*

"You know what, son," I said. "We ain't going to wait for Pap-pap."

I turned around and after much effort managed to climb over the backseat to unbuckle LJ from his harness. Then, exerting myself, I managed to lift him up and put him down on the front passenger seat next to me.

The whole time, LJ was saying, "You got it, Dad. You got it. You can do it."

I somehow pulled the seat section of my wheelchair out of the trunk and into the backseat, then opened the door and put it outside the car. Next, I got a hold on one wheel and slid and snapped it onto the seat. I got the second wheel and slid and snapped it on. My wheelchair was assembled. All I needed to do now was get out of the car and into the chair.

LJ continued to cheer me on. "See. That's it, Dad. You can do it."

I lifted myself from behind the wheel and lowered down into the wheelchair. That done, I rolled around to the passenger door and opened it for LJ. Once he was out of the car, we made our way into the house.

A short while later my dad arrived home. He stood looking at me and LJ with his mouth open, gold tooth showing, surprised. "How did you get out the car?"

"My dad did it," LJ said. "My dad is super cool."

Too often we romanticize children as innocent. LJ has never been sheltered from life's realities. From birth, he was forged in the fires of protest. Before he could walk, he participated in demonstrations with me. Somebody would be holding him while we shouted slogans and threw our fists up in the air. Then when he started walking, he would be sitting on my lap at a demonstration. He always seemed to understand what was going around him. Even as a toddler he was aware.

One day, LJ asked me, "Dad, why did that bad man shoot you?"
The question surprised me.

I said, "Because some white people don't like Black people."

LJ raised an eyebrow. "Really?"

"Yeah."

"That's stupid." Then he said, "But why?"

"Son, I don't know why. I wish I knew why."

"How can we stop them?"

"I'm not sure, LJ."

"Just keep on pushing, Dad?"

"Yes."

"Okay. We'll keep on pushing."

I raised LJ the way I was raised, meaning I never tried to hide him from some of the harsh realities of the world, including my own struggles.

Fathering LJ has reinforced my belief that parents should expose their children to the world as it is and tell their children the truth. That was how my mom and dad raised me, and that is how I am raising my son, too. We should not sugarcoat reality. Tell your children the truth and let them understand to the best of their ability.

24

ANOTHER STAB AT JUSTICE

My civil trial against the city of Pittsburgh started in mid-September of 2017. As strange as it may sound, I never knew the civil case involved money. The entire time I was under the impression that the three officers involved in my traffic stop were going to leave the courtroom in shackles.

From the start, my lawyers put on a strong case. RaShall Brackney, a former Pittsburgh police officer, testified. People often ask, "Where are the good cops who stand up to the bad cops?" For four years chief of police in Charlottesville, Brackney has always been a good cop. She had investigated my shooting and told the court her findings. On several occasions, she attempted to interview the officers involved, but other people always intervened. She conducted the investigation the best way she could, although she kept hitting a brick wall. During her review, she identified several policies and procedures that were broken, and recommended disciplinary action.

Before she moved away from Pittsburgh, she left her investigation with Chief Cameron McLay. Somehow, her report was lost, disappeared. The city tried to take advantage of the missing report by filing a motion to exclude certain evidence in my favor, hoping to silence Officer Brackney. They said they couldn't prove that her report existed, a patently absurd argument.

Lawyers for the city also tried to argue that I dragged the officer with my car. However, we had an engineer who testified that as soon as I pulled off, the front passenger door closed, meaning that Officer Derbish was safely inside the car. In response, the city's lawyers showed photos of my car trying to prove that the car door was open when I crashed.

One of my lawyers stood up and said, "That is not my client's car."

The judge asked the city, "Is this Mr. Leon Ford's car?"

"No, Your Honor, it's not his car. We were using this photo just for the sake of . . ."

The judge shut him up before he could finish his statement. She called all the lawyers into her chambers. Back in the courtroom, she instructed the jury to dismiss the city's photographic evidence. She was pissed.

Throughout the trial, my lawyers proved to be outstanding. Monte Rabner advised the legal team. Fred Rabner was emotional but calm, Ashley Cagle was organized and strategic, while Tom Malone was a firecracker. He would stand up and challenge and object and cuss people out. The judge would say to him, "You don't stand up. If he"—as in Fred Rabner—"is doing the cross-examination, you don't speak." She would warn him, "I'm going to take you off the bench if you keep doing it."

The police officers and the city's expert witnesses often tried to mislead the jury. Each time they lied, my lawyers impeached them and brought up statements they'd made in the past. Their actions were shameful.

We crushed the city. Every day after the court session ended, my lawyers and I would go out into the lobby and start high-fiving.

When the time came, the judge instructed the jury to come up with a decision based on the totality of the circumstances, a preponderance of the evidence, and to challenge the credibility of any witness by the truthfulness of their testimony. I was confident that the jury would rule in my favor. Yet days later, no verdict had been delivered. The jury came back with a question about excessive force. Sometime later, they told the judge that they didn't understand a particular instruction. I found their question confusing. Then a question came up about a warning shot.

"Should Officer Derbish have fired a warning shot and given Leon Ford time to respond before shooting him?"

The judge answered, "If there was a bad storm coming, would you want an advance warning?"

I knew her words would have an impact on the jury in my favor, but she told them that it was up to their discretion.

Then more deliberation. What was taking the jurors so long to arrive at a verdict? It was not lost on me that all the jurors were white. Perhaps they were only able to view the evidence through a white lens. A lens that would lead them to favor the white police officers.

After nine days, the verdict came: one officer was cleared of any wrongdoing, while there was a hung jury on Derbish. The verdict sent a clear message to me: a white lie will always prevail over a Black truth. In the eyes of investigative teams and jurors, white cops and murderers like Michael Dunn, Kyle Rittenhouse, and George Zimmerman are almost always deemed trustworthy and truthful, while Black victims like Rodney King, Amadou Diallo, Jordan Davis, Trayvon Martin, Eric Garner, Philando Castile, Luke Stewart, and me are deemed liars, suspicious, guilty of some crime.

The sad reality is that Black men are the most despised demographic in America. We inspire fear, hatred, and disgust. We are vilified in the media and other spaces both public and private as violent criminals: muggers, rapists, gangbangers, and murderers. As such, we bear the burden of racial profiling that has left many of us dead or maimed, in handcuffs or rotting in prison cells, on probation or denied opportunities for employment and advancement. Then we bear the burden of many other stereotypes: deadbeat, ignorant, loud, angry, weed-smoking, drug dealing, and absent fathers. The simple fact is that, in America, we catch hell.

The mayor told reporters that he had compassion for all parties involved in my case, a false equivalency that I found deeply insulting. How could this progressive white liberal say such a thing? Did he not understand that while these officers were promoted to become detectives, I battled depression, a shortened life expectancy, a loss of bowel and bladder function, and a host of other medical and emotional issues?

I had done everything right in court. I smiled. I was always respectful. I had a solid legal team that put on an airtight case. Even the judge had been fair.

For a month after the verdict, I remained in a state of torment, frustrated and angry about the system. Where were all the Black leaders whose mission was to fight on the behalf of people like me? Why had they not spoken up? Did my life not matter? Had I not been wronged, maimed? Why was it so hard for me to achieve justice? How could I ever come to terms with the lack of accountability for what had happened to me? At that time, I believed justice meant incarcerating Derbish for shooting and paralyzing me. Now I knew that would never happen. I had lost all hope and purpose in my mission. It felt like the life I had dreamed of as an activist and leader, inspired by watching my mentors, would be out of my reach until this was settled.

On November 18, a cop was shot to death during a traffic stop in New Kensington, a small municipality seventeen miles from downtown Pittsburgh. The incident was all over the news. The story hit home. I wanted to kill a cop. I knew what I had to do.

With my plan in mind, I phoned my lead attorney, Fred Rabner. I said, "My friends are very inspired by what happened out there in New Kensington."

"Leon, what are you talking about?"

"I don't feel like justice is a real thing. There's no way I'm going to get justice. Justice is just an illusion."

"Look," he said, "it wasn't a win, but it also wasn't a loss. We still have another shot. Next time, we're going to see if we can have the trial in Philadelphia. We will have a better chance of having Black folks on the jury."

I heard his words, but they didn't land with me. So many conflicting thoughts swarmed around the hive of my skull. It actually hurt for me to think. I asked him, "How would you be able to protect me if I shot a police officer?"

Rabner started pleading with me. "Leon, you cannot think like this. It's not right, you are better than that," he said. "You're like Dr. King. Everyone loves you and you're always talking about love."

"I don't give a fuck about Dr. King. Like I said, my friends are very inspired by what happened in New Kensington, and I don't believe there's any other way to get justice."

"Leon, you need to calm down." He knew that Stephen DeBerry had given me a standing invitation to visit him in the Bay Area. "Leon, just go to California and breathe. Just go out there and visit your friend, and then we'll talk about this when you get back."

"Okay, cool," I said. "I'll go to California. But if I still feel the same way when I get back, I'm doing it."

———

The next day, I flew to San Francisco. On the flight, I listened to Goapele's song "Closer" over and over, which seemed to calm me and help settle my spirit. Although I was still riled up, I was experiencing something else, too, a faint suggestion of hope. In flying out to the Bay Area on the spur of the moment, I was chasing that feeling of peace I'd experienced the night I was shot, that sense of floating outside my body. I felt drawn by the idea of leaving all my troubles behind. Letting go and letting God. Giving up to go up. I longed for a release.

From the airport, I phoned Stephen DeBerry. He told me that he was out of town, but he said I was welcome to stay at one of his properties, a place that locals called Record House. Also, he told me I was welcome to use the car parked in his garage.

I discovered a beautiful, spacious house in East Palo Alto, with wide windows and albums lined up everywhere. Now I knew why the place was called Record House. In the garage I found a black Mercedes S550. With access to the luxury car and house, I felt like a distinguished guest.

Once I was settled, I figured I'd call the one person other than Stephen that I knew in the Bay Area, a woman from Pittsburgh named Candi Castleberry Singleton, who worked at Twitter.

She was excited to hear from me. "Oh my God, Leon. You're in the Bay? What are you doing tomorrow?"

"I don't have anything planned."

"Can you come speak at Twitter? I'll give you five grand."

Five grand? I could barely believe it.

"Sure, I can do that."

I would've spoken there for free.

The following morning, I arrived at Twitter headquarters. Everywhere I looked, I saw platters of fresh salads, barbeque and coconut-encrusted chicken, and rosé on tap. The setup impressed me. I understood the logic here: create a workspace where the employees don't want to leave.

For an hour, I spoke to a group called the Blackbirds, all the Black employees. After sharing my story, I fielded their questions. The experience left me with a good feeling, knowing that I could have an impact on big-brained, hi-tech people. My chest swelled like a superhero. I felt invincible, even thought about springing out of my wheelchair and dancing around the room.

Once the event wrapped, Candi told me, "Hey, my boss wants to meet you. He's in a board meeting right now, but he wants you to come and meet everyone there."

I rolled into the board meeting, and a row of power players looked up at me from around a wooden table, including one woman I recognized as the president of BET.

Jack Dorsey was walking around the room in sandals. He spoke to me. "Leon, I'm super inspired by your story."

We shook hands. I smiled. He started asking me questions about my life, my family, and Pittsburgh. I answered him truthfully.

"How is life for you in a wheelchair?"

"It's not always easy," I said.

"How do you manage? How do you do it and keep that big smile on your face?"

I answered with a joke. "I'm inspired by you."

He laughed.

In a matter of minutes, we had formed a deep friendship, and we've been connected since. Today I can jump on a call with Jack at a moment's notice just to talk or to seek his support for an important initiative or project in my community.

After I left Twitter headquarters, I linked up with Stephen. He's one of the most adventurous people I know, a rescue diver and a mountain climber, a man all about breaking the mold; not a suit-and-tie guy. I was happy to see him because he helped me feel comfortable in unfamiliar spaces by just being himself, a chill, relaxed dude. If he belonged in places of power, so did I.

He was surprised that I'd spoken at Twitter. "How did you pull that off?"

I laughed and said, "Good things seem to happen to me," words I mostly didn't believe. At that moment it seemed to be true. Good things were happening. Externally, many things were going well, but internally, I still struggled with feelings of death and the thirst for revenge.

One reason we bond is that Stephen suffered a spinal-cord injury from a chiropractic session. "Yeah, man," he said. "This dude really messed up my back. I couldn't walk for six months."

"I wish it would be over in six months," I said.

He studied my face. "I know what you mean."

Although he ultimately recovered, the experience allows him to understand a bit of what life is like for me in a wheelchair.

We planned an evening. Stephen invited thirty or so people to the Record House to mix and mingle over wine and hors d'oeuvres, mostly colleagues from his Bronze Venture Fund. They were all good people, friendly and laid-back. I was having a fine time in their company. At some point in the evening, Stephen tapped his wineglass to get everyone's attention.

He said, "Hey, everybody. Get in a circle. I want to tell you all why I invited you here this evening."

People gathered in a circle. The room went silent.

"We're here because of Leon," Stephen said.

I started looking at him, looking around, asking myself, what did he mean?

"Leon was shot by a police officer, and I know a lot of y'all see it on social media or on TV, and y'all don't think it's real. But you all see Leon in this wheelchair, and you all have gotten to talk to him and see how good of a person he is. We need to wrap our arms around him. We need to protect Leon. We need to support him."

Such was my introduction to the group. I smiled. I felt somewhat embarrassed, but it also felt so good to be welcomed, to be part. My status in the world had been elevated big time.

Stephen introduced me to a guy named Brad Gerstner, jokingly saying, "Brad just purchased United Airlines."

"What?" I laughed. "I had to get a Priceline ticket to get down here."

Brad said, "No. Correction. I acquired it."

I admired his humility.

These are the types of individuals who I spent time with at the Record House that night, including people from Apple and Facebook. Later that week, I took a tour of Facebook's headquarters with a good friend, Rachel Coady.

While in the Bay, I also tapped in with the hood, connecting with my "uncle" Derrick Bowman, who always supported me and had my back anytime I was in his neck of the woods. He introduced me to Lil D, a legend in the Bay, who is also like an uncle to me. The love and reverence that community has for them in the Bay is like the love and reverence that many in Pittsburgh have for my father. Through them I connected with people like Mistah F.A.B., E-40, and Marshawn Lynch.

Stephen asked me, "Yo, who the hell are you? How do you know these people, how did you come to the Bay and just figure out how to navigate these spaces?"

I said, "I just know people, and I talk to people."

"Man," he said. "You're so much more than an activist. Have you ever considered tech?"

"Not really, but I'm open to it."

Then he said, "I want you to come on to work with me and become an entrepreneur in residence." As he explained, the residency would involve him connecting me with various entrepreneurs around the country, a great hands-on opportunity.

All I could say was, "Cool." Had those words come from anyone else I would not have believed them. But I knew that Stephen wasn't just blowing smoke up my ass, trying to sell me some pipe dream.

Then, he asked about my case.

"I know it's stressful," he started. "It's hard on you and I know it's weighing you down. You deserve to live. How much are they offering?"

It surprised me that he was so nonchalant in talking about money. For that reason, I didn't hesitate in answering his question. "Five point five million."

"I know it's not much for all that you've endured, but it's enough to build something."

I listened. My mind latched onto the words "build something." If I was hearing Stephen right, I could solve all my money troubles and at the same time build something. More than anything, I wanted to build a legacy for my son, LJ. He would have the best education, his own house, and his own investments.

"Look, I want you to consider just settling it. You deserve to live a life without this stress, without this pressure. We'll help you invest. We'll help you do the right things with your money."

I trust him, I respect him, I appreciate him, I value him, I love him.

I called my attorneys and said, "Let's settle the case." That was it.

Stephen DeBerry saved my life. Had it not been for him, I would have gone down a dark road and potentially committed an act of violence. Stephen opened up a new world of possibility.

He had granted me a rare type of access to a community of billionaires, investors, tech people, high-level problem solvers, people who think differently, out the box. Coming from where I come from, you don't get to meet the world's movers and shakers. Rather than give me a handout, these powerful and influential people would give me information, show me how to invest and build wealth. It made me feel like they trusted and believed in me, that I could do what they were doing.

I received my settlement about four months after that pivotal trip to the Bay Area. In my heart, I felt conflicted about the money, almost as if it had blood on it, my blood. Settling felt a lot like selling out, like putting a price tag on my body, on my life. Still, the settlement was something to build on. I decided that I would keep the money in my savings account until I could figure out the best way to invest it.

Nevertheless, I did decide to splurge on one luxury purchase, a sentimental nod to a promise my father had made to me when I was a child. When I was a kid, he used to rock flashy watches and jewelry, including several Rolexes and a Cuban link chain. A charm in the form of a miniature Mercedes-Benz hung from the chain, the rims on the Benz encrusted with diamonds. While he was in prison, scheming relatives purloined his money and all his possessions. That he could no longer pass the promised objects on to me really upset him.

Luv and I decided we were buying a Rolex. After a few days arguing on the phone over the merits of each model, we finally decided to visit Henne Jewelers in Shadyside, a wealthy neighborhood of Pittsburgh. As soon as we were inside the store, a man greeted us and came to attend to us. Instead of the usual suspicion Black customers face in Pittsburgh, though, this man was warm and welcoming, directing us to a display case filled with a variety of sparkling Rolexes. He introduced himself as John Henne, the owner, as he spoke to the merits of each model. We inspected each watch closely, held them, tried them on for size and feel.

Then Henne asked me a question. "Tell me, what gives you that smile?"

I said, "Faith." For me, that meant that I was starting to see a path back to hope, to living my life as if tomorrow could be better.

From that moment, we hit it off. Instead of leaving the store with a Rolex, I left with a friend.

We met for lunch a week later. John had studied accounting in college, so he is very conscious about investments. He came right out and told me that the watch I was considering buying might not be the best investment for me at that time. He was unusual in that he spoke the plain truth. He gave me a brief history of the store, starting with his grandfather founding the business in 1887. Then we dropped the subject of luxury watches and store history and talked openly and authentically in a way that two people do only after knowing each other for years.

"A few months ago," he said, "a young Black man came into my shop. I was friendly with him the same way I was with you and your cousin when you two came in. That's who I am. I treat everyone with respect. But things quickly went wrong."

He told me that the man had robbed his store, a smash and grab that unnerved him. Seeking to understand, he asked for my perspective on the crime. I obliged him, holding back nothing. We talked about race, about the difference between Black and white, the differences in perception, the challenges that we face as society, and the challenges that John faced as a business owner in welcoming people but at the same time being thoughtful and conscious of security. A deep, difficult conversation, but it felt so comfortable. I was able to be myself with him.

Soon after that get-together, I went on outings with John's family. We went to church together. We went to breakfast together. We went to a Penguins game with his boys. And we spoke several times each week on the phone.

It so happened that the settlement money arrived a few weeks before my birthday. One thing I knew: money and influence bring a different type of power. Before you have money, you have to play the game a certain way. You have to be resourceful, know how to grind in order to survive. You smile, put up with a lot of bullshit, and watch your back. Now I had to figure out the new way to play the game. I faced two choices. Either use it to feed my ego or use it for impact. I decided to embrace the latter.

Luv suggested that we go on vacation to Los Angeles with a few of our male cousins. I took him up on the idea. We had a great time over the course of a week, doing the usual tourist stuff, and partying at night, but also seeking out family members we'd never met. When we were alone in our Airbnb, Rob, Raymon, Luv, and I reminisced and goofed around, having a chance to revert to who we'd been back in our childhood. All the talking and laughing was mad fun. I was feeling good about things. Life was looking up.

On our last day, we got into a disagreement, nothing serious, only a minor dispute between cousins. Luv was sitting in a chair in the living room. I rolled past him in my wheelchair, then once I was behind him, lunged at him and grabbed him around the neck. We hit the carpeted floor. We started wrestling around. Soon we were laughing and joking, mad fun.

I had much to celebrate.

THREE
SOAR

25

THE LEGACY OF ANTWON ROSE

Settling the case was the beginning of my healing journey. It would happen in phases. The first thing I had to contend with was my manhood. After I became paralyzed, I felt insignificant because I no longer played the same dominant role I'd once had in my community. I didn't feel comfortable selling drugs. I could no longer box. I could no longer beat people up or tackle opponents in football.

It took me a while to understand that I was still somebody, a person who could have a powerful influence on others, and by now, I had started defining power in its most positive sense, in the terms of helping a person change their life for the better. Gradually, I started to notice the impact I had on young people when I spoke to them. I recognized the way they appreciated me for who I was and noted how they were happy to be in my presence. There's something about authentic love that transforms you. Connecting with young people helped me begin to make wise decisions and move forward with compassion and grace. I started to ask myself: *If I killed a police officer, what example would that set for these youth who believe in me, who follow me? What example would it set for my son, LJ?* I had to imagine our future together.

When I received my settlement, I was only twenty-five years old, and my son was only five; there was still plenty of time for both of us to live and build a prosperous future. By then, LJ was with me every day. We'd developed a routine that we still follow to this day. He will wake me up in the morning to take him to school. He will come into my room and say, "Dad, you ready?" From early on, his independence and strength shone through.

Like my dad would do with me, I always allow LJ to decide what car he wants to ride in to school, and he will choose between my everyday car or one of my three classic cars. On the drive, we always stop to get him donuts and milk. In LJ, I see myself as a boy. I want him to feel as free and full of possibility as I may have been.

In the immediate aftermath of the shooting, I was all about activism and shutting down the streets. However, after I received the money, my attitude began to change. I started to meet and develop relationships with business titans, experts in finance, philanthropists and others involved in the nonprofit sector, and people devoted to criminal justice reform, along with celebrated public figures like Harry Belafonte, Bobby Rush, Bob Moses, and John Edgar Wideman. I would listen and observe them, determined to learn something about how they navigate through the world.

All my interactions with others seemed to be grooming me for a new leadership role. I did not yet know how I could wield the most influence to create change. But I remained open to growth and possibility.

———

On the night of June 19, 2018, about three months after I received my settlement, I was in my kitchen playing with my son, LJ, when the phone rang. It was Dejohn, one of my childhood friends.

He told me, "Bro, my girlfriend just recorded a police officer shooting this guy, and I think he's dead. Now the police are at her door, and she doesn't know what to do."

I started to think. There was a strong chance that the police officers would take her phone and destroy the video. How to prevent that? I called my attorney, then he called the girlfriend on a three-way. We began figuring everything out. She knew the name of the person who had been shot, Antwon Rose. After some discussion, we decided she should post the video online. I wasted no time in watching it.

I sat before my desktop computer, stunned, devastated.

LJ said, "Dad, don't watch that. It's bad energy."

I looked at him, shocked, so much so that I asked him to repeat what he said and recorded him saying it on my phone.

"Dad, don't watch that. It's going to give you bad energy."

I always wanted to protect him from the evils in the world, and here he was, trying to protect me. The moment reminded me of my relationship with my father. As I prepared to leave the house, I found my father chilling in the living room.

He asked me, "What's going on?" I told him.

"Man, that's fucked up, man."

"I'm going to go talk to the family."

As I headed out the door, LJ asked me, "Dad, are they going to shoot you again?"

I paused, torn inside, for him. "No, they're not going to shoot me."

"Are they going to try to kill you?"

"No, they're not going to try to kill me, son."

Then he asked, "Are they going to try to shoot me?"

His words saddened me. In that moment, I felt more for my son than I did for myself. I took my time in answering. "No, they're not going to try to shoot you. I would never let that happen."

My heart frayed at the seams, as if the stitches of my healing were about to burst.

Once in my car, I decided I would drive past each hospital until I found Antwon Rose's family members. I drove past Children's Hospital but didn't see anything going on. When I got to Mercy Hospital, I saw a bunch of people gathered around crying and figured that must be the family. I got out of the car. They embraced me.

After a while, I realized that this wasn't the family of Antwon Rose but the relatives of someone who had been killed in a non-police shooting in Wilkinsburg within the same few hours. I offered them my condolences. Then I got back into my car, thinking about what to do next.

After a time, I decided to head to East Pittsburgh where the shooting had occurred, figuring I would drive through each neighborhood until I came upon the one where Antwon Rose's loved ones would be sitting in front of the house, a custom in Black communities. I set out on my quest through the streets of East Pittsburgh. In a few short minutes, I chanced upon dozens of people standing outside of a house. I told myself, *This is it. I know this is it.* I parked, opened the door, and started assembling my wheelchair. People were watching me, curious. I transferred into my wheelchair and rolled toward them. I could hear the whispers, and someone saying, "Go get his mother." A few seconds later, a tall woman stepped out the front door. She seemed completely broken. However, when she saw me, she lit up.

She looked at me and said, "Well, if you're here, I know this shit is real."

I said, "Yes, ma'am, it is."

She walked toward me, bent over, and hugged me, and held on tightly, crying. She talked into my shoulder. "Leon, I followed your story all these years, and I felt so connected to you and your family, and I never knew why. I never thought that I would be in this position. I never thought I would feel this pain."

I just held her and let her talk herself out.

Once she composed herself, she invited me to come into her

home. We made our way through the small house, every room jammed with people. After we reached the kitchen, she suggested that we go outside into the backyard to talk. So, we did. It was a cool spring night filled with the smell of grass.

She asked me, "How in the world did you find me?"

I said, "I'm from the city. I can find anybody."

We both laughed.

Then we had a serious conversation, holding back nothing. I told her what to expect, told her that she was only at the beginning of a never-ending battle. She needed to be mindful of the people around her, including her family, and be on guard against people who pretended to have good intentions, especially the activists. Despite appearances, many activists have no other goal than building their brands and their platforms. I advised her to be skeptical of the attorneys and others who would develop clever schemes to exploit her. In a nutshell, they would present her with projects they claimed would benefit her when, truth be told, those projects would ultimately benefit them the most. The best thing she could do was give herself permission to grieve, then to focus on healing.

From that moment on, we had a connection that has lasted to this day. I understand her and she understands me. When we're together, we can have a conversation and not have to keep saying, "Do you understand?" or "Do you know what I mean?" because we both know, we both get it. When we're together, we can be completely ourselves, say whatever we're thinking or feeling, a rare kind of connection. I've never had a moment with her that I haven't been grateful for.

———

Local activists staged a large demonstration in downtown Pittsburgh a few days after Antwon Rose was murdered. I didn't want to attend because I feared the demonstration might trigger memories of the night I got shot, but Brother Victor from the Nation of Islam said to me, "Man, we need you here."

The street was packed with a crowd of thousands. People started to notice me and shout, "Get Leon to the front!"

I made it to the front of the stage. Then everybody started asking me if I was going to speak.

"No," I said. "Absolutely not. I don't have it in me to speak today."

A football coach I knew came over to me. He had his son with him, a boy around twelve years old. "We got to get you up on stage so you can speak," he said.

"I ain't speaking."

Then his son said, "But you have to." His shiny smooth face floated before me like a balloon.

That settled it. I couldn't disappoint this kid. "All right, I'll speak."

They lifted me up on stage. I had nothing prepared in advance, so I simply spoke from my heart.

"Six years ago, a police officer mistook me for a criminal and shot to kill. Now it's happened again, and only a few miles from where I live.

"This time, the victim was seventeen-year-old Antwon Rose Jr., a young man that many of you gathered here today knew and loved. The police shot him three times in the back as he ran from a stopped car.

"Unlike me, it cost him his life.

"When I met his mother, all I could feel was a mix of rage and regret. In the six years since I started traveling around the country to tell my story, nothing has changed.

"I feel guilty to be alive. We all failed Antwon Rose.

"Though I am grateful to have survived the shooting and to have received compensation, my pain and anger continue to grow.

"It breaks my heart that such a young life was extinguished because our community hasn't found a solution to police brutality in the past six years. Tuesday night was a wake-up call for me, and it should be for everyone concerned about police violence.

"It's not enough to tweet, protest, or hold vigils. We need to elect new leaders who will push for accountability and consequences in police shootings. Stephen Zappala, the Allegheny County district attorney who charged me with aggravated assault, will also handle Rose's case. He's up for reelection next year.

"While millions of dollars are awarded regularly for police abuse throughout the country, we need to remind people that victims of the police are not simply looking for a payout. We are fighting for fairness, equity, respect, and love for Black life.

"Many of my peers have opted out of the system by disengaging from the political process, believing that there's no chance for it to work. Social media activism stops at sharing stories like mine with friends and projecting rage. But rage is not enough.

"If more of us register and vote, Antwon Rose's mother will have a better chance of securing a jury of her peers, which will increase her chances for justice. If more people of color had been registered to vote in Allegheny County, I might not have faced two all-white juries.

"If we want to change the system, we need to register and vote or, better yet, run for local offices that affect the justice system. If you're called as a juror, don't shirk the opportunity to serve. We must engage the justice system at all levels if we ever hope to position ourselves for change. We owe as much to Antwon."

At one point I started crying, my whole face wet with tears. I had tried to be strong for so long that I couldn't hold it in anymore. It was a tremendous moment of release; any notion of crying as a weakness had long faded for me.

Once I got off the stage, I felt like I was coming apart, my thoughts racing, nothing seeming to connect. It was as if my brain were encircled by a dark cloud where questions fired like streaks of lightning. *Could I go on another day? How should I kill myself? Who would find my body? How would my death affect my family and friends? Perhaps no one would care. No, they would. They had to.*

Nobody else at the demonstration seemed to recognize that I was on the verge of a nervous breakdown. Instead, people in the crowd started saying that I should run for mayor. And people were already on Twitter and Facebook posting "Leon Ford for Mayor." Those posts planted an idea in my mind: perhaps I should run for public office, not mayor but city council. I began mulling over the possibility.

During the funeral later that week, Antwon Rose's mom, Miss Kenney, was in bad shape, her entire body undone by grief. She struggled to remain standing and kept dropping to the floor. It pained me to watch her, but I knew there was little I could do to help.

Before the funeral, I had looked at the program and seen that I was scheduled to give the eulogy. This posed a bind since I didn't know a thing about eulogies despite the many funerals I'd attended over the years. Desperate for some pointers, I did a Google search. Fortunately for me, I made it through the eulogy, repeating some of what I'd said at the protest.

A funny thing happened at the cemetery. Having somehow made it through the funeral, Miss Kenney did not seem mentally able to handle the burial and appeared to be hiding out in the backseat of a limousine. Most people had already gathered around the gravesite, but the terrain made it difficult for me to maneuver over there in my wheelchair. Still, I was giving it my best effort when I heard someone knocking on the window of the hearse. I rolled back over to the car. Only then did I realize that Miss Kenney was trapped inside, the child locks in place. I opened the door and let her out of the vehicle.

Sometimes, I will get a feeling, an inkling, and a little voice in my head telling me "Call Miss Kenney." Upon calling her, I will discover that she is going through a lot. I will help put things in perspective.

I always remind her that she needs to give herself grace and formulate a plan on how long and how much she wants to endure. From my own experience, I know that it is difficult to maneuver in a world where most people truly don't understand the battle you face.

I try to always tell people that police shootings come with baggage. The families of the murdered can't grieve in the normal way. You're a target of the police, of law enforcement, and of supporters of law enforcement. Both you and your family are being judged.

Sometimes Miss Kenney will be doing a public event, and I will just show up unannounced, out of the blue. Given the bond that we have, I know that my being there helps her to make it through another day, and she helps me. But I still had to learn how I could address on a larger scale the brutality that bound the two of us.

26
A LIFE IN POLITICS?

O nce I connected to the idea of running for public office, I couldn't let go. It seemed like the logical next step. After all, many noted activists—John Lewis, Bobby Rush, James Clyburn, Alexandria Ocasio-Cortez—had advanced into politics. Public office would afford me the opportunity to represent my community in Pittsburgh, people for whom I cared deeply, who understood and nurtured me back. With a seat on the city council, I could help bring jobs, housing, health care, and other desperately needed resources to my community.

At the time, I believed public office was the avenue for change. It didn't bother me that I knew nothing about policy. Surely, my honesty and passion would make up for any civic and administrative shortcomings. Of this I was certain: I was destined to lead, and so I would.

My friends and family were largely supportive. But Brother Victor had major reservations about it.

He warned me, "Don't get involved in politricks."

My father expressed similar feelings.

Because I admired both men, I could not simply dismiss their doubts. Seeking further guidance, I reached out to Lenny McAllister.

"Child of God," he said, "you have given me such wonderful news. I always knew you would take this path. Politics are difficult, but you are capable. One day you'll be running against me for political office. I can see you being a state senator or even our president one day."

These were the words I needed to hear. Perhaps the predictions he'd made about me from a few years earlier were coming true. I might be mayor someday, or even governor.

On a mission, I spent the summer of 2018 hitting the streets, getting the word out, letting people know that I was running for city council. Everyone I told seemed overjoyed at the news. Their enthusiasm further inspired me, convincing me that I was of the people and for the people. The district I would represent consisted of all the neighborhoods I had grown up in in Pittsburgh: Homewood, Garfield, Lincoln, East Hills, Larimer, and East Liberty.

However, I didn't quite look the part of the traditional politician. I wore sweat suits instead of the traditional suit and tie. I had to live within the district and quickly realized that it was a challenge finding a disabled-accessible apartment. I soon realized that there were only two options for wheelchair users who wanted to live in my district: subsidized housing or the new developments. I decided to rent a posh one-bedroom apartment in an upscale building located in a section of East Liberty in the thick of gentrification. The flat rented for $2,400 a month, a fortune in Pittsburgh. I assembled a seven-person team, some with years of campaign experience while others were new to the campaign trail. They began working around the clock to generate interest in my candidacy.

We launched my run for city council on October 25, 2018, at a venue in East Liberty with the media heavily in attendance. We shot a catchy campaign video filmed on the streets of Homewood and in my new apartment. My campaign seemed to be off to a good start. The only issue of concern was that money was slow to come in. Despite our best efforts, we never raised more than $3,000 in donations. To keep the campaign afloat, I drew on $19,000 of my own funds. I spent most of my money on Leon Ford for City Council merch and yard signs that I gave away for free. Instead of learning about policy, I spent most of my time going to community events, even those organized by my new political rivals.

I felt fortunate to have my old friend Turahn Jenkins also running for office. Everything seemed to be going well with his campaign.

But then, he made a controversial statement to the press, and his campaign was over. It was a foreshadowing of things to come. Regardless of whether I agreed with him, I respected that he spoke his truth, but I would soon learn that politics involved much more than truth telling and inspiration.

Once I received my settlement, every bank in Pittsburgh, in addition to several financial advisors, started reaching out to me. They never let up, overwhelming me. Every phone call became a conversation about money. I was raised never to tell—or ask—people how much money I had. Now, these experts were pitching every investment under the sun. They would inundate me with puzzling information.

Luckily, I met someone who helped me find a new framework. We met one summer day in downtown Chicago, outside the hotel where a conference called Breakout was being held. I was rolling down the street on my way into the hotel when another Black man started walking next to me. He was a cool brother in his early thirties, slim and trim in a casual outfit, and well-groomed, the epitome of debonair and smooth. We greeted one another.

I asked him, "What do you do?"

He said, "I'm a financial advisor." He went on to introduce himself as Richard Murray from New York.

We struck up a conversation that continued throughout the conference.

In an informal way, he started giving me some useful facts about investments. I really appreciated him for not trying to sell himself and his services, which he could have easily done.

In January of the new year, 2019, Trabian Shorters brought together in Bermuda about thirty African Americans for a gathering called SOAR. This was a carefully selected circle of like-minded individuals, some of whom I knew, including Stephen DeBerry, Terry Williams, and Dorian Burton, people I love and respect. To my surprise Richard Murray was also there, our second encounter.

Over the next few days, I enjoyed my stay in Bermuda, a balmy and beautiful island. I would strip down to my swimming trunks and bask in the weather, take in the sights and sounds; even if I could not fully enjoy the white-sand beaches, the crew would assist me. Dorian, Steve, Trabian, Denmark West, or one of the other fellas had no problem carrying me to the beach to relax. Usually, I don't trust people to pick me up. However, this vibe was different. I could feel that these men genuinely wanted to help me.

Aubrey, my girlfriend at the time, came with me on the trip. Aubrey and I had met a few months earlier in Orlando, Florida, while I was on vacation. We were in a committed relationship, and I thought I was in love. Even then I longed to be a good lover despite not truly having a clear definition of what that entailed. In his book *The Road Less Traveled*, M. Scott Peck says, "I have defined love as the *will* to extend oneself for the purpose of nurturing one's own and another's spiritual growth." I believe that. I'd be willing. I'm still trying to figure that part out.

At all times I try to be compassionate and thoughtful to my significant other and create an environment for us both to succeed and thrive.

Looking back, I realized that I really liked her, but I did not love her. I had not made what Peck calls the "choice to love." Instead of being more attentive to her needs, I was focused on my future. I didn't want to be like the many affluent people that Rich told me about, the NBA and NFL players who made the wrong decisions and ended up losing money and getting into tax problems. Their first mistake: they didn't know how to build a financial team.

After listening to him, I decided to open an account with his firm, Bernstein Private Wealth Management, right there in his hotel room.

In time, like Stephen DeBerry, Richard would help me see myself as more than an activist. He would help me understand that progress requires money, and he would show me how to leverage my platform in Pittsburgh to bring people and resources together to solve problems and have a positive social impact. He showed me how to work with other investors to block the construction of a new prison in Pennsylvania. Money provides access. Money opens doors, gets you a seat at the table so you can have a say in decisions that impact the communities that you care about. More and more, I was starting to think about how I could use money in my capacity as a leader trying to bring about change.

———

In February 2019, one month after the retreat in Bermuda, I attended another retreat, in Mexico, at the invitation of Dina Kaplan, the founder of The Path, an organization that "teaches meditation for the modern mind." Speaking on the phone one day, she asked me if I had ever gone away from home to meditate. I had not. She thought my doing so would provide a period of respite from the pressures of the city council race.

The retreat certainly provided me time to relax and reflect. The landscape was beautiful with wide views of mountains and flora bright with colors I had never seen before. The participants were warm, friendly people, quick to smile and engage in conversation. Each person I spoke to was surprised to learn that I was running for city council. The news did not meet with everyone's approval. Some found my run inspiring, while others warned that politics would trap me in a box.

In particular, I remember a conversation I had with a guy sitting next to me at lunch in the hotel restaurant. He said to me, "Man, you're brilliant. Why do you want to run for office?"

I said, "I want to do good for the people I care about, my community."

"City council is cool, but you're a shark in the fish tank. You belong in the ocean with us. That political cesspool can be catastrophic to your growth."

Even though he didn't support me taking a leap into politics, he still wanted to support me and gave me a donation for my campaign.

His words provoked some serious reflection on my part.

Meditating that week, I started to have second thoughts about assuming public office. Perhaps that world wasn't for me. I was starting to realize that, honestly, I didn't have any specific goals. I had paid lip service to the usual promises: housing, gentrification, jobs, education, and police brutality. But what I really wanted was to shake some shit up. As a person outside the political establishment, I felt my getting elected would give a big middle finger to those traditional leaders who didn't respect and who had never supported me. The city had taken so much from me. I felt that this was my moment to shine. But, as I meditated, I started to reflect on one of my favorite movies, *The Count of Monte Cristo*. The main character loses everything and comes back as a wealthy man seeking power— and revenge, only to realize that "only God could give him justice." This message hit home. Only God could give me justice. Running for office had seemed like the right thing to do at the time. However, I now knew that my heart wasn't fully in it. Although I might do good, my race was more about me than about the people. Running for office was all about my ego. A way to flex power. A way to get revenge. It turned out, some of my demons were still working their dark influence over my decisions.

I talked through my feelings with the other participants at the retreat. I shared with them how I felt politics was messy. I watched politicians who were once friends say the worst about one another. I experienced elders in the community who have been advocates for youth voices argue that I was not qualified. I became discouraged and felt that politics was toxic. By then, we had all become friends, and they encouraged me, telling me they'd support me no matter what decision I made.

By the time I boarded the flight back to Pittsburgh, I had decided to drop out of the race. I remember driving home from the airport and passing through East End where I saw one yard sign after another saying "Leon Ford for City Council." This broke my heart. I had selfishly got the community's hope up, just to walk away. They were counting on me to be the change. Instead, I changed my mind about being their leader.

The following day, I was leaving my house when a car pulled up and stopped. The person inside said, "Hey, bro, we got your back, man. We're so happy." This made me feel like a failure. I thought, *How do I tell these people that I want to drop out of the race?* I began to battle and think deeply about my next steps. I thought maybe I would stick it out, but the thought of being a councilman for four years sounded exhausting. Then I thought maybe I stay in the race and not campaign, but again I thought, *I still may win.* I was conflicted and felt like a disappointment to those I was serving. I wanted badly to put myself first but could not break this tie with my people-pleasing side.

What happened next could have made it easy for me to drop out. Although I had a campaign team, I wanted to run the race my way. But my team had a firm strategy in place, one that I felt would have required me to be someone other than myself. They wanted me to dress differently, learn about issues that I didn't understand or have any real connection to, and play the political game. My initial plan was to mobilize the community by using the authentic voice that I had been for years. Instead, I was slowly becoming more polished, representing parts of the community that I wasn't familiar with and didn't feel comfortable speaking on. Politicians are all about policy, but I was not a politician, and I didn't care about the policy side of holding office the way that they did. Instead of going to the community football games, I was now being invited to meetings with community groups that were active in the political spaces but not active in the community. It became apparent to me that my vision was being hijacked. Or perhaps I was simply not fit for office since I couldn't walk the walk and talk the talk of politics.

———

I'd collaborated with a friend from New York to produce a short film about me as a survivor of police brutality who ran for city council and won. At the time we made the arrangement, I was fully confident that I would win the race. The plan was for me to stage a campaign event for my friend to film. He kept reaching out to me, but for weeks I avoided answering his phone calls. Finally, I gave in and spoke to him. He told me that he was ready to come to Pittsburgh to begin the shoot. I informed him I hadn't put together a campaign event, thinking that would be the end of the matter, the film.

He said, "We'll find something to shoot."

A few days later, he and his team drove to Pittsburgh and started filming my mentoring sessions at a community center. After one session, I felt drained, physically and mentally exhausted, nothing left in my body, then something came over me, a feeling even today I find hard to describe, my thoughts spinning as if I were inside a machine. I was angry, confused, afraid, and worried. I was now a millionaire, trying to find my new normal. I wanted to live a normal life but couldn't see an identity outside of activism, which I found to be triggering and exhausting. I was feeling lost mentally, emotionally drained.

In the quiet hallway of the community center, I said to a friend,

"I need to see a therapist. My mind is just racing right now. I feel like I'm going crazy."

She responded, "The joy in your smile doesn't match the pain in your eyes. You deserve to be happy and healthy. You deserve to heal."

I simply couldn't hold it all in anymore, all the trauma I'd endured year after year, dating back to my cousin Darnell's murder. That very day, I made an appointment to see a therapist.

27

THE REAL HEALING BEGINS

My entire life, I protected my outer self, while on the inside I felt like I was dying. Since going to my first funeral for my cousin Darnell, it had been a long string of funerals for the rest of my life: Steve, Leona, Grandma Flo, the funerals of friends and cousins. Then my shooting, my struggle to survive, my journey to come into a new sense of identity as a paraplegic, only to face a criminal trial, and, always, always, more funerals. Between 2015 and 2016, four of my childhood friends, Carlos, Buddha, Kerrese, and Poppa, all died. I never had a chance to properly grieve because of more death, more drama, more chaos, more crises like my civil trial, on and on. So many layers of brokenness.

In and of itself, the loss of my sister Leona was devastating. After she passed away, holidays that had once been days to celebrate, to be happy together, became days that we dreaded. My mother and I would think of her, and those special days became saturated with loss. My entire family suffered through the memories. Even now, certain dates are heavy for us: Thanksgiving, Christmas, Easter, Leona's birthday (June 26), and the most dreaded day of all—September 30, the day she passed. As these dates approach, we become very emotional, sad, angry, snappy, and irritable with people.

For years, all the suffering built up inside until it reached a point where I could no longer function, where I started to unravel. The coping mechanisms that I used—listening to music, writing, and acting like the pain didn't faze me—would no longer sustain me. My cup was completely empty. I often found myself just one blink away from crying. Nobody could see it. Everyone focused on my being a hero. Nobody focused on my healing.

I started therapy on March 12, 2019. With the agreement of my therapist, Erica, my friend from New York filmed the first session, hoping to use some of the footage as part of the campaign video.

Erica asked me why I had come to see her.

I said, "I'm addicted to the chaos."

She asked me to explain what I meant. I tried my best to put my feelings into words. I'd fought the city for years, a fight that kept me going, fueled mostly by anger. After I had settled my case, I sunk into a deep depression because I no longer had anybody to fight. I was coming to realize that I'd only decided to run for city council because I needed a fight. I craved chaos to keep me going. After receiving a settlement, most people would have simply ridden off into the sunset and gone about their life. I could not.

Erica listened attentively. Then she assured me that I could get better with an open mind and an open heart.

I dropped out of the run for city council the next day. Although I felt that I was giving up on my community, Erica assured me that self-care was a necessity, a courageous act. She would say, "Seeing a therapist is courageous." She affirmed that I had a right to create space to heal and that self-care is a revolutionary act. What I didn't know was how much pain and hard work that revolution would entail.

———

Through therapy, I have come to recognize that trauma was blocking me from reaching my full potential as a person. In hindsight, that realization has helped me to understand much about my life up until this point, and much about the community where I grew up and where I still live. Therapy helped me realize that, for my entire life, I had been so stuck in a war zone mentality, always preparing for the next attack, that I couldn't understand how to effect change. As I started to understand my own motivations, I grew more compassionate to myself and to the world around me.

For the most part, my friends who still battle in the streets are good dudes simply trying to survive. However, society paints them as monsters. We should understand that they live in a war zone. They don't want to fight, but they have no choice. It's like when you're a kid, and you're afraid to fight somebody you know is tougher and might do some serious damage to you, but you must still swallow your fear and square off. The situation is similar for these men, but they're fighting with guns, not fists. Under constant stress, they fear dying while losing friends to violence. Therefore, they feel they must kill before they get killed.

In middle school and high school, I thought a male reached the ripeness of manhood at age twenty. However, once I made it to twenty, I realized that you have experienced so little, your brain is still developing, and your life hasn't even begun. Little Steve and all the other people I'd lost never got the chance to experience life. When he was thirteen, Little Steve boasted about his many accomplishments, but I later realized he hadn't had the opportunity to live. He hadn't seen the world. At thirteen, he hadn't even learned to drive.

When you are only exposed to death, and when you live only to survive, you can't see life beyond that. The Everytown for Gun Safety policy and research group notes that "Black children and teens in America are 14 times more likely than their white counterparts to die by gun homicide. Black children and teens are 13 times more likely to be hospitalized for a firearm assault than white children." They go on to say that "children exposed to violence, crime, and abuse are more likely to abuse drugs and alcohol; suffer from depression, anxiety, and posttraumatic stress disorder; resort to aggressive and violent behavior; and engage in criminal activity. Exposure to community violence, including witnessing shootings and hearing gunshots, makes it harder for children to succeed in school."

In our communities, kids often assume the burden of survival. On top of worrying about how you're going to feed yourself, many young men and women have to consider how they will take care of their families. When my father was in prison, I felt responsible for him. I also felt I needed to help my mom financially. These are heavy obligations for a child.

On top of that, as Black people in America, we struggle with grief, the loss of parents, siblings, cousins, aunts, grandparents, friends, and classmates. The American Medical Association reports that on average Black people experience over 74,000 "excess deaths" each year compared with white people. Death is our everyday reality. We bear it and go on. In doing so, we become desensitized to death. Traumatized, we start to suffer from the symptoms of posttraumatic stress disorder.

Although there is little research about the impact of grief on the African American community, we do know that most Black people never receive grief counseling. In contrast, should a student at a white school die in a car accident, the deceased's classmates receive grief counseling for an entire year. Such is life in our country. Black people in America suffer an ongoing mental health crisis that largely goes undiagnosed and untreated.

———

Through therapy I was afforded the opportunity to review my life and experience breakthrough moments of clarity. I came to understand that I had grown up with a limited definition of manhood based on how my father and other men around me interacted with the world. A man provided, protected, and possessed power. Manliness was defined by how much money you had, how many women you slept with, how much influence you wielded, and how strong you were.

Then I got shot. When I woke up in the hospital, none of those things mattered. I could no longer physically beat up anyone. I couldn't even stand up and look another man in the eyes. People were now looking down on me in my wheelchair, which made me feel inferior.

I have a cousin who made it to the NFL, and I can remember his father calling my father one day. Both men screamed and laughed on the phone, their happiness ringing through the hallways. I remember sitting with my head down in my wheelchair in the living room of the house I shared with my father and thinking, *I'll never be able to make my parents proud like that. They will always have to take care of me.*

These feelings didn't serve me. Frustrated, confused, and insecure, I had to redefine manhood.

After I started speaking at schools, some of that pressure eased. Observing the way other men, young and old, could relate to me boosted my self-esteem. With this new sense of purpose, I started to build my identity around being a community leader and activist. That was my sole purpose for years. I didn't have an identity outside of those roles. When I wasn't organizing, protesting, or speaking at community events, I did not know what to do with myself. I was very one-dimensional. I began experiencing burnout to the point where I started to disconnect from the work.

My biggest breakthrough in therapy came when I realized that I am a multidimensional human being. Now, after being in counseling for more than four years, I no longer feel the burden of putting community first, although I am still committed to helping people and planting seeds. I learned that true leaders don't exhaust themselves trying to heal people. Instead, they assist and encourage people to find the healing power within themselves.

Using a wheelchair, I felt like a burden to everybody. For that reason, devoting myself to community made me feel like I was adding value to the lives around me. Though it's not often discussed, many activists give so much of themselves that they burn through their internal resources and motivation—essentially killing themselves from the inside out. We must move past the martyr mentality and realize that we can make significant changes without sacrificing our lives.

Activism can also take a toll on activists' families. Several community leaders I look up to have children my age but have no relationship with them because they are never present or available to them. I refuse to be that person. I value my relationship with my son above all else. What's more important: Saving somebody else's child or saving my own? Building a bond with somebody else's child or strengthening my bond with my own? There was a time where mentoring youth and activism came first in my life. However, through therapy I was able to let go of my savior complex. I now understand that I didn't have to make being a hero my identity. I embraced the fact that I am a father first. I add value to the community whenever I can. However, I am intentional about being fully present with my loved ones.

My time in therapy has made me realize that it is okay for me to express my emotions. I had been culturally conditioned not to feel pain I should have felt. The first two lessons that I remember learning as a child came by way of my father, lessons I learned probably even before I could speak. One, "Big boys don't cry." Two, "Fight." Hurt and be hurt, but hold your feelings in. These lessons resulted in me carrying around for years a tremendous amount of trauma, dating back to Darnell's funeral, where I proudly told my father that I had withheld my tears.

Recently my dad called me, upset, on speakerphone. He is remarried, and his wife has a five-year-old grandson.

"Leon," my father said, "what did I used to tell y'all when y'all was little, when y'all used to cry and shit?"

"You used to tell us big boys don't cry."

"Yeah, that's right. And if y'all going to cry I'll punch y'all in the chest."

He'd never punched me in the chest, but he had punched Reese and Dale.

"I'd tell y'all I'd give you something to cry for."

I took a moment to think about what to say. "Well, why is he crying?"

"It don't fucking matter. Ain't nobody die in this family."

This was the message my father wanted to send to the little boy. Only a dead family member justifies tears.

I spoke to the boy. "Look, it's all right to cry. Pap-pap just doesn't want you to be crying for no reason. He doesn't want your grandma to baby you."

Angry, my dad said, "What?" Then he hung up on me.

We no longer share the same perspective, and that's okay.

Toughness is my father's form of compassion. In some ways, especially when I wanted to kill myself, it inspired me to persevere. Everybody may not agree with his approach. I recognize that he has bottled up his pain and was teaching me what worked for him. Only recently has he been able to talk about Leona's death. He still doesn't say much; he simply does little things to keep her memory alive.

––––––

Therapy has completely changed the way that I view and interact with myself and the world. Therapy has helped me trust myself, which has, in turn, taught me how to trust other people. Often, we carry emotional baggage—including fear of abandonment and rejection, overwhelming guilt and anxiety—that shapes how we make decisions. I encourage people to be mindful of what they are carrying and to become aware how that emotional baggage affects their daily lives. Think about some things that you may be struggling with internally, then consider what it will take to heal.

I have learned that acceptance is a huge part of healing. I may not want to admit it, but I am a paraplegic, I've lost my ability to walk. I can live in denial, or I can choose to accept this reality while working hard to change my circumstances mentally, physically, and emotionally. Healing is a choice and a choice that can significantly impact our lives and the lives around us.

My efforts to heal have transformed the way that I operate as a leader. For one, I've gotten to a place where I no longer let people trigger me. To reach common ground, I can listen with a clear head, and I can also communicate my position in a clear manner. Leadership is about finding common ground, solving problems, getting results, leveraging influence and resources to meet the needs of the people you're representing.

To many of us, activism never goes beyond self-expression, articulating hurt, articulating pain, speaking out against institutional and systemic injustice, and being a voice. We get lost in the struggle. Our voices have been ignored for so long that we have a strong desire to be heard. Being heard is essential, but it is even more important to evolve and demand more. There was a time when my strongest desire was to be heard. As an activist, my focus was to create awareness about the daily violence that young Black men like me experienced, not only from those sworn to protect us, but among ourselves in a high-stakes, kill-or-be-killed environment.

Through relationships with different leaders, I learned that there are many ways to systematically reach goals. Instead of focusing solely on being a voice, I now focus on the goal. Being a voice is simply a tool I can use to reach my goals. We should acknowledge the struggle and focus on achievable goals. We should know how to express ourselves in such a way that we welcome others to the table. Ultimately, activism should aim for unity, togetherness, wholeness, and healing. We can be very effective when we embrace the spirit of collaboration.

I try to help people reach their goals by working together, despite their differences. This is my aim. After I learned about the impact of lack of affordable housing, education, and poor health on communities like mine, I decided to run for a representative position in the county I was raised in. But now, I realize that my role can go even deeper than that. Politics often gets mired in ego, conflicting values, bureaucracy, and overblown rhetoric. When I ran for office, I wanted to bring people who would never even sit in the same room together to solve socioeconomic problems. That is now an achievable goal.

28
WAKE-UP CALL IN DUBAI

Although I had started therapy, I was still feeling burned out and uncertain about what I should do next. In April of 2019, I decided to decompress and take a trip overseas to visit one of my mentors, Heath Bailey. A lifelong educator at high schools in Pittsburgh, Heath had been working for a decade as a principal of an international school in Dubai. He'd married a beautiful Ethiopian woman and enjoyed life there. He hates America and vows that he will never return. We speak by phone from time to time, our conversations always revolving around his belief that every Black person should leave this country.

Before my trip to Dubai, Heath had long been set on convincing me to emigrate there. "You need to come over here. You can marry an African woman and get on with your life." In a dramatic voice, he would issue me dire warnings and say things like, "Man, listen. If you stay in America, you're going to die. Shit is going to go down. The white people over there are crazy. Donald Trump's in office. There's going to be a civil war. You need to leave."

His son Cam and I had grown up together. I decided to buy Cam a plane ticket so that we could fly over and surprise Heath. The three of us spent a few pleasant weeks together. It was a relaxing getaway, although I found Dubai a bit artificial and strange with its immaculate streets, palm-shaped islands, and overabundance of skyscrapers. Heath, Cam, and I made the most of each day and had many meaningful conversations.

One night, the three of us went out to get some ice cream. We sat down in front of the shop to eat. We had been doing so for only a few minutes when a loud sound ripped through the air. The sound startled two of us, jolting Cam to jump up from the table. After a few seconds we realized that a motorcycle had backfired. Heath broke down and started crying. We were so used to gun violence in Pittsburgh that the sound of a motorcycle backfiring had triggered us.

Heath said, "Man, this is why I want you all to leave America. We don't have that here. Nobody has a gun over here. You never hear anything about shootings." He was so heartbroken about our reality back home.

A few days later, I had the opportunity to speak to students at his academy, a hundred or so middle and high school kids, a cool, receptive bunch, who listened attentively as I shared my story. Their faces became bright with looks of surprise. They couldn't believe they were meeting somebody who'd been shot, let alone shot by a police officer.

One student asked me, "Are you afraid for your son while he's in school?"

"No," I said, confused. "Why would I be?"

She responded, "Because they kill students in school in America."

Another student piped up: "People get shot in America and all kinds of stuff. I would never come over there."

I found her statement ironic because my whole time in Dubai, my parents had been texting me, "Be careful over there. It's dangerous."

I thought about her words and what that meant to me as a father. What it meant for LJ. Somehow, I had never considered how risky life in Pittsburgh could be for LJ. I wanted to move him to a country where neither he nor I would have to worry about being shot, either by a government official or someone who looked like him. Facing this threat, I desperately wanted to escape the country with my son.

My experiences in Dubai left such a strong impression on me that I decided it was time to leave. For the first time in my life, I found myself in a foreign land contemplating what life could be like outside of America. It was inspirational to see someone who ran the same streets of Pittsburgh living well as an expat. As had happened so many other times in my life, I was exposed to something different and began to dream. I also reflected on the many conversations with my grandfather and Aunt Koko about life abroad. Going into exile seemed to me the only surefire way of protecting LJ from all the violence, racial and otherwise, that might befall him in the land of our birth. No way would I let LJ suffer all that I had suffered or endure all I'd had to endure. Time to make moves.

29

AROUND THE WORLD
AND BACK AGAIN

After considering my options for moving overseas, I signed up
for a program called Remote Year that would make it possible for me to spend a year traveling around Europe. Bags packed,
I left for Split, Croatia, in early July 2019. Split did not disappoint
with its cobblestone streets and Old World sensibility. I visited a
two-thousand-year-old castle. Never in my life had I been inside a
structure so ancient. Croatia also offered some amazing food. Black
people were noticeably absent from the city. Little did that matter to
me. Being there, the weight of America was lifted.

I had been in Croatia for only a short while when I started experiencing a sense of liberation from American racism, a feeling akin to
what others like Richard Wright and James Baldwin had felt before
me. A burden had been lifted. I lived each day to the fullest, taking in
the sights of the Old World—cathedrals, monuments, ancient ruins—
and eating great food. Wealth had given me the opportunity to travel,
just as wealth has cushioned me somewhat from everyday racism.

For the next six months, I traveled throughout Europe. Altogether, I spent almost six months there, an important period of

learning and reflecting, and thinking about myself and the world. My whole time there, I had my grandfather in mind and experienced some of the relief from American racism he must have experienced during the years he lived in Europe. Although racism exists all over the world, those six months in Europe were a relief for me. I was exhausted from losing friends to gun violence, seeing videos of police shootings, the political divisiveness, and from being seen as a martyr to the antiracist movement. All in all, I had a phenomenal time in Europe from the perspective of someone who was running from a tremendous amount of pain back home.

My grandfather always says, "You don't teach people what to think. You teach them how to think." In Europe, I was learning how to think. In cities like Stockholm, Venice, and London, I met individuals who began to change my understanding of activism and leadership, helping me develop a global perspective. In these cities I met teenagers who knew more about international politics than I knew. They could tell me in exact detail about what was going on not only in Europe but also in Africa, Asia, and the United States. I was shocked to meet nineteen-year-olds who knew more about American politics than I ever knew at that age. Through conversations with many young and old, I gained a new sense of politics and the social justice movement. I came to realize that as activists, we can accomplish more by having intentional dialogue with opposing sides. As my new friend, Alby, would put it, "We must think global but act local."

———

Viewing my country from afar, I realized that activism in America today is mostly about building a brand and antagonizing rather than solving problems. Many players in the social justice movement simply perform for social media, a platform that waters down everything. What then is genuine social and political engagement?

The "social advocacy" around police brutality in America is a lucrative enterprise for some. Top tier "advocates" have Twitter followers by the thousands, earn millions of dollars in speaking fees, book deals, and consulting fees as media pundits and commentators. Then there are the billions of dollars raised by Black Lives Matter activists that goes unaccounted for.

In Pittsburgh, I'd heard some people talk about building a stronger sense of community, others talk about building relationships with local government, still others speak about building relationships with the state government, or with attorneys and police officers, nonprofits and foundations. However, no true dialogue takes place because activists talk to activists, politicians talk to politicians, police officers talk to police officers, teachers talk to teachers, and entrepreneurs talk to entrepreneurs. I started to wonder: what would it look like if all these leaders from these groups put their differences aside and came together to solve problems like police brutality and gun violence?

Though I longed for a respite from racism that Europe offered, I know I had to go back to America to help change things. Could I bring a global perspective to Pittsburgh and help bring about positive change in the Black community? Could I channel my affluence into a new platform for dialogue? The settlement money might serve as a tool to get me into rooms with the powerful—people like bankers, CEOs, and tech giants. A tool that would persuade the powerful to trust me. My lived experience, family, and community relationships would keep me in touch with grassroots movements. I could position myself as the man in the middle of a vast social network. I didn't have a particular plan, but I knew that I had to use my platform to bring people together. I would return to Pittsburgh and give it my best shot.

Another important matter factored into my decision to return to America. I knew that LJ's mom, Avery, would never allow me to take him overseas to live. I was starting to understand one of the tough realities about parenting. Our efforts to protect our children only extend so far. Although I fear for LJ's life and do my best to protect him, I am not in control of what he faces once he steps onto the street. I still find it hard to accept.

By the start of November, I was back in Pittsburgh. I wasted no time in resuming therapy. As I would discover, therapy would not only further my process of self-examination, but it would also play an integral part in my efforts to bring people together in my city. Striving to be a consensus builder, I would check in with pastors from my community and ask, "What do you want to see happen in our community?" Many of the church leaders would bring up the ideals described in scripture, and then I would ask, "Hey, I'm familiar with biblical scripture, but what do you want to see change right now? What can we do right now, to make things better on our streets? What is the solution?" I would talk to business leaders, and they would tell me, "Well, I don't trust this person. I don't like that person." I would respond, "Okay, I understand that. But what is the solution?" Often, I would leave a meeting feeling frustrated.

After concentrating on my own personal healing and development, I was able to find the patience to listen to people different from myself—politicians, lawyers, preachers—in meetings and imagine the issues from their perspective, while also challenging them to focus on the solutions. If my platform puts me in a room with powerful and influential people who can impact the way my city operates, especially Black lives in my city, I look to fulfill my purpose. I understand that I wouldn't be in these rooms if I were an angry person. I'm not saying I don't have anger, only that I have learned how to redirect my anger and deal with it privately, in healthy spaces.

I go to therapy every Monday. There, in my therapist's office, I'm able to deal with some of my anger and disappointments, which in turn helps me to go out and do the work that I do. I get frustrated with police officers. I get frustrated with activists. I get frustrated with local government. It's not a one-way street. I'm a human being with a full range of emotions, but I've learned how to deal with my emotions and manage them. I am then able to focus on my purpose and get things done.

I tell my therapist. "I've been carrying so much weight and I just want to let it go."

She says to me, "You're sitting in here doing therapy. From my standpoint, I think that is courageous. I think it's strong to be willing to have that level of transparency, that level of vulnerability. Maybe the slogan is, 'I choose me. I would like you to choose you.'"

"As I'm deciding to walk away from this chaos, I'm fearful because I don't know who I am without chaos."

"Now that's an honest assessment. You just took the mask off."

I lay my head back on the couch and let her words sink in.

She tells me, "Now, breathe. Breathe."

I breathe.

"You just held your breath."

I release.

———

One thing I have come to understand is that ideology divides people, that it serves only as a roadblock. Often, we make assumptions about people based on their group identity, Democrat, Republican, Baptist, Catholic, etc. I'm so grateful that I didn't grow up with an allegiance to any political party or religious group. My older brother Dale is a Jehovah's Witness. I have uncles who are Muslims. I have Catholic friends. I have friends who are Republican, others who are Democrats, some who are independent. In my circle I know people who never vote. I don't judge them. They're human beings, and they all have value. The more that I worked on myself in therapy, the more I became able to remove triggers, which has helped me to meet people as people, and to hear their stories. I'm connected to certain individuals—investors, CEOs, tech people, entrepreneurs, business owners—that I probably wouldn't have connected to as an activist, and these same individuals are really helping me push things forward in Pittsburgh. Had I gone with first assumptions—"These people are not like me and won't listen to what I have to say"—I would have presumed that we don't care about the same issues.

I also discovered that therapy allowed me to reframe my conversations with other allies in the social justice movement who are important to me, people like Miss Kenney. Not long after my return to Pittsburgh, we found ourselves seated next to each other at a fancy dinner with other activists from the city. She didn't seem well to me. I could sense it.

We started talking. Thirty seconds into the conversation, I said to her, "You need to decide how long you're going to be in these kinds of spaces. You should make your rounds and then dip out. You gotta protect your own peace."

She looked at me, smiled, and took my hand into her own. We were both learning about what it means to heal.

30
PRESIDENT BARACK OBAMA'S LESSON

The country and the world erupted during the summer of 2020 in the wake of George Floyd's murder in Minneapolis. While many people tuned in to the media coverage or demonstrated on the streets, the unrest triggered me. I tried my best to guard my mental space, even if much that troubled me caught my attention. Needing a safe outlet for what I was feeling, I spent many hours on the phone confiding in Alby, sharing my frustration with the narrative around the Black Lives Matter movement. As I explained to Alby, Black Lives Matter is three things: a phrase, a movement, and an organization. I support the phrase and the movement, but I don't support the organization. It does not surprise me that the organization has become embroiled in controversy around mismanagement of money.

As for the movement, much of the discourse and action seemed divisive to me, coming from a place of anger. I had reached a point in my life where I knew that once you move past anger, you encounter a more productive place. Many people involved in the BLM movement don't realize that they are traumatized because it's easy to mask trauma with purpose. It's easy to overlook pain when you're doing something positive like following in the footsteps of great people like Fannie Lou Hamer, Martin Luther King, and Stokely Carmichael.

Thinking back, I remembered how I'd been triggered by a statement the mayor made after we agreed upon a settlement. He'd said, "Officers and families can now heal and move on with their lives." Only after therapy could I understand both the meaning and truth of his words.

Alby encouraged me not to become despondent or to give in to hopelessness. He felt that I needed to find a way to remain connected and involved, despite the pandemic. I confessed that the isolation was taking its toll. Giving the matter some thought, he remembered that he'd met a woman named Sarah Hurwitz, who worked as a speechwriter for President Obama and Michelle Obama. He introduced us, and she in turn put me in touch with people at the Obama Foundation. Shortly thereafter, I received an invitation to participate in a virtual panel entitled Mental Health and Wellness in a Racism Pandemic, a program that would be presented under the auspices of the My Brother's Keeper Alliance at the foundation. I instantly filled with excitement.

The podcast aired on June 5, 2020, with a panel consisting of President Obama, Congressman John Lewis, Bryan Stevenson, Laquan Muhammad, moderator Darnell Moore, and me. I felt honored to be in such auspicious company and only wished that I could have met the four other men in person. I felt like I had arrived, that I had reached the pinnacle of leadership. The decisions I'd made in the past, including choosing not to retaliate against the police, had finally paid off. Here I was on this tremendous platform. I thought about what Lewis had overcome, and I thought about what Obama and Stevenson had achieved.

Lewis was frail and weak from cancer, but he summoned the strength to share an inspirational moment from his storied life.

When it was my time to speak, I did what I always do; I spoke from the heart. I began my segment by saying, "I had to believe that the world wasn't as bad as my experience." Real talk.

I marveled at the eloquence of Obama and Stevenson and felt humbled when Obama spoke of his admiration for me and my refusal to give into bitterness. He described me as a "phoenix who had risen from the ashes." For all the poetry of his words, their meaning escaped me. What was a phoenix? I hadn't a clue, but I planned to find out since Obama is a man of deep insight and understanding. Indeed, in time I would discover that he had given me a new way of thinking about my life.

Obama's words helped me to reframe the way I thought about myself. He made me realize that the fire was meaningful and the ashes purposeful. Many people reject the fire in their lives and become consumed by the ashes. None of us asks for trials and tribulations, but we have a choice in how we respond. Obama's words made me realize that rising is a choice. To be on the stage with four of the world's great political figures was confirmation of my purpose. Healing and leadership had brought me to the world stage.

John Henne and I had formed a deep bond and often worked together on projects we thought would better the communities we cared about. Like myself, he had deep Pittsburgh roots. His great-grandfather, Rudolph J. Henne, had started the family jewelry business one hundred thirty years earlier, making the establishment a well-known fixture throughout the city. A deeply Christian man, Rudolph had strived to use the store to do good. John put a lot of work into carrying on this philanthropic mission.

John started to hire some of my friends at the shop, a well-intentioned effort that hasn't always gone well for him. Sometimes, my friends don't show up for work. John finds their behavior and the absenteeism perplexing. After all, he pays a good salary. I would explain to him that these are men and women who have endured a life of trauma. They need to heal. I suggested that he hold them accountable as employees but also find a way to encourage them to seek help.

In the same way that John has tried to better the lives of my friends, he has also strived to connect me with powerful individuals whom he thought would engage in dialogue around healing. He would often ask me, "Leon, do you know so-and-so? Oh man, you two need to meet."

I had my reservations when he suggested that I have a sit-down with the mayor of Pittsburgh, Bill Peduto. I fully trusted John's judgment, but Peduto didn't strike me as a man who knew how to get things done. Like many politicians, he talked the talk but never walked the walk. I heard all the usual political platitudes and promises—he would bring jobs, houses, and opportunities to Pittsburgh—but I saw no results. Also, we had a history. I had been unkind to him when I was running for city council. I had taunted and harassed him and had even called him a racist. Still, I was open to the idea of meeting with him if John could make it happen. True leadership demanded that I always keep my eyes on the bigger picture.

To my surprise, Mayor Peduto accepted John's offer for a sit-down, with John serving as the mediator. We met on a hot July day inside the air-conditioned office of John's store. Accompanied by his chief of staff, the mayor looked a bit uncomfortable. His face mask could hardly contain his full gray beard that seemed to have a life of its own. Each button on his blazer was fastened. The four of us maintained social distance so that we could speak without having to wear face coverings.

The mayor and I talked for a good hour, enough time for me to realize that I'd read him wrong. He seemed to want the same things for the city that I wanted: peace and prosperity for all. I realized that he was traumatized from the pressures of the office. At the end of the meeting, he asked for my help in serving as a mediator between the Black leaders of the city and his office.

As much as I tried to serve as a mediator, a consensus builder, I discovered that the Black leaders were also traumatized, so much so that they couldn't articulate what they wanted. No progress could be made. How could I create a space to help tailor solutions to everyone's lived experience? Going forward, I would make that my mission.

Laura Ellsworth was another person John thought I should meet. For about twelve years, he had sat with her on the board of Imani Christian Academy, a school that served mostly African American and underprivileged youth in Pittsburgh. He'd found Laura to be the most dynamic and impactful board member.

Although originally from New York, Laura has lived in Pittsburgh for forty years. She holds a prominent position in the city as a well-known attorney for a law firm that has offices in several parts of the world. No stranger to philanthropy, her father opened the first Ronald McDonald House in America.

On August 22, 2020, we met at a little restaurant in Shadyside. I would learn later that she walked into the meeting with a great amount of skepticism. Because her husband was a drug prosecutor for the US Attorney's Office for thirty years, my family was known to her. Her husband knew my father. He knew my great-uncle Rocky and other members of my family. In fact, he knew the entire history of the Ford family. However, Laura and I quickly became comfortable with one another.

I still recall the first question she asked me: "If at this moment in time, you could have one thing that you really wanted, what would it be?"

I said, "I would stop everybody on all sides from victimizing the traumatized."

"I don't understand. What does that mean?"

I told her that when somebody has been shot, or they've lost a family member, what we do now in this country is we put a microphone in their face. "Everybody on all sides exploits these people who are victims of trauma. Instead of exploiting them, we should put our arms around them and help them heal."

She said, "Wow, well, what else would you do?"

I started talking about my ideas for workforce development programs, for helping people released from prison, and for mentoring kids: constructive, creative ideas that were based on knowing real people and wanting the best for them.

Then she told me something about the good work she'd tried to do for the past thirty years in Pittsburgh, leading organizations, working with foundations, serving on the Chamber of Commerce and the Workforce Development Board. Serving as president of this, vice president of that. A life spent designing and funding many programs.

In the nicest possible way, I smiled and said to her, "You want to know why none of that worked?"

"Tell me."

I said, "You said this, people heard this, and nobody showed up."

She asked me dozens of questions during lunch—about leadership, police-community relations, and other topics. I answered each as truthfully as I could.

Then she said, "We have to work together."

Almost immediately, Laura began setting up meetings with the president of the Pittsburgh Foundation, the president of the Hillman Foundation, the president of the Carnegie Foundation, this federal judge, that federal judge, this attorney, that attorney, this bank, and that bank.

Over another lunch, she asked me, "Have you ever thought about starting a nonprofit organization? Because you're brilliant."

I said, "I don't like managing people."

"Well, maybe you should think about a foundation."

We began to discuss the idea, although I was largely against it. I didn't want to keep simply talking about the same things to the activists. One foundation had tried to get me to join a coalition, the

Coalition to Reimagine Public Safety. I had declined their offer before later reluctantly making the commitment. I ultimately didn't find my time participating in the coalition to be rewarding.

I said to her, "I'm really not feeling these activists because they all move the same way. I don't see what we'll come up with that's different. There would be more value in me talking to the police chief, or commanders, or the people from the Fraternal Order of Police, the mayor's office, the district attorney's office." I realized that I had evolved into more of a power broker.

She nodded, affirming that we saw eye to eye. We began to work on our own foundation.

31

HOW TO HOLD A MEETING

I'm not a fan of starting a conversation addressing serious issues. Instead, I like to meet people as people and find out how we are similar. For instance, the first time I met with the chief of police, Scott Schubert, I didn't start off by saying I was shot. David Derbish might be his friend. We might come at odds over my shooting since I believe the shooting was unjustified, while Derbish still believes that it was. We would have already hit a brick wall, making dialogue impossible.

Once the chief and I sat down to meet, I asked him, "What's your story? How did you get here? How did you become a police officer?"

The chief began telling me about his father, a man he admired greatly, and how he wanted to emulate his work as a police officer. My father wasn't a police officer, but I loved him, and I also wanted to be like him. We had common ground around our fathers.

Then the chief told me about his wife, his love for his family, and his love for the community. I also love my family and love my community. After that, things got deep.

I asked him, "When was the last time you cried?"

His eyes began to water a bit, although he never answered the question. From that moment on, I was no longer having a conversation with him as a police officer but as an individual. To my way of thinking, when we have conversations as individuals, our differences don't matter.

Some people will be surprised to learn that I have white friends who have Blue Lives Matter signs in their yards and stickers on their cars. When I first met them, I didn't start the conversation by telling them that I was shot by a police officer. Instead, I made sure that we connected and let them take a liking to me as a person. Some would look at my wheelchair and assume that I was a veteran. Then when I told them I was shot by a police officer, their entire perspective changed because they like me for me. Now they might start thinking, *Well, if this happened to Leon, it could happen to anybody. Maybe police officers are not doing what they need to be doing. Maybe there is something wrong with policing in our country.*

We can change our world for the better through dialogue and collaboration. Nobody is coming to save us. There won't be another Martin Luther King who will lead us to the promised land. It is up to us. What we can do as individuals is engage in progressive conversations and find common ground. Be it police violence or community violence, everyone has a role to play. No one can afford to turn a blind eye to public safety or politics. We all want our communities to be safe and prosperous, so we must be involved.

Confrontation is a dead end. Some Black Lives Matter activists try to shame white people into feeling guilty. Some people reject that intrusion. The people accused reject that judgment. They feel like, "Hold up, you don't even know me." Experience has taught me a far more productive approach. A mutually respected individual should bring the two opposing sides together. For instance, when I wanted to meet with the mayor, John Henne made that meeting possible. The mayor respects John. I also respect John, so I wouldn't dare insult the mayor in John's presence. Nor would the mayor insult me. A similar thing happened when I met Chief Schubert. Laura brought the chief and I together. The chief respects Laura, and I respect Laura. Real dialogue could now take place.

There's a certain level of power when two people with opposing views are connected by somebody that they both love, respect, and appreciate. That's how you get things done. I use this approach all the time to bring together individuals who disagree with one another. With me in the middle, both sides know they're in a safe space where neither will get violated.

32

SITTING DOWN WITH THE MAN WHO SHOT ME

You may be shocked to learn that I had a face-to-face meeting with the man who shot and paralyzed me, Detective David Derbish. Not long after my first conversation with Chief Schubert, I started to feel that a sit-down with Derbish was something I had to do, although why I felt that way was unclear to me at the time. Perhaps it began with a desire to send a message to him: "You didn't just shoot a Black boy walking around the neighborhood. You shot Leon Ford." Indeed, that was part of it. But there was more. I spoke a lot about healing and even facilitated a meeting between my mentor Jason Rivers and my childhood friend Anton, who was convicted for murdering Jason's brother. As hard as it was for the two, the meeting was necessary to help a community heal. In many ways Jason and Anton modeled what restorative justice could look like in my life.

I'm a very curious person. If somebody says, "I hate Black people," I don't say, "Well, fuck you. I hate you, too." Instead, I want to ask questions such as, "When did you start hating Black people? What was your lived experience? How are you culturally conditioned to hate Black people? You do understand that you weren't born that way?" I'm genuinely interested to know and understand how people think. My personal experience has instilled in me more grace for complicated individuals. Accepting that I was complicated helped me to be more understanding. I was raised in a very gender-specific household with strong views about gay people. Through the years I've become more informed and accepting. However, I'd be lying to say that my neighborhood didn't raise me to look down on people who chose to date the same sex. If cell phones were more accessible when I was in high school, there is a good chance that a video of me using derogatory terms about certain groups could have gone viral. Therefore, I've learned to own my past ignorance while creating space for other people to own theirs. That way we can grow together and create a more accepting society. For that reason, I wanted to talk to Detective Derbish and learn how he thought and what made him pull the trigger. As a leader, I thought it could inform my work moving forward to know, from a psychological perspective, why Derbish had shot me.

I made my feelings known to some of my closest friends, including John Henne and Laura Ellsworth. Laura wanted to know why. I stretched the truth in answering her, saying that I wanted to forgive Derbish and also wanted to afford him the opportunity to apologize, motives that had not made their way into my conscious thoughts—although they would in time.

Being protective of me, Laura decided that she would test the waters and speak with Derbish. She did so in November of 2020. I never found out what transpired during that encounter. Laura simply told me, "He isn't ready to meet with you." I figured her motherly instincts kicked in, and she decided to protect me. From what? I didn't know.

However, that did not put an end to the matter. We decided to keep the possibility open, affording Derbish the opportunity to become worthy in Laura's eyes. After much back and forth between several parties, Laura thought it was time. We scheduled the sit-down for the afternoon of July 12, 2021, at the Penn Hotel downtown.

In the lead-up to that day, a powerful urge came over me one morning, pushing me to open my Bible and read about David and Goliath for the first time. Turning to scripture is rare for me since I associate the good book and church with funerals and death. Be that as it may, people often told me that my story reminded them of David and Goliath. I was David, and the city was Goliath.

Captivated by what I read, I then turned to the conflict between David and Saul, also a compulsion. In the pages I was both delighted and surprised to find parallels with my own life. Saul had tried to murder David, and yet David had forgiven him. Perhaps I was struggling to forgive Detective Derbish, and I wished that I could be like David. I even spoke the words, "Let me be like David. Let me have grace like David." Despite Saul's shortcomings, David didn't kill him. He was still able to view him as a child of God.

The day of the meeting, I woke up feeling nervous, anxious, and a bit uncertain, although I was prepared for any outcome, including for Derbish to justify himself, to say, "You deserved to be shot." I was also aware that the outcome would reflect his heart more than mine. One thing was certain, Derbish would meet the Leon Ford I'd become since that night nine years earlier when he'd shot me five times. How he reacted to this Leon Ford was up to him. I'd told a dozen people about the scheduled encounter and articulated a dozen different motives for why I wanted it to happen. This might seem disingenuous on my part. It wasn't. The truth of the matter is that on a personal level, I still didn't know why. I simply *felt* it was something I had to do, something beyond my control, from deep within me. It was spiritual.

I was experiencing the same sensation of peace I had felt on the night when Derbish shot me and my spirit left my body, then proceeded to hover in the air above my corporeal form bleeding out on the street.

In everything I do, I let that sensation of hovering, of tranquility, guide me. Many people look at my life and assume that I am a big planner. I'm not. Experience has taught me to follow my intuition, chase that feeling of peace, and trust that all will work out. I'm the type of person to jump out of an airplane and build a parachute on the way down. That is the level of faith I have.

Once, when I was a kid, we took a family trip to Disney World. My father wanted me to get on the water slide although I wasn't tall enough. He stood in the pool with his hands up, saying, "Jump. I got you." I did because I trusted him.

Although I don't go to church on a regular basis, I'm a firm believer. I can feel the hand of God at work in my life. When I decided to go to California instead of retaliating against the police, I knew that God was directing me there, although I didn't know for what purpose. Now I know it was for me to meet people as I had Stephen DeBerry.

————

In the hours leading up to the meeting, I continued to feel unsettled. Seeking spiritual reassurance, I decided to phone one of my mom's best friends, a deeply religious woman affectionately known as Aunt Yolie. I told her that I would soon be meeting with Officer Derbish.

She said, "Let's pray."

I bowed my head, closed my eyes, and listened to her prayer:

"Lord, I thank you for the safe space that we have with one and other, to be able to talk about anything. Lord, I thank you for giving Leon wisdom. I thank you for giving him a heart of forgiveness, despite everything he's been through. I just ask you to go before him now, Lord, as he prepares for this meeting with the officer that attempted to take his life. Lord, I pray that my nephew's spirit will illuminate every corner of the room where the officer sits.

"I pray for a spirit of conviction that will become so overwhelming that this officer will seek to know how to get to know the God that saved, that spared my nephew's life. I pray that this officer will begin to transform his life, that he stand up and become a leader, not a follower, that he share the story of his vices that were either taught to him or that he learned over the years, Lord, that he share his traumas and that there be a healing balm released in the atmosphere, and that it descend on my nephew and the officer.

"Lord, thank you for allowing my nephew to be an example of how to walk in love and forgiveness. Many of us wouldn't be able to do what he is doing.

"Lord, we pray for the city of Pittsburgh, and for all the victims. Continue to be with their families. Continue to heal their grieving hearts. Continue to lift them up. Increase in them the Holy Spirit. Provide resources to those in the city and who seek to serve you, Lord, so that they can carry out your agenda and purpose.

"Lord, we thank you. Lord, we love you. In Jesus's name we pray, amen."

Laura was the next person I called. She said, "I'm praying for you. I love you. I know it's going to be okay because it's you." I became more confident with every call.

Then I reached out to some of the Voyagers, an international group of travelers I'd hooked up with in Portugal. They also prayed for me and sent good wishes. Now I was ready for the meeting.

As I drove toward the hotel, I selected a gospel station on my car radio, an unusual choice since I don't listen to gospel that often. The first song that came on was "God Chaser" by William Murphy. I thought, *I'm not only chasing peace. I'm chasing God.* I felt absolute calm.

I finished listening to the song, then found a place to park near the hotel. I removed my wheelchair from the car and assembled it on the sidewalk. Fully relaxed, I swung down into the chair, rolled to the corner, and angled up onto the curb, only for the doorman to rush over and assist me. I made my way into the spacious and ornate lobby of the hotel. Several years earlier, I had come here more than once for my lawyers to take down my deposition for my civil case.

Commander Eric Holmes and Reverend Cornell Jones stood together in the middle of the lobby talking. The time it took me to roll over to the two men afforded me a good view of both. Bespeckled and brown-skinned with curly hair above a cherubic face, Commander Holmes only looked the part of a police officer because he was in uniform. I'd met him through Chief Schubert and had found him to be sincere and committed to making the community better.

Unlike the commander, Pastor Jones was bald and heavyset although well-groomed, a roundish-looking man in a neat suit. He sported eyeglasses and an immaculate goatee. I knew him through BMe. Socially committed, he works very closely with the Pittsburgh police and hails from a distinguished background; his father founded one of the first Black nonprofits, POISE Foundation, in Pittsburgh forty years ago.

I shook his hand and was about to shake Commander Holmes's hand when I saw Detective Derbish enter the lobby in suit and tie through a door fifty feet away. The sight of him startled me. I had once wanted to murder him, and somewhere in me those feelings still existed. The anger, frustration, and confusion that I had suppressed surfaced for a second or two. With each step that he took toward me, my heart became unguarded. It was not anything that I intentionally did or tried to do, just a spirit of healing. I realized that all I had to do was show up and allow the spirit of God to work through me. His face was as I remembered it from a few years earlier in the courtroom, but he now looked more like an average guy than a police officer, no vest, no badge. He wore an ordinary haircut, neither too long nor too short. And he was also much slimmer. I had to take a moment to collect myself, although I didn't feel afraid. In fact, I felt powerful. I was in alignment with myself, and the universe. The lobby and every object in the lobby seemed to affirm my existence. I could feel that affirmation in my body like sore, growing muscles.

My legs began to tingle, almost as if an electromagnetic field covered my body. So, when he walked up to me, I looked him directly in his face and shook his hand. The very moment I did so, I felt something move through his body, a slight tremble, as if his soul shook. Then it was gone. His eyes became watery.

We all stood there for a moment, Pastor Jones a little taller than the other two men.

Then Derbish asked me, "Can I hug you?"

Without thinking, I said, "Sure."

He embraced me, and I embraced him.

The last time I saw him was in a courtroom. He was cocky and seemed to have no regard for my life. This time, it felt like I had the upper hand. I was confident. Although he had taken my ability to walk, I was sitting before him, walking in my purpose. I took in the scent of his cologne, remembering that the last time a police officer had touched me, he was grabbing my hoodie, while he fired several bullets into my torso.

A look passed over the faces of Commander Holmes and Brother Cornell like, *Whoa. What the hell just happened?*

Commander Holmes suggested we all go sit down.

The three men went to sit at a small table next to a wall. I struggled as I rolled up a ramp and rolled over to them.

I was the first to speak. "I don't know why I called this meeting."

None of the men said anything.

I continued. "Look, I've articulated why I wanted to do this meeting several times, but the truth is, I don't have a reason, and that is why I know this is more spiritual than anything." The men watched me and listened. I told them that I had no desired outcome, no expectations. Derbish sat without speaking a word. I wanted to hear more from him, but he looked as though he was in the midst of a dream, wanting to speak but unable to find the words.

I spoke some about my mental health journey and why I decided to take this path of reconciliation instead of retaliation. Then

I related a parable from Paulo Coelho's novel *Aleph*. The narrator of the novel walks into a "beautiful building where, in 1754, a man killed his own brother. The brother's father resolved to build this palace as a school, as a way of keeping alive the memory of his murdered son. I say that surely the son who had committed the murder would also be remembered" (Coelho).

The narrator's guide, Samil, responds:

"It's not quite like that . . . In our culture, the criminal shares his guilt with everyone who allowed him to commit the crime. When a man is murdered, the person who sold him the weapon is also responsible before God. The only way in which the father could correct what he perceived as his own mistake was to transform the tragedy into something useful to others."

Through it all, Detective Derbish seemed a bit aloof. His pale skin was a mask, reluctant to share his vulnerability.

So, he surprised me when he said, "I admire you."

The other two men looked at him.

"You inspire me to be a better human being."

Derbish went on to say, "You inspire the way I police and the way I mentor people within the department."

I did not know what to say in response.

He continued talking. "I'm now a negotiator. I talk people out of SWAT situations and other tough situations like that." His eyes were bright in his face. "You inspired me to go after this position because I didn't want to be a regular police officer anymore. I wanted to really do something meaningful and save people."

I told him, "I also want to save people. To start, I have a responsibility to my son, LJ. One day he will be sixteen years old and driving his own car. How might I best protect him during a traffic stop?"

Derbish grew silent.

I continued with conviction in my voice. "Rather than raise my voice against the police, I prefer to know the mayor, know the police chief, know all the bankers, know the small business owners and the corporations, know the owner of the Penguins, and the vice president, president, and executive director. I prefer to know all these individuals in order to create a bubble and insulate LJ and other people that I care about in my community."

Derbish looked confused.

I shared more. "My parents prepared me for the world. I did everything they told me to do during a traffic stop and still I sit before you without the use of my legs." I could sense this was an awkward conversation for everyone at the table, but I continued. "I realize that it's not enough to prepare my son for the world, giving him advice, insight, and education. I must also prepare the world for my son. For me, I do this by building relationships and making society a better place for him and all children to thrive without parents feeling they could be murdered by a police officer or anyone in the community. This meeting isn't about you, it isn't about me, it's about my son and little Black boys like him. I'm willing to put my ego aside and work to prepare the world for my son."

My words seemed to push the other three men back in their seats.

I shared with the other men my view of power. "You know, I used to think that power came from the barrel of a gun. Now I realize that anybody can pick up a gun and shoot another person if they get angry enough. From my perspective, a true warrior is somebody who can control their emotions and do what's best for their tribe. Like my grandfather would say, 'It's chess, not checkers.'"

I looked over at Reverend Cornell. He smiled.

I told Derbish, "I'm doing what's best for my tribe, and I understand that you're also doing what's best for your tribe."

He agreed. Then he said, "I want to be a part of whatever you're working on." I was surprised. The energy in the space felt like we were all touched by a higher power.

I made it known that I was open to collaborating with him. We could do some innovative things together. Was that not the whole point? I said healing and reconciliation isn't just about this moment of us meeting, but about what we do next, how we go forward. "I don't have the traditional perspective of forgiveness, the Dr. King 'turn the other cheek' perspective. Nah, I just know what I am capable of and would rather create a legacy of love rather than death and destruction. Even in my lowest moments I realized that I wanted to live more than I wanted to die."

He nodded his head in agreement.

I was a vulnerable boy the night that he shot me. Now I was a grown man, sitting before him and looking him in the eye. I felt so proud. Hard work had brought about this evolution. In shooting me, the system had stolen my dignity. Through this meeting I had reclaimed it. That was more than enough. No apology was necessary.

Our conversation continued. Among other things, I told him that I know many people in my community who are open to working with police officers, but because they're loyal to me, they won't do so until I give them the go-ahead. "I'm sure the same is true for police officers."

"Absolutely," he said. "There are people who told me that I shouldn't come to this meeting today."

Pastor Jones spoke up. "Well, can I ask you? Why did you come?"

Derbish replied, "Because I believe in it. I believe in the work."

By "work," I took him to mean all that Pastor Jones and Commander Holmes had told him about me, the work that I'm doing in Pittsburgh, trying to bring the city together, trying to get us all to heal. Chief Schubert and I were already hard at work putting in many hours each week on the foundation. Much to do still. Most important, the foundation will be a bridge between the police and the Black community.

Derbish went on. "I feel free. I feel like a weight has been lifted."

In that instance, I experienced a similar feeling. Then, too, I was feeling more. "I feel like I'm living out a Bible story."

"You are," Pastor Jones said. "You're leading us, you're leading a nation. This is a very historic moment, and this is happening because of you." His eyes swelled with tears.

We all seemed to spend a few minutes considering his statement.

Then Pastor Jones said, "So, where do you all see yourselves in five years as far as working together?" He looked at Derbish first.

"I'm not sure," Derbish said. "Just working together and just doing good things."

I said, "Well, you're a negotiator and this is restorative justice at its highest level." Then I said, "I see us traveling the world negotiating between countries, resolving conflicts and wars."

They all chuckled.

"Yeah," I said. "I'm a big thinker." I smiled.

Commander Holmes had remained quiet throughout the conversation. Now he took a moment to bring the dialogue to a close. "Fellas," he said. "I'm so sorry that I didn't speak. I'm just overwhelmed with emotion." He paused. "I've studied restorative justice, I've done restorative justice workshops, but I have never imagined being a part of something like this. I don't even have the words to describe what I'm feeling right now, but I thank you all for your willingness to make this happen and for your trust in me." He wiped tears from his eyes. It was such a profound moment.

We shook hands, and that was it.

Derbish never apologized. The surprise, admiration, and respect I saw in his eyes was better than an apology. Someone had told me that this meeting wasn't for me. It was for Detective Derbish, a chance for him to heal. At the end of the day, he is a person, another human being, another child of God, with his own lived experience in this country, his own hurdles, his own trauma.

Some things in life we are destined to do. I left the meeting feeling as if I'd just lived out one of those moments.

The next day, I drove to New York to spend some time with Alby. Over dinner, I gave him a full report about my sit-down with Detective Derbish.

Alby looked at me and asked, "Do you love him?"

I said, "Don't push it." We both smiled.

33

MENDING THE UNFIXABLE

People would often ask me, "What happened to the officer who shot you?" Seething with anger, I would answer, "Well, he still works for the police department." One reason I decided to sit down with Detective Derbish is because I had reached the point where I didn't want to be pissed off anymore. In his book *The Four Agreements*, Don Miguel Ruiz says, "You will know you have forgiven someone when you see them and no longer have an emotional reaction. You will hear the name of the person and you will have no emotional reaction. When someone can touch what used to be a wound and it no longer hurts you, then you know you have truly forgiven" (Ruiz). I would add: when someone can touch a wound and it no longer hurts, you know you have healed.

The wound will remain, it will scar over. I'm not saying I'm healed; I'm healing, involved in an ongoing process. Part of getting better is knowing my window of tolerance, knowing what triggers me. I can't watch videos of people getting shot by the police. I don't like being around anyone who complains and has a victim mentality. For me, healing is all about taking your power back.

Healing is not a passive form of forgiveness where you turn the other cheek. Rather, it is the type of forgiveness where I don't have to tell you I am a human being. I show you. I don't have to tell you to respect me. I show you.

In therapy, I learned that everybody wants three things: security, connection, and personal power. Healing involves all three elements. How do you get to a place where you feel secure within? How can you become connected to others in a meaningful way? How do you gain a sense of personal power? I truly believe that, with some work, all of us can heal no matter what we have been through in our lives.

It's important for anyone who has been oppressed, violated, disrespected, or abused to find their voice in a healthy way, to get to a place where they are not triggered, to get to a place where they don't feel like victims, where they can instead feel proud and live with dignity, despite hardships.

I know how hard it is for Black and Brown people in America. I've experienced it. I write about it. I talk about it. My question is: What are we going to do collectively as a people? How can we navigate the struggle for peace, justice, and equality with pride, dignity, and integrity? How can we embrace our personal power and heal?

———

I had many personal reasons for sitting down face-to-face with Derbish. However, I also had a larger purpose in mind: to serve the community and to discover a higher good. Perhaps our connecting could be a bridge for Pittsburgh to heal. Perhaps cops and community can start a dialogue that will lead to fewer Black men getting shot by cops. On the night that Derbish shot me, something inside him made him feel afraid, made him jump into my vehicle and fire five bullets into my body. The solution to fear is safety. However, safety for a police officer looks different than safety for a nineteen-year-old. One of the ways we can reach common ground is through dialogue.

The solution to create safety for both sides involves talking to both sides and getting those people to talk to each other. We can find out from young Black men and women what will make them feel safe when engaging with a police officer when they're alone on the side of the road at the darkest hour of the evening. We can ask a police officer what will make him feel safe when he's conducting a traffic stop on the side of the road with a Black kid at the darkest hour of the evening.

As a leader, I can bring both sides together. I have evolved from shouting "Fuck the Police" and wearing T-shirts that say "Criminals on Patrol" to creating spaces where I can bring the community and the police together for true dialogue. We can't afford for the city to go up in flames. I understand the protests, the outrage, the frustration. However, if the city goes up in flames, we all lose. As a businessman, my business loses money, my employees lose jobs, my property value goes down. When someone loses their business, they can't afford to feed their family and pay the rent. Losing a family-owned business is like an inheritance going up in flames. When there is chaos in the community, everyone suffers.

I'm trying to prevent that. I want the city to grow, to prosper. For me to help make that happen, I need to be a part of a process to make the city safer. I must talk to the police and make sure they're not shooting people. I must talk to the people in the streets to make sure they're not shooting each other or the police. I must help all people in my city understand their true value so they can tap into their potential and thrive. Brother Victor would say it like this: "A man cannot rise above the conditions of his people." For me to rise, I must assist in uplifting the quality of life for my people.

From working with cops, I'm learning things about them. We need to remember that police officers are human beings just like we are. They are not simply a group of individuals with a "police mentality." The police officers I know are regular people. They have thoughts, feelings, trauma, guilt, regrets, just like everyone else.

34

THE TROUBLE WITH "JUSTICE"

Those of us working to change the world for the better should eliminate the word *justice* from our vocabulary. When I think about justice, I picture scales. The problem is that the scales never balance. When someone is murdered, brutalized, or violated, the loss cannot be replaced; hence, there can be no justice. If the cop who shot me was paralyzed and confined to a wheelchair, that punishment would not erase or balance out all the pain that I've endured. If the cop who killed George Floyd lost his life, George Floyd would not be resurrected from the grave. Justice as we know it is an illusion.

The tragedy that I suffered has transformed me into a new person working for a larger type of transformation in my community. My transformation is akin to the caterpillar evolving into a butterfly, an embryo developing into a baby, a seed growing into a tree, which sprouts fruit to nurture others, a phoenix rising from the ashes. My transformation involved connecting with a deep part of myself to become someone other than a man who had his flesh pierced by bullets.

To me, that transformation is more powerful than justice, a new stronger self that nobody could give me—not a court, a district attorney, a judge, the mayor, or the police officer who shot me. If you're waiting on justice to heal, you never will. The world we live in can never restore what you've lost, but you can choose to transform the tragedy into triumph by making a conscious decision to acknowledge your pain, accept the loss, then use all that hurt you as a tool to change the world around you. I've seen women who were raped leverage their pain to create awareness and support other women. I've seen victims of drunk driving become huge advocates. Instead of soaking in pain, they've found a voice and used it for good.

As Black people, our communities have been so traumatized, from hundreds of years of slavery to Jim Crow segregation to our conditions now, that many of us don't know how to get out of a victim mentality. No outside force will be able to restore us to our full humanity. There's no way to properly compensate Black people for hundreds of years of slavery, rape, murder, and systemic oppression. Money cannot erase history. Investments in underprivileged communities should be front and center in our policy to improve quality of life and outcome. But even billions of dollars won't restore all we've lost. We must go within ourselves, show up, and take back our dignity, the same way that I had to go deep within myself and show up for police officers like Derbish to respect me.

———

Despite the numerous demonstrations worldwide following George Floyd's murder in the summer of 2020, the *Washington Post* reported that police in America shot and killed at least 1,055 people in 2021, the highest total since the newspaper began tracking fatal shootings by officers in 2015. So much for the supposed racial reckoning. The facts underscore the difficulty of reducing police shootings and eliminating racial profiling and other problematic and discriminatory practices despite sustained public attention to these issues. Changing the way law enforcement operates in our country is an uphill battle. We will not change policing with a PR campaign, and policy alone will not be sufficient.

America has over 18,000 police departments, and they are all governed differently. While I empathize with what's happening around the country, I recognize that I am in a perfect position to directly impact the way policing is done in my city.

I'd met with the chief of police, the mayor, bankers, activists, the heads of all the major foundations in Pittsburgh, and many other powerful and influential individuals in the city; now was the time to bring them all together in a formal way, through The Hear Foundation. Our goal is to build a stronger and safer community for both police and residents. Our mission is: "To convene, fund, and implement initiatives that build police and resident relationships and strengthen Pittsburgh's neighborhoods."

What does that really mean? The overall goal of the foundation is to find constructive opportunities for citizens and police officers to work together and form actual, legitimate relationships with one another. Not programs where you sit in the same room, then everybody goes home. Rather, programs where both sides make a commitment to being an instrument of change. That's what we're trying to build. How? By implementing a series of initiatives that involve workforce development, athletics for kids, mentoring programs, educational programs, policing reform, civil and criminal justice reform, and mental health.

We want to build a stronger sense of community. No matter how you cut it, the police officers work in our neighborhoods, even if they don't live in them, which is a major part of the problem. They're still part of the community because they're in it every day. There's no reason why we shouldn't know every officer on a first-name basis. There's no reason why I shouldn't know who my neighbors are. I should know what businesses exist in my neighborhood and in the neighborhood over. Ask yourself, What can I do to add value to my community?

We want youth to be assets to the community. At the foundation, one idea involves a public safety initiative where we teach youth about civic duties, policing, and effective leadership. The young people who go through this program might then decide that they want careers as police officers. Through attractive homeowner's packages, we will provide them with incentives to live in the city. Rooted in Pittsburgh proper, they add value to the tax rolls.

We want everyone in the community to feel safe. Pittsburgh utilizes ShotSpotter technology in many neighborhoods to notify police at the sound of gunfire. The Foundation would like to see a social services team accompany the responding police officers. Within a two- to five-block radius of the shooting, the team would provide counseling to any person who feels upset or traumatized. Counseling should also be made available to the household of a shooting victim. Therapy can play an important role in breaking the cycle of gun violence. My friends who are shooters have either been shot themselves or lost people to gun violence. Counseling might have helped them think and act differently.

Everyone in the community is safe when each person is well. Through the foundation, we will encourage mental health awareness and treatment. Many people I know suffer from clinically diagnosable PTSD, because they have lived in incredibly difficult situations, have been victims of abuse, have been shot at, or have shot people. Many of the police officers I know also suffer from clinical PTSD. Here is a commonality we need to recognize, a mutual vulnerability that can be a catalyst for violence. Unfortunately, both Black people and police officers tend to be hostile to mental health initiatives. Wouldn't it be great if they could heal together? Both groups can learn to respect each other, grow from there, and help one another.

———

A small city, big town, Pittsburgh is a growing, dynamic municipality, small enough that everyone is one degree of separation away, but large enough to possess many financial resources. Deeply rooted in the city, I can have my biggest impact here. In Pittsburgh, I'm not just Leon Ford. I'm also Little Bit's son, Tawn's son, Miss Flo's grandson, Miss Green's great-grandson. I'm Stefon's cousin, Drama's cousin, Luv's cousin, and so on. I am a man who became a leader not by choice but by circumstance, through a baptism of fire.

My settlement, my national and international connections, as well as the support I receive from my community puts me in a perfect position to become a power broker in the city. My primary goal is to directly influence how power is distributed in that community and to the benefit of that community. I don't get involved in politics, rhetoric, or PR campaigns. I'm in rooms with thought leaders solving problems.

In putting the foundation together, I thought it was crucial for Chief Schubert to serve as cofounder and board member. He knows and respects many people on the board and won't act in such a way as to let them down. As cofounder and board member, he will be held to a high level of scrutiny and accountability. The trajectory of his career will change. How he's looked at in the community will also change, as will how law enforcement views me. Our foundation will change the culture of policing in Pittsburgh. It will also influence how activism is done.

Instead of protesting to help end police brutality, we should focus on mental health. More money must be provided for counseling and other therapeutic services for both citizens and cops. We must also address the root causes of violence in our society. If we invest in building a stronger sense of community, we can reduce both crime and police violence by a significant amount. While I am a huge advocate for strong policies, I believe relationships can accomplish some things that policy can't. When we fix the divide between the haves and the have-nots, we can maximize impact, increase upward mobility, strengthen our economy, and leverage more resources to resolve societal ills.

Seeking to truly understand how law enforcement thinks, I meet with police officers and listen to their ideas. I've never heard them use words like *reform* or terms like *defund the police*, although many of their ideas end up being connected to reforming toxic police culture like the blue wall of silence and reallocating funds from police departments to social services like counseling. However, if I used those words in their presence, they would shut down and not talk to me. From a psychological perspective, we should consider this fact in our discourse about law enforcement. Policing is their identity. We can't try to strip them of that identity and expect them simply to go along with it.

Oftentimes, people ask me, "Why do you want to work with police officers? They're this and they're that." When you have a goal, and you know what you're willing to sacrifice to get what you want, then you know how to maintain your integrity. I'm not really concerned with a police officer trying to leverage my platform to make himself or herself look good. I know what I'm doing. I lost something that most wouldn't even consider giving up. My why is to prevent bodies from falling in the street.

I'm a chameleon who can blend into different environments. I'm able to go in the hood and talk about supporting Black businesses. I've also made significant investments in Black businesses. I'm able to go to banks and say, "I think it's important for us to lower the credit requirements so that we can help more people do this and that." Then I can go to the city and say, "I think we need to partner with this organization to get this done." I'm taking the same message into different spaces but tailor my language to fit the ears and minds of a specific group.

The way some radicals in the past framed Black economics made white people afraid, made them believe that they would lose money if Black people made money. White people turned a deaf ear to slogans like "Support Black businesses. Fuck white businesses. We don't need them." We must frame the narrative differently, must let it be known that supporting a Black business means supporting America, since those businesses bring more money into the overall economic infrastructure. Those who believe in America should support Black businesses.

Money talks. Activists must learn to engage in conversations across the racial, political, and financial divide, for only the sharing of widespread resources can bring about change. To eliminate systemic and institutional racism, we must put money to work to create new opportunities and to build new institutions. Putting money to work requires leveraging our relationships with wealthy and powerful individuals who want genuine progress. If we build more businesses, if we generate more jobs, if we grow the economy, everybody wins.

35

OVERCOMING THE BARRIER BETWEEN PUBLIC AND PRIVATE

True leadership involves solving problems, and before all else, leaders understand that progress requires money. I learned that truth coming from the streets. A drug dealer recognizes that certain people need to get high. They need a product. He will say to himself, "Here's an opportunity for me to fulfill a need and I can make money off of it." It's how our economy works. If people are hungry and you have access to food, you provide the food to them, and you make a profit in the process. People want to wear clothes or jewelry, and you fulfill that want and make money in the process. That's how America works.

We should also have that same mind-set from a social justice lens. My financial manager at Bernstein Private Wealth Management, Richard Murray, has been showing me different ways to use my wealth to solve problems in Pittsburgh. He and his colleague Eric Glass showed me how we could leverage municipal bonds to switch out 20,000 lead pipes in the city. The firm switched 18,000 lead pipes in Newark, New Jersey, in 2019.

That's the type of activism I'm doing now. Although important work, I'm no longer shutting down streets. Instead, I'm leveraging my platform to better the quality of life by making an impact on the drinking water. By understanding how systems work and by collaborating with people to solve problems, I'm helping to create change on the institutional level. In doing so, I am bettering the quality of life for everyone. We must not underestimate the power of shared knowledge, resources, and collaboration.

When you have money and influence, it's easier to get things done. Instead of saying, "I need this" or "I want this," I'm now able to say, "This is how we can make this happen for the benefit of the community." As an activist, I would complain endlessly. "The tap water is messed up. They're trying to poison us, and our kids are getting lead poisoning." Now I can say, "I know it's messed up. Here's a solution. The wealth management firm that I use is worth $600 billion. We can buy municipal bonds from all over the world. Through such bonds we can rebuild infrastructure in Pittsburgh."

The firm that I use provides me with access to knowledge and resources that strengthen my platform. I do recognize my newfound privilege and how most people don't have the access that I have. My goal is to enlighten you to the possibilities of what can be done. We don't have to be helpless. I'm no longer an activist protesting, "This is fucked up. Y'all are wrong." I'm a leader saying, "We acknowledge that there's a problem, but here's a solution. Here are the connections and resources to make change possible. It's not just a dream. It's not just an idea. These are the experts who are ready to come to the city right now and help us. All we have to do is talk and figure out the logistics."

Barclays was going to broker a deal to build a prison in Alabama. Eric Glass reached out to me because this is an issue he knows that I care about. Strategizing, we were able to get a group of investors at the firm to sign on to a letter opposing the deal. As a result, all the financiers pulled out. I won't have my money tied up in anything that goes against what I stand for. Richard discovered that the 401(k) retirement packages of many teachers help fund companies that perpetuate the school-to-prison pipeline. Now we are working on an initiative to incentivize teachers to invest their funds responsibly.

As activists, we can leverage money to build schools or to oppose mass incarceration and the production of new prisons. The public and private sectors can and must work hand in hand to construct a better world.

———

Growing up I always wanted to punch in the face those who hurt me. Perhaps I wanted to be respected and feared the way my father was. That was my definition of strength. Now people often tell me I'm the strongest man they know, words I never heard when I was fighting all the time. Now I hear it almost every day from strangers, mostly from dudes my age.

When I go out to the club, dudes want to shake my hand, hug me, and say, "Bro, you're the realest thing I know."

Judges who've been sitting on a bench for thirty years will say to me, "You are a real man. I respect you."

People from every walk of life see the same force in me. What they're seeing is God working through me to help me live out my life's purpose. Each day when I wake up, I ask myself, How can I add value to the world? How can I help people? How can I add value to relationships, friendships, an organization, my community? Sometimes all it takes is a smile. As my grandmother would say, "The million-dollar smile."

We all need to be assets to our community. You can't just live somewhere and go to work. No matter what you're going through, you must be involved. Get to know all the institutions that engage with your community and what their budgets are. Know what they spend their money on. And stay committed to your purpose despite adversity.

Whether you're white or you're Black, whether you're in Germany or in South Africa, life will present you with adversity. Rather than let it discourage or deter you, allow it to build your character. As we know, coal under pressure transforms into a diamond. Yes, we face inequality, racism, and systemic oppression, but we cannot give up. Have faith and stay committed whatever your religious background or belief system. You are at your strongest when you believe in something, even if that something is yourself. The thing driving you must be more powerful than the thing that's trying to drive you into the ground.

Ask yourself, Who am I? What is my purpose? Why am I here?

36

LEARNING TO PROTECT MYSELF

Over the years, Miss Kenney and I have built a strong bond. As the mother of a son murdered by police, she has gained a certain level of celebrity, appearing on BET, hanging out with Jay-Z, Beyoncé, and Meek Mill, attending the Super Bowl, and other high-profile engagements of that nature. People see her, and they want to take pictures with her. Publicly, all looks well for her.

However, I've learned that, behind the scenes, she and many of the other mothers and relatives of victims of police shootings on the Black Lives Matter circuit are suffering in silence. Obviously, we know they're grieving, so what have we done to help them heal? Everyone around them focuses on the movement. No one focuses on their healing process, which, to me, is the most important thing.

Miss Kenney and I often discuss how we didn't ask for the limelight, the celebrity. For one thing, being in the public eye can have a triggering effect, such as when we hear some activists say things that we don't agree with. Attending public events may trigger us, for even at a nonpolitical gathering such as a community day, people will start talking about "victim of a police shooting" Antwon Rose or Leon Ford. Although we want to have a positive impact on their world, we are more than what happened to us.

In 2020, I attended a Father's Day event where I was asked to speak. In the lead-up to my taking the microphone, my mind was filled with positive thoughts about fatherhood. I reflected on how amazing it is to have a son, and how amazing it is to have a great father. However, the guy introducing me began talking about Antwon Rose and me getting shot and said he can't imagine how hard it is for me because I'm in a wheelchair, and so forth, heavy stuff that caught me by surprise.

Because his introduction set a certain tone, I felt reluctant about speaking, although I did so anyway. I told the audience, "Most of y'all already know my story. I'm just here to talk about fatherhood," which is what I did.

After I got off the mic, a preacher came up to me and offered me advice about what he called "the thirty percent rule." He said, "When you speak, tell thirty percent of your story, tell thirty percent about how you got through it, and end with thirty percent about what you're going through now, because everybody here doesn't know your story. You have a testimony."

I said, "Bro, I'm not trying to talk about being shot."

It was so hard for him to understand where I was coming from. Many people don't understand how even their support can trigger us.

After that event, I went to a graduation party for the son of one of my mentors. I was the only Black person there. Ironically, I felt safe. No one expected me to talk about anything traumatic, partially because most of the partygoers there had never experienced anything traumatic. The victim mentality of some Black people causes them to be addicted to a type of trauma porn. At public events, people often say to me, "Tell me about the details of your shooting." Would you ask a woman who has been raped for the details about her violation? Miss Kenney and I both have experienced this type of insensitive questioning.

The next year, we attended a two-day event, a black-tie gala event on a Saturday night, then a gospel explosion on Sunday. Tamika Mallory was scheduled to speak at the gala. Because she was running late, the organizers asked if I would take the mic and say a few words. I agreed to do so, although on such short notice, I had only about five minutes to prepare something. The organizers asked me if I would share my story.

I said, "No, I'm absolutely not going to do that." I knew it would traumatize me.

Disappointed, they tried to convince me to change my mind.

I said, "I ain't trying to talk about all that."

I got up on stage and spoke about my admiration for the young people who had organized the event, and how proud I felt to have watched them over the years develop into leaders. My words were genuine because I had mentored these young people.

Once Tamika Mallory took to the podium, she started talking about activism, cop killings, and related matters. As I started listening to her, I wondered if she had people in her life who cared about her as someone other than an activist, someone related to a victim. I continued to listen. Once I heard her say the name of her murdered husband, Jason Ryan, the words triggered me. I am often triggered by videos of police shootings and firsthand testimonies or the testimonies from the victim's family members. I could take no more. I left the event.

Miss Kenney sent me a text. "How did you have the courage to leave?"

I texted her back. "Because of my whole self-care routine, I know what my window of tolerance is."

The next morning at the gospel explosion, I was sitting next to Miss Kenney, and the sister of Botham Jean, the man who was killed in his apartment by a police officer in Dallas, sat next to her. We started talking about the day before. She said to me, "Wow, you're so brave."

I told her that it was important for her to take care of herself and understand her window of tolerance, because people will exploit her pain. They don't understand how heavy it is to lose a loved one. They demand justice, but they fail to understand that once you suffer a loss, it's a loss. The best thing you can do is go deep within yourself and heal. Sometimes you just have to take a deep breath. Inhale peace, love, and gratitude. Exhale frustration, resentment, and brokenness.

Miss Kenney and I have had many conversations of this type.

The following day, Monday, July 12, Antwon Rose would have turned twenty-one years old. Miss Kenney was hosting a pool party celebration and asked me to be there.

Almost pleading, she said to me, "I really want you there."

I told her I couldn't be there because I must practice what I preach. "Miss Michelle," I said, "it's going to be mighty heavy for you to have this public event for everybody else to enjoy your son's birthday. You'll have a lot of people around you during the day. That's going to be triggering, and then that night you're going to be alone."

She smiled. "I love you so much. I respect you and your process."

Early the next morning, she sent me a text. "Leon, you are definitely right about everything that you said. This is probably my last public celebration. Nothing has happened. It's just too much, and it hasn't even begun. I love you so, so much."

I received that text before the party. After the party, she sent me another text. "Leon, you have no idea how much your words stuck and impacted me yesterday. Nobody else in the world can tell me what to do. I don't listen to them, but I listen to you. Thank you so much. I love you."

I replied: "I'm always going to tell you what you need to hear, not what you want to hear, because you have a lot of people around for the sake of being around, and they just want to go along to get along. I really care about you and your well-being."

Those conversations represent the full circle of our relationship, from us having that first conversation in her backyard to her finally realizing that she needs to take time to heal.

About a month after the gospel explosion, we found ourselves together at another gathering. We sat and talked.

She said, "I want to give up, but I don't know if I should."

I asked her, "What's giving up?"

"I'm tired of all this organizing, but I feel that I have to do it."

"That's not giving up. If you're tired, you should take a break, and taking a break is not giving up."

The thing is, when you're burnt out, when you're triggered, it's hard to make good decisions. For some activists, activism is their entire life. They become locked in to a limited way of thinking. Once a mayor or a governor says, "Here's what we're willing to give you," or "Let's have a meeting," they're like, "No, that's not enough" or "Fuck you. I ain't meeting with you."

They don't have the capacity to be objective and negotiate. Even getting some of what they want might be a step in the right direction. However, when you're triggered and react to past traumatic experiences, all you see is fire.

37

A BETTER WORLD FOR LJ

When I think about LJ, I think about my parents and how they gave me tools that I could use to prepare for the world and to protect me from the world. They gave me many valuable lessons. They gave me unconditional love. They instilled in me a sense of pride. They made me believe that I could achieve anything. Despite their efforts, I still got shot.

I have decided to take a different approach when it comes to my son, LJ. As I told Detective Derbish, I'm not only going to prepare my son for the world. I'm going to prepare the world for my son. Preparing the world for my son means changing the environment he lives in.

Motivational speaker Alexander den Heijer gives this often-quoted phrase of wisdom: "When a flower doesn't bloom, you fix the environment in which it grows, not the flower." If you fix the environment that gives the flower everything that it needs to thrive, you won't have to give so much attention to an individual flower. In other words, fix the environment, not the child. I work each day to create an environment that will nurture my son, that will allow him to bloom.

I start with my neighborhood, Larimer. When I first moved

into my house, trash lined both sides of the street. The moment I started remodeling my home, my neighbors also started fixing up their homes and picking up trash. We all know each other. And we all work to look out for one another. That's what it means to build a strong sense of community. A kid on my block can go to a neighbor and borrow sugar, or soap, bread, or anything else.

What it looks like to protect other people's children is to engage other parents and other grandparents in a process to work together to build a strong sense of community. That means providing people with mental health services and other resources. It means being intentional about and innovative about how we solve problems.

I don't feel unsafe driving through any neighborhood in Pittsburgh because I know all the police officers. I want to create that same feeling of safety for every resident of the city, especially the children. When children grow up in an environment where they feel safe, where they feel seen and heard, they're more likely to be courageous and audacious in how they interact with the world. The love and support my mother and father gave me as a kid helped me see the world in a different way.

My son, LJ, teaches me so much about life. As adults, we disempower children by thinking they can't do things. At nine years old, LJ washes his own clothes, cooks his own food, and cleans the house. In addition to being a responsible kid, he teaches me that life goes on. No matter how you're feeling, no matter what troubles you face, you have to make the best of it. When I'm down, he will say to me, "Don't give up, Dad" or "Don't worry, Dad. You got this." He reminds me about the lessons I teach him.

LJ makes me mindful of the future. I'm sure that my parents and grandparents, when they see me, become hopeful about the future. To put so much into a child mentally, emotionally, and spiritually, then to see your efforts pay off, see that child come into his own as a person, be confident and talented and express that confidence and talent in ways they find pleasing—it means so much to see that happen as a parent.

LJ loves to play football, and he's good at it, far better than I ever was. I played football primarily because my dad wanted me to. He thought it would help me become a man, a way to fulfill his own notions of masculinity. Whenever I got the ball, people rejoiced. When I tackled another player, people said my tackle was the best tackle of the game, although fifteen other players had performed better tackles. Everyone said I was good at the game, but I wasn't. I was simply that guy, a popular kid.

LJ has his own mind. I always thought I would be the kind of father to be super hard on my child. "You're going to do this; you're going to do that." As a parent, I've discovered that's not me. LJ is self-motivated and discovers what his interests are. I simply try to create a healthy environment for him to explore himself and to figure out what he wants to do, who he wants to become. As a kid, I was always free to express myself, and my parents, grandparents, aunts, uncles, and cousins supported me. I have tried to re-create that environment for my son. I connect him with the best people, like a personal trainer who can help him with strength and conditioning. If he one day decides, "I'm done with football. I want to try something different," I will support his decision.

On more than one occasion, I have taken LJ with me to have lunch with a police officer or to sit in on a business meeting. He has listened in on my conference calls, participated in meditation sessions, and heard me speak before an audience. My son has even been present at some of my therapy sessions. John Henne and I have a standing agreement that once LJ gets of age, he will start working part-time in John's jewelry shop. I'm doing everything I can to provide LJ with access, with social capital. As parents, we must train our sons and daughters to become self-actualized human beings, never limiting themselves as they strive for their goals.

Anyone who spends time around me knows I have a lot going

on each day. Still, parenting remains my priority. Growing up, my parents made me and my siblings feel like we were a priority, and I do the same for my son. I never felt like my mom's job was more important than me. I never felt like my dad valued whatever he had going more than me. My mom never made me feel like dating came before me; the same with my dad. My parents always made me and my siblings feel like we were everything to them, which made us confident.

I value family. If I had to choose between going to ten events in one day or hanging out with my family or going over to my grandma's house, I'm going to choose to go to the latter. If more people were intentional about spending time with their children or families, they wouldn't need to seek external validation. My advice to activists: prioritize family, prioritize children, because if you have healthy relationships with them, they'll never turn their back on you. Heroes become villains overnight in the media. We see it all the time. You can be the most sought-after speaker, the most committed activist, and then you say one wrong thing and everything you've built disappears.

Be authentically yourself in any space that you show up in. Because I've built real relationships, I can have a difference of opinion without getting into an argument. I didn't tell my father about my sit-down with Detective Derbish until after the meeting. On hearing about it, he told me holding the meeting was one of the most powerful things I'd done; he told me he was proud of me. However, on the flip side, he said, "I could never do that. I'd kill that mutherfucker."

My father and I could have two completely different perspectives but still respect each other. Why? Because the love is real. Strangely enough, it was my father who taught me to be open to opposing attitudes. I'm trying to pass this lesson on to LJ. Two people can hold different opinions but still love one another.

I also want LJ to understand that racism and bigotry will always be with us. For that reason, we must be strong within, firm in our sense of self. I won't get bent out of shape because some racist doesn't like Black people. In fact, I'm willing to tolerate that attitude as long as they don't put their hands on me or try to disrespect my mother or hurt my son. Somebody else might not like people in wheelchairs. Their dislike won't offend me. Words don't hurt me. Another person's perspective is not going to change the way I think about myself. Now, if you put your hands on me, if you disrespect me, that's something different.

As a father I don't have all the answers. I'm a work in progress, as is the world. What I do know, the world must become a safer and better place for my son, LJ, to reach his potential.

38
THE REBIRTH OF LEON

In my youth, I put my father on a pedestal. He could do no wrong in my eyes. I soon realized that he was a human being, a mortal man who made mistakes, a man who, as he would put it, "is a work in progress." Many of us reject our parents because they make mistakes. I have always viewed my parents for who they are without judgment. Even a bad example is a good example of what not to be.

Often, we expect leaders to be perfect people. This is unrealistic. The truth is, we are all complex, and we don't always do everything the right way. Some leftists today criticize Gandhi because he harbored racist attitudes toward Black people at one time in his life. I understand that point of view, but Gandhi's racism doesn't negate the fact that he added value to the world.

I always recognize the wisdom of people who fail, who have made mistakes, and who might be down on their luck. We can miss out on insights by overlooking that homeless person because we instead want to talk to a CEO, not realizing that the homeless person, or that person just getting out of prison, has a wealth of knowledge. I look for wisdom anywhere.

I still rely on my father for guidance. Often, when I'm mulling over an important decision, I will talk things through with him and get his input. However, if he can't answer my questions, he'll call his father, my grandfather, Big Leon, and get him to weigh in. A knowledgeable man, my grandfather is guaranteed to answer the question. This is life as I know it: three Leons putting their minds together. A legacy of knowledge, passed down through generations.

My father will still drop in on me. He plays the role of the protector. Once a week, he will come to my home while I'm away and pull the trash cans to the curb. He will cut the grass or shovel the snow, fix anything that's broken, and restock essential items like water, rubber gloves, and toothpaste.

His actions are a form of wisdom, teaching through showing, practicing what he preaches. What I know about the world starts with all that I gleaned from my father and my mother, what they have taught me and continue to teach me as loving parents. Our parents should be our first gurus and philosophers.

In *The Fire Next Time*, James Baldwin has this to say about his brother: "I know what the world has done to my brother and how narrowly he survived it." Thinking about my father, I echo Baldwin's words: I know what this country has done to my father and how narrowly he survived it. I'm aware of all the pain and suffering he carries on the inside even as he appears to be brave. Even as a fearless man, there's only so much he could take on. He is a protector, but who protects him? Like my father, I'm trying to protect my son, but who protects me in this country where all Black men are under attack?

Being a Black man in America is to be afraid. However, in order to survive, you have to suppress this fear and move through life with confidence. That confidence sometimes takes on the appearance of radicalism. Many philosophers and historians draw a polarity between Dr. Martin Luther King Jr. and Malcolm X, suggesting that the former was an integrationist, while the latter was a radical. To me, they were simply two Black men trying to survive, trying to protect their families and the people they loved. Still, they both ended up dead, felled by the bullets of assasins.

Who was the better leader? I can't say. To me, the answer is not an either/or but a both/and. Each man was a good leader. Each man died trying to figure out the best way forward in this racist country. Honestly, as a Black man in America, sometimes I don't know which path to follow or what to believe. I'm certain that most Black men feel this way. Sometimes we don't know what we're doing other than trying to protect what's ours and be respected in the process. Across the country, many of us die every day over respect. If you disrespect somebody, you might lose your life. If someone disrespects you, you might take a life. Because we are continuously disrespected, all we have to hold on to is our pride.

In so many ways, this country strips away your pride, no matter how wealthy you are, no matter how much you have accomplished. As someone who is both learning from the past but also trying to pave my own way, I must confess that I don't have all the answers. Although I have achieved a level of wisdom through life experience and hard work, I'm also still learning.

I'm often asked, "What's the future for Leon Ford?" I aim to become one of the experts in public-private partnerships. My ability to have authentic relationships within the community and with various individuals in the public and private sectors provides the perfect opportunity for me to leverage those relationships to solve real problems. That process requires a level of involvement where I continue to build bonds with investors and bankers, partnerships with foundations, that involves me knowing all the politicians and people involved in law enforcement, not just the chief of police but many police officers on patrol, along with all the commanders, the sergeants, the detectives.

In practical terms, expertise in public-private partnerships in Pittsburgh means figuring out how I can work with the mayor's office. How do I work with the superintendent of the school board? How do I work with the presidents of foundations? How do I work with the local banks? How do I work with the Pittsburgh Steelers? How do I work with the Penguins? How do I work with the Pirates? How do I work with utilities? How do I get all these people to work together? We're all committed to making Pittsburgh a safe and prosperous place for everyone. On a national level, how do I go to cities and get their power brokers and influencers to collaborate and work together the way I have decided to work and collaborate with people in Pittsburgh? If we could put our egos aside and collaborate in every city, in every state, in every country around the world, we would have the remedy for world peace.

Authentic power cannot be taken away. How can we empower every human being on our planet? We do so through love. Love begins with the healing and evolution of self, which then serves as a catalyst to heal, evolve, and strengthen your family. Healing and strengthening families will lead to community peace. That level of peace can expand to include every individual, family, community, city, state, country, our entire world. This process starts with the self.

We should not look at the world in terms of different tribes, races, ethnic groups, creeds, economic classes, and religions in a way that judges people before we've gotten to know them. Start with a conversation. Before all else, get to know a stranger as a fellow human being. Put a high value on selflessness, for when the ego gets introduced to your life, gets introduced to the way you love and the way you lead, that is when you experience unhealthy attachments and turmoil.

Also, we sometimes make the mistake of holding family to standards that we don't hold others to. I made this mistake with my brother Reese. For a long time, Reese and I didn't talk because we were not mature enough to have courageous conversations. We were both misguided, caught up in youthfulness and greed, and couldn't see through our dysfunction. What I didn't know: he longed for a relationship with me, so much so that he purchased a handicapped-accessible house, hoping that in time we would reunite. Reese has become the big brother I have been looking for. He has a wisdom from lived experience. Reconciliation with family is important because family is our foundation.

On the morning of Thursday, November 11, 2021, the ninth anniversary of my being shot, I received a text message from Detective Derbish. We had not communicated since the meeting the previous July.

He wrote: "I know this is a hard day for you."

I wrote back: "Yes, it is. Thanks for thinking about me."

Although I appreciated his reaching out to me, truth to tell, I still can't say if his message made me feel better or worse. I had already been thinking about the night of the traffic stop. Hands gripping me. Flashes from a gun. The smell of gunpowder. Warm blood oozing out of my chest. My face pressed flat against a cold street. Already certain dark emotions had resurfaced taking me back to those many days, months, and years when I fixated on death. Some people see me smile and think I don't have dark moments. The reality is that dark thoughts find me more than one may think. However, I still choose to love, I still choose to smile. I remembered the way I used to sit in my car, feeling like a caged bird, wings clipped, feet tied, peeking out at the world through bars of rage, unsure about how I could continue living.

November 11 will forever represent a line in the sand demarcating my life from being a man who could walk to being a man in a wheelchair. Whenever that day comes around, it will forever be a reminder of loss.

Along with Derbish's text, that Thursday held another surprise for me. At a Heal America event I had helped organize, I received a declaration from Allegheny County naming November 11 Leon Ford Day. That act of renaming has not been lost on me. After years of growing and healing, I now recognize November 11 as my second birthday, the day of my rebirth. The shooting was both the best and worst thing that ever happened to me. Pittsburgh built a monster, Little Bit's son, then turned that monster into a giant. I was never supposed to be in the position I am in now. I rose above the life that was scripted for me and so many other Black men in this country: an ordinary dude from the neighborhood living a life of no significance, doing a little bit of this, a little bit of that, selling drugs, shooting people, getting into beefs, in and out of jail, maybe a little dead-end job. Then on November 11, 2012, I got pulled over for a traffic stop and everything changed.

When I was a boy, my father used to tell me, "If you want to be big, you got to think big." I think big. A part of me believes that, had I not been shot, I would have been indicted or even killed. After all, I'm still Little Bit's son, although I have also evolved into the person I am today. The moves I'm making now in Pittsburgh, in offices and boardrooms, my father made when he was younger in the streets. I'm taking all that street knowledge and using it to have a positive impact on the world around me. When I think about my life in the simplest terms, I have taken the enterprising qualities of my father but use them to do good in the world. I truly believe that he would have turned out differently if he'd had the information I have, if the environment that he grew up in were conducive to his needs.

I think back to the letter he wrote me from prison more than twenty years ago, where he hopes that I will become the "better part" of him. Leon Ford today embraces the best qualities of both of my parents.

The world knows me as a happy person who greets every person I encounter with a smile.

In large part, I smile because I am an optimistic person. Some days I feel wholly optimistic, other days less so. Some days I feel hopeful. Other days I'm more of a realist, looking at things as they are, shaking my head at this broken world we live in. Regardless of my perspective I try to be positive. I don't think that optimism and positivity are synonymous in the same way that I don't think negativity and pessimism are synonymous. You can be positive but also have a little pessimism, especially when considering certain facts and circumstances that come with being a Black person in America.

Each day, I wake up smiling and happy, but that doesn't mean that I never have negative thoughts. When an abusive cop goes to trial, I expect the worst outcome and tell myself, *This dude is definitely going to get off.* That is a realistic expectation, based on our country as it is today. Sometimes we hear the things our elders say and think, *Yo, this cat is really cynical.* However, we should wonder if that person's cynicism stems from life experience. Black people in this country continue to long for justice and equality, only to be disrespected, devalued, humiliated. Recognizing the world as it is, I give myself permission to go through the full range of emotions. When I'm optimistic, I'm optimistic. When I'm realistic, I'm realistic. Either way, I'm committed to the work. I never feel defeated. I think that commitment is what's most important. Whether you're an optimist or a pessimist, you must remain in the struggle and keep your heart beating for change.

I'm living proof that change is possible. We can all be reborn. We can all discover the true self within. I testify to that fact. I refuse to let the world define me. I'm not defined by the five bullets that entered my body on the night of November 11, 2012. I'm not defined by what other people want me to do in terms of public service. I'm not defined by being in a wheelchair. I'm defined by my humanity in the way that I engage with other human beings. I am the phoenix that rose from the ashes. For President Obama, the ashes symbolized the shooting and my subsequent paralysis. Although I do not disagree with that interpretation, the ashes hold a broader meaning for me. The ashes are how I saw the world as a young man, wanting to be 'bout it 'bout it, King of the Streets, that mind-set of destruction that came from trying to survive in a hostile environment and from being culturally conditioned to see the world in a negative, dog-eat-dog way.

The shooting was the catalyst that helped me to rise above that mind-set. However, it first pulled me down into a dark, sunken place of anger, despair, and self-doubt, an almost total negation of self. With the love and support of others, I was able to lift myself up, a long and painful process of recovery, restoration, and rebirth. It was important for me to acknowledge my pain, work through the triggers, and ultimately move forward with my life. One of my biggest accomplishments was not allowing myself to become stuck in that pain. I deeply understand how trauma can paralyze you. Although I lost my ability to walk, I gained so much more on my spiritual journey.

I discovered that my wheels have wings. Know that I'm still rising. How high I go is up to me.

BIBLIOGRAPHY

Akbar, Na'im. *Visions for Black Men.* Tallahassee: Mind Productions and Associates, 1991.

Baldwin, James. *The Fire Next Time.* London: Michael Joseph, 1963.

Coelho, Paulo. *Aleph.* New York: Knopf, 2011.

Everytown for Gun Safety. "The Impact of Gun Violence on Children and Teens." December 28, 2021, https://every townresearch.org/report/the-impact-of-gun-violence-on-chil dren-and-teens/.

Island Health. "Caring for the Spirit in Island Health." *Numa,* Summer 2018, https://www.islandhealth.ca/sites/default /files/2018-08/numa-summer-2018.pdf.

Jenkins, Jennifer, Lati, Marisa, and Rich, Stephen. "Fatal Police Shootings in 2021 Set Record Since the Post Began Tracking, Despite Public Outcry." *Washington Post,* February 9, 2022.

MeMe. https://me.me/i/stef-starkgaryen-stefisdope-you-cant-truly -call-yourself-peaceful-unless-26d8cf984ff34e9cbeb68d 575e7db71e.

Muhammad, Khalid. November 29, 1993, speech at Kean College in Union, New Jersey, https://www.youtube.com/watch?v=E7M VbwVwrmI.

Peck, M. Scott. *The Road Less Traveled*. Toronto: Touchstone Books, 2003.

Reilly, Wilfred. "Black Lives Matter's Missing Billions." *Spiked*. February 14, 2022, https://www.spiked-online.com/2022/02/14/black-lives-matters-missing-billions/.

Robeznieks, Andis. "Inequity's Toll for Black Americans: 74,000 More Deaths a Year." American Medical Association. February 22, 2021, https://www.ama-assn.org/delivering-care/health-equity/inequity-s-toll-black-americans-74000-more-deaths-year.

Ruiz, Miguel. *The Four Agreements*. San Rafael: Amber-Allen Publishing, 1997.

ABOUT THE AUTHOR

LEON FORD, a native of Pittsburgh, is an accomplished entrepreneur, author, international speaker, community organizer, and former city council candidate for Pittsburgh's District 9. A well-respected activist, mental health ambassador, and social advocate for change, he has devoted his life to the betterment of his community, working with police officers to help provide clarity on cultural competency and with Pennsylvania legislators to draft policies that modify the use-of-force laws. He executive-produced the Cannes Film Festival Award–winning documentary *Leon* in 2019, and his long-form video *Breaking Bread: A Conversation on Race in America* (2021) is the recipient of a Shorty Award for Social Activism. He serves as an entrepreneur in residence for Bronze Investments, focusing on investing in social impact companies. In 2022, Leon, together with Pittsburgh Bureau of Police Chief Scott Schubert, founded The Hear Foundation to foster collaboration between the public and the police. The recipient of President Obama's Volunteer Service Award (2017), The Root 100 (2018), Pittsburgh's 40 Under 40 (2019), and a member of The Aspen Institute's Inaugural Civil Society Fellowship, Leon is a devoted advocate for community healing, individual empowerment, and social change.